THE
Heartache
NO ONE SEES

OTHER BOOKS BY SHEILA WALSH

All That Really Matters
A Love So Big: Anchoring Your Child to the Heart of God
Living Fearlessly
Stories from the River of Mercy
Stones from the River of Mercy
Life Is Tough but God Is Faithful
Gifts for Your Soul
Honestly
Bring Back the Joy

Children's Books

In Search of the Great White Tiger (#1 in the Gnoo Zoo series)
Chattaboonga's Chilling Choice (Gnoo Zoo #2)
Einstein's Enormous Error (Gnoo Zoo #3)
Miss Marbles's Marvelous Makeover (Gnoo Zoo #4)
Big Billy's Great Adventure (Gnoo Zoo #5)
Hello, Sun! A Morningtime Tale of God's Great Care
Hello Stars! A Sleepytime Tale of God's Loving Presence

Coauthored Women of Faith Books

Women of Faith Devotional Bible
The Great Adventure
Irrepressible Hope
Sensational Life
The Women of Faith Daily Devotional
The Women of Faith Study Guide Series

THE
Heartache
NO ONE SEES

CHRIST'S PROMISE OF HEALING
for a
WOMAN'S WOUNDED HEART

SHEILA WALSH

NELSON BOOKS
A Division of Thomas Nelson Publishers
Since 1798
www.thomasnelson.com

Published in Nashville, Tennessee, by Thomas Nelson, Inc.

Published in association with Yates & Yates, LLP, Attorneys and Counselors, Orange, California.

Library of Congress Cataloging-in-Publication Data

Walsh, Sheila, 1956-
    The heartache no one sees: Christ's promise of healing for a woman's wounded heart / Sheila Walsh.
     p. cm.
    ISBN 0-7852-6290-3 (hardcover)
    1. Christian women—Religious life. 2. Suffering—Religious aspects—Christianity.
3. Consolation. I. Title.
    BV4527.W35 2004
    248.8'43—dc22

2003023680

Printed in the United States of America

04 05 06 07 08 QW 9 8 7

CONTENTS

CONTENTS

ACKNOWLEDGMENTS

*S*heila would like to thank the following people for their invaluable input into this book:

Mike Hyatt. It's a gift to be part of your author family. Your vision and passion for truth have inspired and challenged me.

Jonathan Merkh. You use your tremendous skills to give wings to the dreams God places in the hearts of your authors.

Brian Hampton. Thank you for your encouragement, wisdom, and insight as you worked with the manuscript. Every one of your ideas have made this a better book.

Kyle Olund. Thank you for your careful and gifted editorial work.

Lisa Guest. Thank you for your work on the Bible study. It is my heart's desire to take women to the deep well of God's Word, and you have joined me in that pursuit.

Thank you to Mary Graham, Marilyn Meberg, Luci Swindoll, Patsy Clairmont, Thelma Wells, Nicole Johnson, and all the Women of Faith family.

Thank you to Amy Chandy. Our gifts are different, Amy, but our hearts are the same. We want to put books into the hands of women that will change their lives forever. Thank you.

Sealy Yates. Thank you for your love, character, and guidance.

Barry Walsh. It is a rare gift to be able to share your heart, your home, and your calling with your husband, but I am one of those blessed women. Thank you!

Praise the LORD!
For it is good to sing praises to our God;
For it is pleasant, and praise is beautiful.
The LORD builds up Jerusalem;
He gathers together the outcasts of Israel.
He heals the brokenhearted
And binds up their wounds.
—PSALM 147:1–3 (emphasis added)

This is Christ's promise for us!

An Introduction

OUR HIDDEN PAIN

*F*rom 1987 until 1992 I was a very visible presence on religious television. I was the cohost of the daily show *The 700 Club* with Dr. Pat Robertson and the host of my own daily show, *Heart to Heart with Sheila Walsh*, on the Christian Broadcasting Network. Then one day it was as if I disappeared off the face of the earth. I was there one morning, and by the next morning I was gone. Very little was said about my disappearance. A reference was made on one show that I had taken some time off to rest, but if you missed that day's broadcast, you had no idea where I had gone or why. Had I gone back to my family in Scotland? Perhaps I'd been fired?

A month later I bumped into a woman in a mall.

"Sheila, is that you?" she asked. I imagine she was used to seeing me in a tailored suit, and I looked a little different in my jeans and ball cap.

"Yes, it's me," I replied.

"Where have you been? My family watches the show every day, and we miss you. What happened to you?"

I looked into her eyes for a moment. She was a stranger to me and yet I longed to connect with someone as I felt so alone.

"Do you have a moment to grab a cup of coffee?" I asked.

"I'd love to," she said.

We got our coffee and sat down in the food court.

I took a deep breath and said, "I was released from a psychiatric hospital this morning."

I waited to see what her response would be. She reached across the table and took my hand.

"What happened?" she asked. "I saw the show the day before you disappeared and you seemed fine."

"I was diagnosed with severe clinical depression," I replied.

"But you didn't looked depressed," she said. "I would never have known."

We talked for a while and then she left. I stayed at the table, tears falling into my tepid coffee. Her words rang in my heart: *I would never have known.*

That was a big part of my problem. I had become used to hiding from others what was going on inside myself.

A COMMON PROBLEM

I have written about my experience with depression in my book *Honestly*. But over the last few years I have begun to realize that what I was dealing with is not unique to me or even just to those with depression. There is an epidemic of broken hearts that are being carried around in private. I talk to women every day who, because of my decision to be open about my pain, feel that I am a safe person to risk sharing their story with. I count that a holy privilege. That's why I am writing this book. I believe that Christ wants to heal our broken hearts and free our crushed spirits to love and worship Him.

If you are like me, it will take some time to open up to this process. Some of us have carried our wounds for so long, we no longer see them; they are just part of who we are. At times in the past we might have looked for healing and been misunderstood, so we hide our pain.

Let me ask you a few questions that might help you focus on some of the reasons you chose to hide.

Are you a victim of well-meaning friends who have told you to *get over it*? Sometimes those who are closest to us don't understand the depth of what we are feeling. As far as they can tell, everything is going smoothly in your life, so why do you keep harping about old stuff? Your ensuing sadness causes you to hide rather than deal with the pain of not being understood.

Have you tried to do it yourself, to tidy up what's going on inside with a quick fix? Some women starve themselves in an effort to feel in control over something. Others eat and eat until the wall around them seems enough to protect them from a cruel outside world. Some turn to alcohol, relationships, or soap operas in an attempt to dull the ache. Some try to lose themselves in a frenzy of ministry that can be as addictive as substance abuse. I have been there.

Do you struggle with shame? Is there a voice inside you that tells you that you will never change, that you are not worthy of God's love, that you will always be stuck as you are right now?

Have you listened to those who come in Jesus' name, promising healing for your wounded soul? Perhaps you prayed with someone on television and sensed that God had done something in your life. But even as the light flickered off the television screen, so did the hope in your heart. You longed for an instant miracle rather than the painful process of walking through whatever you needed to face to be whole. A quick fix was offered, but nothing permanent remained.

Whatever the source of your disillusionment, the residual pain is the same. You tried something but it didn't work, and you are left with more questions and no answers.

I tried for years to hold myself together. I worked harder and harder to be the perfect Christian woman, but it never worked. There were too many painful wounds under the surface that festered in the darkness. Some wounds are so deep and have been present for so long, it seems as if they will never heal.

MY ROAD TO CHANGE

I have been in relationship with God since I was a young girl of eleven growing up in a small town on the west coast of Scotland. My desire to please Him and respond to that love led me through Bible college to roles as a youth evangelist, contemporary Christian artist, and television host on the Christian Broadcasting Network.

But after working side by side with Dr. Pat Robertson and the staff of *The 700 Club* for five years, I was admitted as a patient in the psychiatric wing in a hospital in Washington, D.C., diagnosed with severe clinical depression. I felt as if I was drowning, dragged under the water by rocks of despair, sadness, and hopelessness. I had no issue with God. I believed then and believe now that God is good and loving and kind. The issue was with me. I was disenchanted with all the efforts of Sheila Walsh. I was dizzy from years of trying to keep all the plates spinning in the air in an attempt to show God how much I loved Him. Nothing I did felt as if it was enough.

Have you been there? Are you there right now?

For years I had taken comfort in the omission of the "big sins" in my life. I thought that if I were a "good girl," then God would love me more. I was sexually pure and abstained from anything that was on my long list of things to avoid if I wanted God to be happy with me. As I moved into my thirties, that comfort blanket had worn thin. I saw in myself the potential for disaster of every kind. I saw hypocrisy and fear; I felt anger and resentment. I had worked so hard to be approved by God and by others. I was finally tired of it all.

The plates began to smash around me. Depression seemed to invade my body like the beginning of a long, dark winter. By that fall of 1992, I felt as if I was getting colder and colder inside every day. My decision to check into a psych ward was based on the simple fact that I had tried everything else that was familiar to me, everything I knew to do, but nothing made a difference.

I had tried to eat better and exercise more. I had fasted and prayed for twenty-one days. I had worked harder and longer than ever. Yet this invasion of frosty hopelessness gained ground. The hospital was a last resort and a dreaded one. When he was in his midthirties, my father died in a psychiatric hospital, and I wondered if I had inherited his fate just as surely as I had been gifted with his brown eyes.

Some of my friends were horrified that as a Christian, I would consider reaching out for this kind of help. They offered the more traditional remedies. Perhaps you have received a similar prescription.

People told me to pray more, confess any unconfessed sin, listen to more praise music, get involved in helping someone who was in a worse state than I was, paste verses of Scripture to the dashboard in my car— the list went on and on. What some of my advisors didn't know was that I had tried all of those things many, many times. I found the list heartbreaking. The implication was clear: the problem was with my spiritual life. That only added to the guilt that I already carried.

My family was very supportive. My mom urged me to have courage to walk through this dark night. She assured me that God was with me and would walk with me every step of the way. I heard her words but they slipped through the cracks of a broken heart.

Just before I was admitted to the hospital in Washington, I was driving home from work when a storm appeared out of nowhere. The sky turned black, and lightning slashed the sky in two. It was as if an aqueduct opened in the clouds and dumped plague–like rain on the tarmac. I thought that it was my fault. I thought that God was angry with me. Even as I write that, I find it hard to imagine myself in such a place, but when I was overwhelmed with guilt and shame, it seemed as if everything that was wrong with the world was *my* fault.

Some of my friends told me that what I was doing was spiritual and professional suicide. They said that when people learned that I had been in a psychiatric institution, I would never be trusted again as a broadcaster or as a believer. I was sure that they were right, but I didn't need a public relations company at that moment. I needed a place to fall on my face before the throne of God and hear what He had to say.

I don't know what I expected from this temporary prison, but I could never have imagined what God would do in me in this place of my undoing. Even as I ran out of mercy for myself, His mercy overwhelmed me, and His compassion began to change my life moment by moment, cell by cell. I discovered that the faint hope I had in the solutions my friends offered me was nothing compared to the absolute hope offered by Christ. I want you to know that Christ has changed my life. It didn't happen overnight. I am not a fan of quick fixes or imagined healing. What Jesus has done for me has totally changed everything in my life. He taught me how to live. That is what I pray for you as we journey through this book together. It is hard to articulate for others that very personal work of the Holy Spirit deep in the internal life. What I can say is that I became convinced of the love of God based on nothing commendable in me; it was based solely on who He is and His commitment to me.

My life changed. It was the beginning of my healing. I began to read God's Word and hear Him talk to *me,* not just find a verse that might encourage someone else. As I read verses that talked about God as Father, I took comfort in that name. It was such a relief. For years I had worked harder and harder to make God like me. Finally I began to understand not only does He like me but how passionately He loves me. As my life moved on I began to see how others struggle with the very same issues.

LONGING TO BE HEALED

In 1994 my husband, Barry, and I were married in his hometown of Charleston, South Carolina. After the wedding we set up home in Southern California where I had enrolled as a student at Fuller Theological Seminary. Two years later I turned forty and became a mom in the same year! Life seemed as if it could not get any better. Then one day I received a phone call from a woman I'd never met asking me if I would be interested in joining a team of speakers who had begun to travel together across America under the banner of Women of Faith. I told her that it was impossible. I had a brand-new baby; I was trying to finish off my degree and barely had the stamina to make it through the supermarket never mind the airport. She was persistent. She told me that although she was putting the team together, my friend Steve Arterburn was the founder, and he had suggested she call. She asked us to pray about it. Even though it seemed an unlikely time to start traveling again, I sensed that God had opened a door and invited me to walk through it.

The combination of being a mom and a women's speaker was a marriage made in heaven for me. The first time that I looked into the eyes of my son I felt as if God had kissed me. I talked to Christian, sang to him, and told him that God loves him in all the moments of his life. In arenas all across the country, I sang the same song to women who came together for two days to laugh and cry, to be encouraged, and to remember or discover for the first time who they are in Christ.

But there was something that I couldn't ignore. I saw it in the mirror. Even though I was several miles down the road on this new way of living, I still reacted badly at times to innocent comments my husband would make, or I felt devalued by an unfavorable review of something I had written or recorded. Those things still pierced my heart and tripped me up.

I saw it in the life of my well-loved son. Even though Barry and I pour our hearts into his life, a comment from another kid at school—"Do you know that your ears are too big?"—can pull the rug from underneath him.

I heard it again and again from women as we traveled from Los Angeles to New York.

We are wounded by life, by each other, by our poor choices or the poor choices of others.

We long to be healed from those wounds, to be free, to be

At moments we experience a glimpse of healing from God

we seem to be able to lose it in a moment—another careless wo

appointment with ourselves or with others. So what are we to d

The key question of this book is this:

Is there lasting healing on this earth, or are we doomed to si

patch ourselves up as best we can until we finally limp home t

arms of our Father in heaven?

I am learning that God's overwhelming love gives us the cou

grace to look at our wounds, no matter how deep or painful the

to bring them out of the dark into His light. Perhaps as you thir

wounds, God's love seems absent. You might ask,

"Where were You, God, when these things were happenin

"Where were You, God, when some of life's deepest wou

being inflicted?"

"Do You see?"

"Do You care?"

These are valid questions and ones we will think about tog

let me say at this point, the same God who holds the univers

loves you. Perhaps that is where you struggle, not wondering v

was, but questioning that God could love you in spite of where

been. I believe that God loves you right now with all that is

your life—externally and internally. That's my life message. It's

that we can never hear too many times, for it contradicts the t

voices of dissent in our heads. Those voices tell us that it can't

true, not with all we know about ourselves and all that has be

us. We know that we have failed to reach God's standards. We

we have failed in our relationships with each other, so how can

pure God possibly love us with no reserve?

It took me a long time to be able to receive God's love, to b

His love is as constant on my bad days as on my ducks-in-a-r

believe it now with all my heart and soul.

That may be hard for you to accept for yourself right nov

I began to ask God to help me understand how we are to

world with all the potential for hurt, pain, and fear and yet e

eep healing that we are able to hold onto, no matter what life throws at
s. I'm realizing that there is a reason that some of us are able to access
nd maintain this healing and move on with life while others lose it like
ie morning mist or are unable to receive it in the first place. It is my pas-
on and heart to study what God's Word says, and then together we can
ve in the liberty of all He promises.

That may seem to be an overwhelming thought in an already over-
ommitted life. As I have said, I don't believe in quick fixes, but I do
elieve that Christ has left a path for us. We can listen to what the world
iys is true about our lives—that we are victims of all that has happened
> us and we can never be free—or we can listen to what God's Word says
true:

> May the God of all grace, who called us to His eternal glory by
> Christ Jesus, after you have suffered a while, perfect, establish,
> strengthen, and settle you. To Him be the glory and the dominion
> forever and ever. Amen. (1 Peter 5:10–11)

: the end of each chapter you will find application points. It is my
ayer that these will help to bring the message of that chapter into focus
r your own life. I want us to walk though these questions together. Take
much time as you need. Don't feel obliged to move on quickly. You
ight want to have a journal with you as you read so that you can write
iwn your thoughts and questions. Also, at the back of the book I have
cluded a Bible study. You can do this by yourself or in a small group.

The Lamb of God gave everything He could give to restore our bat-
red souls and place joy and light back into the darkened rooms of our
arts. It's time to come out of the shadows, remove the masks, and stop
ding. He invites us now to walk with Him, dance with Him, fight side
side with Him, and love with Him. I remain your grateful traveling
mpanion.

Listen to His invitation:

> Come to Me, all you who labor and are heavy laden, and I will give
> you rest. Take My yoke upon you and learn from Me, for I am gen-
> tle and lowly in heart, and you will find rest for your souls. For My
> yoke is easy and My burden is light. (Matt. 11:28–30)

APPLICATION POINTS

- Why have you picked up this book? What do you hope to learn and/or gain from it?

- What feelings that I shared or statements that I made did you readily identify with? Let them be a touchstone for you to look back on and see what healing work God has done in your life.

- What hope and encouragement did you find in this Introduction? Highlight those points so you can easily find them when you need them.

Heartache

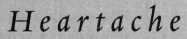

1

BROKEN HEARTS AND
SHATTERED DREAMS

A merry heart makes a cheerful countenance,
But by sorrow of the heart the spirit is broken.
—PROVERBS 15:13

Though I speak, my grief is not relieved;
And if I remain silent, how am I eased?
—JOB 16:6

*I*n this first chapter we will discuss the reality that our hearts have been broken in many ways at many times. We have become used to living with our pain. We almost don't notice it anymore; it's just the way things are. That would be fine if the heartache remained in a back closet somewhere like an old school photo album, but brokenness is never quiet or completely in the past. The pain that we experienced as children or in other relationships as we have grown casts long shadows over the present. It affects the choices we make and the way we respond to life, to God, and to others.

THE UNHAPPY GHOSTS

In a *Christianity Today* article, Tim Stafford addressed the issue of the vast number of people in the church community who are in deep pain. He described them as "unhappy ghosts." That's an intriguing picture. It conjures up images of those of us who are barely there, hovering on the sidelines. We don't leave—perhaps because we have unfinished business, we are immobilized by sadness, or we have nowhere else to go—but we are not really present either. We don't contribute to the life of the church or enter into worship; we are stuck in a no-man's-land of darkness and despair.

Perhaps that's where you are. It might be why you picked up this book in the first place. Your heart is broken, you feel dead inside, but no one else seems to notice your pain.

I have received hundreds of letters from women who feel as if the church or a parachurch organization has let them down. What has been delivered to them falls far short of the advertised special. We are told to come to Jesus and He will carry our burdens, but no one tells us how to do that. If you walk into church next Sunday with a broken arm, chances are, you will be asked several times, "What happened?" But *what if you have walked into church every Sunday for the last ten years with a broken heart and not even one person noticed?*

Then perhaps someone gets up to sing and tells her story of how God met her when she was battered and bruised and now she is whole and happy. You sit and listen. Sure, you are glad for her, but what about you? Her answered prayer makes you feel more alone.

WHAT IS WRONG WITH ME?

I struggled with that awareness when I was cohost of *The 700 Club* with Dr. Pat Robertson. Every day we presented stories of marriages healed, physical health restored, and children redeemed from bad life choices. I interviewed men and women whose lives had been at the edge of a cliff, and then God intervened and directed their steps to a safer path. They were not left with unanswered questions, disappointment, and a broken heart. The stories we told were true, but they were not true for everyone in our audience. In reality they represented the experience of a minority of people.

Marriages are not always restored. The divorce rate in the church rides side by side with the statistics of those outside our doors. People who love and trust God die of cancer every day. Many parents don't live to see their children redeemed from the bad choices they have made.

Not everyone can find a safe place to share a broken heart, a place to receive love, understanding, and care. Most people do not. Watching the joy of those who have received the answer they were seeking from God is an encouragement to many. To others, it is rock salt pressed into an open wound. What compounds the pain is realizing that others do not understand, or hearing them say, "Get over it."

Telling someone who is internally broken to just get over it is as ridiculous as giving a child with a broken leg a Band-Aid. It might seem like an immediate solution, but it won't hold.

LIFE IN THE REAL WORLD

I received an e-mail from a woman who had attended a Women of Faith (WOF) Conference in the spring of 2003:

> Do the cries you hear at the conferences from women's hearts about things that have happened to them in the past or are going on now really hit any of the ladies of WOF seriously? Do you all ever answer any of the notes given to you at these conferences? Do you all ever realize that you may sometimes be the link between life and death in a woman's life at one of these conferences?

I understood her questions. At our conferences we get together for twenty-four hours with thousands of women. We sing together, and it's hard not to be inspired by the sound of eighteen thousand women singing "How Great Thou Art." Each speaker's message is fine-tuned to convey God's love and grace to every woman present. But at 5:30 on Saturday afternoon it's all over. Women leave the arena, pile into waiting cars and buses, and head home. We return to our real lives and the challenges and struggles that exist on a daily basis. In many ways the same thing happens on Sunday mornings. We are buoyed by the atmosphere of faith and community, but then the service is over and life continues. One thing remains apparent: *Broken hearts are much harder to heal than broken bodies.*

We have spent a lot of time in the church discussing physical healing. We are split along denominational lines, with some exceptions, about whether God still breaks into our human experience with miraculous physical healing. That is not the subject of this book. My passion is the realm of broken hearts and crushed spirits.

Can God heal what was broken years ago?

Can God heal a pain that is so old you almost forget where it began?

Can God heal you when you no longer have a prayer left inside you? Can God heal your heart when the unimaginable has happened?

A MOTHER'S CRY

My husband, Barry, had a friend from high school who died in 2002, leaving behind two young children. Her mother is destroyed by this loss, her heart in a million pieces. Imagine, one moment her daughter is fine, loving her family, getting ready for Valentine's Day, and suddenly a strange, strep-type virus robs this young woman of her life in a matter of days. This brokenhearted mother and grandmother came to hear me speak on the Friday night of our Women of Faith Conference. It had been a year since her daughter's death.

"How could God allow this?" she questioned bitterly with tears pouring down her cheeks. "No mother should have to bury her own child. Her children cry for her every night. They want to put on their shoes and join Mommy in heaven. Do you have any idea how that makes a grandma feel?"

GRIEF IS NO RESPECTER OF AGE

The one person who was able to really connect with this grieving woman during that weekend was my six-year-old son, Christian. During the Saturday of the conference, he spent some time with her at her home. He saw a picture of her daughter and asked who it was.

"That's our daughter, Susan. She was a friend of your daddy's."

"Is she not still a friend?" he asked.

"Yes, but Susan is in heaven. She died last year."

"My papa died too," he said.

"I know, darling. I knew him. He was a good man."

"Shall I tell you what happened?" he asked.

"I'd like that," she replied.

"When I came upstairs, he was lying on the bathroom floor beside my mommy. It was like he was sleeping. I sat beside him. I think it helped. Mom and I went to the hospital, but when we got there, Papa was already in heaven. He couldn't wait. My dad didn't get to say good-bye. That must have made him sad. At least I got to say, 'Good-bye, Papa.'"

For a few moments a small child and a grandmother shed tears together—two generations apart but brought together by the bond of a broken heart and a common question, "Why, God?"

What about the woman who e-mailed me, crying out to know if the speaker team at Women of Faith Conferences, of which I am a part, really care about what is going on in the lives of those in our audience? Or is it just talk to sell books or tickets for the next event? Do we deliver our messages of hope and healing, and then return to our hotel rooms, indifferent to the pain that has poured out of open wounds into a sports arena? We care more than I can express in words. Each of us on the team has walked through moments of heartache and devastation. That's why we are committed to extend hope to those who have lost hope. We understand that barren place, for we have been there.

I have wondered what happened to this woman to prompt such a cry from her soul: Had she cried out for help before and been ignored or been perceived as one of those "difficult" women? Perhaps she had lived through the kind of nightmare where everything that you thought you could count on changed in a single day. Had she encountered the bitterness tasted by a man we know by the single name Job? His story is found in the Old Testament but in many ways it reads as if it had been written yesterday. The pain he experienced caused him to wish he had never been born.

A GODLY MAN WAS DEVASTATED

At his lowest, Job was so wretched that he questioned why God ever gave him life in the first place:

> Why is light given to him who is in misery,
> And life to the bitter of soul,
> Who long for death, but it does not come,
> And search for it more than hidden treasures;
> Who rejoice exceedingly,
> And are glad when they can find the grave?
> Why is light given to a man whose way is hidden,
> And whom God has hedged in?
> For my sighing comes before I eat,
> And my groanings pour out like water.

For the thing I greatly feared has come upon me,
And what I dreaded has happened to me.
I am not at ease, nor am I quiet;
I have no rest, for trouble comes. (Job 3:25–26)

We don't know who wrote the book of Job, but whoever wrote it has given us an in-depth account of the unusual life of this man. He had ten children, seven sons and three daughters. He was wealthy, described as the greatest man among all the people of the East. We are told Job was "blameless and upright, and one who feared God and shunned evil" (Job 1:1). In a rare endorsement of a man's character we hear God's personal commendation of Job's life: "Have you considered My servant Job, that there is none like him on the earth?" (Job 1:8).

So what happened? What took this man from the place of acclaim in the courts of heaven to the man who would cry out in such bitter agony, "I am not at ease, nor am I quiet; I have no rest, for trouble comes"?

Here we have a man who lived centuries ago and a woman sitting at her laptop in 2003 separated by time but united in the human experience of suffering and plagued by similar questions:

God, I don't understand.
Is there anyone who will reach into this black
hole of despair and pull me out?
Why is this happening to me?

WOUNDED BY GOD

Let's travel back down the centuries and take a look. It started out as tragedies often do. It was a good day. All Job's children had gathered at his eldest son's home for supper. It must have been a comfort to Job to know that his children got along well with each other, but into the peace of this moment came three of his servants with news that would change everything. As each one told his devastating story, Job realized that businesswise, he was wiped out; his livestock and servants had been slaughtered. While he tried to absorb this information, the one last remaining servant arrived and told him that an unusual wind had attacked the house where his children had gathered. The wind—in what seemed to be an act of vengeance—had battered the house at all four corners and the roof caved in. His children were dead, buried beneath the rubble.

Can you imagine such a personal holocaust? Within ten minutes everything that is precious to you in life is gone. As you try to absorb the horror of losing your livelihood, you hear news that makes that decimation insignificant. Your family, all your children, are dead. Where was God when that was happening to Job?

How would Job have survived if he had overheard the conversation that took place between Satan and God before this personal disaster, realizing that God allowed Satan to do that to him, His faithful servant?

Then the LORD said to Satan, "Have you considered My servant Job, that there is none like him on the earth, a blameless and upright man, one who fears God and shuns evil?" So Satan answered the LORD and said, "Does Job fear God for nothing? Have You not made a hedge around him, around his household, and around all that he has on every side? You have blessed the work of his hands, and his possessions have increased in the land. But now, stretch out Your hand and touch all that he has, and he will surely curse You to Your face!" And the LORD said to Satan, "Behold, all that he has is in your power; only do not lay a hand on his person." So Satan went out from the presence of the LORD. (Job 1:8–12)

"All that he has is in your power; only do not lay a hand on his person." This is a hard passage for us to understand. A God who is good and loving, powerful and just, allowed Satan to decimate His servant. Job's pain was intense. It was the agony that no parent ever wants to face, the death of a child. As I listened to Susan's mom at our conference I heard Job's voice:

"There is no relief for me."
"I never should have been born."
"I will never be all right again."

One thing is crystal clear; people are in deep pain and have been for centuries. Perhaps it's because of the vast cavern that seems to exist between the belief in a good, loving God and the heartache and sorrow that invade the lives of those who love Him. A further death blow is delivered by those we expect to be able to help heal our wounds, yet they often create a deeper pain. Job believed that God was good and just, but how could a good and just God allow Job's children to be killed, his property destroyed, and then to add misery to wretchedness, his own body became so debilitated that it became a prison of pain?

The woman who e-mailed me stands like a sentry at the gate of the arena calling out, "Do you see what's happening? Do you feel the pain? Do you care? We're dying here."

WOUNDED BY THOSE WE TRUSTED

Most of us, thank God, will not live the nightmare of Job. Most of us get to see our children grow and marry. Few of us lose absolutely everything overnight. But many of us face the heartache of longing for connection, for relationship, while feeling desperately alone. The pain seems more intense when we experience that in the house of God.

I love to listen to audiotapes in my car. My mom and my sister regularly send me British comedies and dramas. One of my favorite modern playwrights is Alan Bennett. He is a man fascinated by human nature, and he has a gift that enables him to pull back the drapes for a moment and let us look inside someone else's soul. His monologues in particular permit us to sit with a total stranger for a while and listen in to the person's internal conversation.

One of the most illuminating is about a pastor's wife disillusioned with her husband, with God, and with His people. She wonders, *If God is indeed a loving God, then why does everyone in the church appear to be so miserable? And why, if God sees all, do His people take great pains to hide the truth about their lives from one another?* It seems to her that her husband wears the perspiring mantle of the used car salesman, not quite sure that what he sold you will get you all the way home. She is acutely aware of the disapproval of many of the women in the church. When she tries to arrange the flowers on the altar, they are never quite right. When she undertakes visitation, she doesn't say the right thing. She encounters one slight after another, little wounds that collect in her heart and soul, causing her to close down inside. Brutalized by those who claim to love God, she finally turns away from faith and finds companionship and compassion in the arms of another man.

It's just a play, but when I listened to it for the first time, I wept. I wept because what is fiction in Alan Bennett's play is reality to too many who have been wounded by God's people. It is one of the most painful experiences in life to be isolated or stigmatized by a fellow believer.

SUFFER IN SILENCE

During a radio interview, a woman called in and asked me, "How can God ask me to love others when there are people in my life who have lied about me and hurt me deeply? It would be painful enough if they were unbelievers, but these are people who claim to love God. That's what makes it hurt so much."

Job knew that feeling too. In the second chapter we read, "Now when Job's three friends heard of all this adversity that had come upon him, each one came from his own place—Eliphaz the Temanite, Bildad the Shuhite, and Zophar the Naamathite. For they made an appointment together to come and mourn with him, and to comfort him" (v. 11).

That may well be what they set out to do, but that was not what ultimately happened. It is common in sermons and books to rip Job's three friends to shreds because of their frustration with him and their assumption that there must be some problem in his personal life to have brought such catastrophe on his head. But it's worth noting that when they first saw him, they wept and sat with him for seven days, saying nothing. It was apparent to them that his suffering was unspeakably intense. We would struggle in our culture to find many who would keep silent vigil with us for seven hours, let alone seven days. The trouble began, however, when Job ended his silence. As long as Job was quiet, they were with him, but when he opened his mouth and began to curse the day he was born, that was more than they could handle.

Have you been there? As long as you are silent about your pain, sympathy is given, but if you allow the poison to flow from your wounds, then the raw edges cause others to back away from you or attempt to contain you again. Surely the church should be the place where we can come and let the anger and disappointment flow out of our veins until it is washed away by the blood of Christ.

One of the most poignant passages from the book of Job illustrates the agony of crying out for help, but no one hears you. He was a man who had been there for others when they were in trouble, but no one was there for him.

> Have I not wept for him who was in trouble?
> Has not my soul grieved for the poor?
> But when I looked for good, evil came to me;
> And when I waited for light, then came darkness.
> My heart is in turmoil and cannot rest;
> Days of affliction confront me.
> I go about mourning, but not in the sun;
> I stand up in the assembly and cry out for help.
> I am a brother of jackals,
> And a companion of ostriches. (Job 30:25–29)

I find it hard to read that passage without weeping. I know a little of that despair. During my stay in the psychiatric hospital, I received a letter from a friend that broke my heart. In it he accused me of being used by Satan to discredit God's work. He called me a hypocrite and a liar: "How can you sit on television every day and talk about the miracles that God can do and now you have run away from everything you believe? I thought I knew you. I don't know you at all."

I wept bitter tears when I read those words. I remember lying facedown on the floor, wishing that it would open up and consume me. I felt as if I was in a wasteland surrounded, like Job, by the scavengers of the night. When your heart is broken, you want to be held, to be comforted. You want someone to tell you that everything is going to be okay. When those you turn to for help add to the weight of brokenness, it is hard not to give in to despair.

Add to this weight the pain and woundedness we carry not for ourselves but for those we love. It is a terrible thing to watch our loved ones suffer at the hands of someone else, knowing that there is nothing that we can do to help.

HOW COULD THEY DO THIS?

I am in touch with several pastors' wives whose faith has all but been destroyed by the way congregations have treated them, their husbands, or their children. One woman wrote, "I never knew that I could hate so much, but I do. I have watched the way that my husband's congregation has slowly and methodically annihilated his spirit. When we came to this church, it was with hearts full of love and faith, but as I write to you today, my husband is on anxiety medication and I carry around a lead weight of hatred and unforgiveness every single day."

I read her letter and I heard Job's voice:

> "Why is light given to him who is in misery, and life to the bitter
> of soul?"

WOUNDED BY OUR POWERLESSNESS

For the first few years of Christian's life, Barry and I decided who came into our son's life and who did not. We were with him all day, every day. Then he started school and the circle of those he interacted with became much wider. I had an acute awareness that first day as I dropped him off in his classroom and watched as he found his name tag and sat down at his desk that life had changed for our family. From that point on I wouldn't know all that was said to him or share in all of his experiences. I would not be able to shelter him from hurt.

One day as I waited in the carpool line I saw him standing alone in the playground with big tears running down his cheeks. Parents are not supposed to get out of the cars. We are to wait for a teacher to bring our children to us, but I ignored that and got out anyway. When he saw me, he rushed over and buried his head in my sweater.

His teacher saw us standing there and came over. "He's had a rough day," she said. She told me that an older boy had hurt his feelings.

My first instinct was to find the kid and flatten him. By God's grace I suppressed that desire and headed for home. He was very quiet in the car. I have learned to let him choose his own timing to share what's going on inside. We stopped off at his favorite ice-cream store and sat outside on the grass with our multicolored selections of pure sugar.

"A boy said I had big ears, Mom," he whispered.

"You have perfect ears," I said.

"He said they stick out like wings!"

"They are my favorite ears in the world," I told him.

"Thanks, Mom," he said.

But every now and then I still catch him looking at his ears in the mirror, two years later. Something was etched into his spirit that day that is not so easily erased.

In *Telling the Truth*, Frederick Buechner wrote, "You do not just live in a world but a world lives in you." From the first moment that you opened your eyes and the glaring light of planet earth invaded your mind and soul you have been recording information. Some of it is accurate and factual: "I have brown eyes." Some of it is hurtful: "People would like me more if I was thinner or taller or funnier."

As a parent I ached for my son that day. I felt so helpless to protect him from the inevitable scars that life inflicts. Part of the world of being a parent is walking with our children through the harsher moments in life. We feel as if we should be able to make it all better, and sometimes we simply can't.

I watched Christian one morning as my husband, Barry, was shaving. "Not like that, Dad. You're doing it wrong."

Barry kept shaving.

"Mom, Dad's doing it wrong."

"How do you think he should shave, O Wise One?" I asked.

"He should do it one simple stroke at a time. Look at him! He's always cutting himself."

That's the trouble, though, isn't it? We're always cutting each other or ourselves. We are human and we make mistakes. We have done things and things have been done to us. There is indeed a world inside each one of us. There are moments in life that carve their pictures into our souls: cruel words, heartbreak, rejection, abuse, pain, or loneliness. What comes to your mind when you take time to look at the snapshots that your heart holds, those pivotal moments of sorrow and pain that make you cringe when you remember them?

SNAPSHOTS

I picture a day when I was ten years old. I was at summer camp, and it was parents' day. A girl in my dorm looked out the window and said, "Sheila, there's your dad!" She knew that my dad was dead, but for a moment I forgot and turned to look out the window. Even as my mind caught up with my heart I looked at her, and she was laughing. I felt such a fool, such a lonely fool, that I locked myself in the bathroom and cried bitter tears into a cheap camp towel that offered little comfort.

I picture a day at college. I was nineteen and dating the most handsome boy I'd ever met. I went to his room to return a book that I had borrowed, and as I stood by the window with the sunlight on my face, he said, "You shouldn't stand so close to the window. It shows off your bad skin." I knew that I had bad skin, but I had hoped that it wasn't as bad as I thought. That morning I knew that it was worse than I could imagine, and every time he looked at me that was what he saw. That event affected me for years. I would never sit at an outside table in a restaurant. I looked for dark places to sit and shied away from photographs. I'm sure at times it seemed that I was simply being difficult when I would refuse to get into a shot. No one knew that I was dying inside at the idea of being captured on film, a permanent record of my imperfections.

What are your snapshots? What are the moments that are etched into your soul and psyche and cast such long shadows into the present?

As you consider your life today, do you feel like a ghost weighed down by the shame you drag around with you everywhere you go? Perhaps it's been so long since you felt alive, you can't imagine things changing.

HE STILL CARRIES THE SCARS

When I was thirty years old, I privately believed that I would always walk with a deep sadness inside. I became used to it. It was who I was. Then I read a book by Dr. Henry Cloud called *Changes That Heal,* and something that felt like *hope* began to stir deep inside me. It was very faint at first, then the message got louder and louder. My initial surprise was that anyone would be able to put words to what was going on inside me. I thought that I was the only one who felt as I did.

Then I recognized that I was being shown a way out of the pit. That is my prayer for you. I want you to know that you are not alone, that hope and healing are to be found in Christ. There *is* a way out of your pit. It's not an immediate thing; it is a process, but it is available to you.

You begin by simply being open to healing. I believe that because of God's grace and mercy, you can bring each one of the painful snapshots of your past into Christ's light. You can put them on the table and look at them with Jesus right by your side. That's where you begin. I don't believe that the Holy Spirit simply takes an eraser and removes all the marks of pain from your heart but rather He gives you the grace to face each moment in the company of your Savior.

Christ carried the scars of the Crucifixion with Him as He rose from the dead but the wounds were healed. They were not festering in the darkness. Wounds that are left untreated or covered over don't heal as they should.

I have had the thumb on my right hand broken three times. The first time it happened I was working on a summer youth mission in England and didn't bother having it looked at. The bone healed but it healed crookedly and has remained vulnerable to further damage and pain if someone accidentally twists it.

The wounds on Christ's hands and side healed in such a way that He could offer them to Thomas, the one who doubted, as proof that He was indeed Jesus, the risen Christ. He didn't hide his wounds or have them erased. They are part of his identity.

I will always carry the scar of the loss of my father, but it is no longer a weeping wound. Christ has removed the poison and all that is left is the mark. Jesus wants you to bring your festering wounds into His light so that He can heal them to be touched by others.

There are many negative images to erase along the way, but you can start. You can take just one step and ask God to help you to be willing to have your wounds brought into His healing light.

When I am afraid or uncertain I turn to God's Word.

> You, O GOD the Lord,
> Deal with me for Your name's sake;
> Because Your mercy is good, deliver me.
> For I am poor and needy,
> And my heart is wounded within me. (Ps. 109:21–22)
>
> Restore to me the joy of Your salvation,
> And uphold me by Your generous Spirit. (Ps. 51:12)

Father God,

I thank you for the gift of Your Son, Jesus. I thank You that He embraced His wounds so that I can be healed. Give me grace and courage to bring my wounds into Your healing light.

In Jesus' name, amen.

APPLICATION POINTS

- When, if ever, have you felt like a "walking ghost"? What led to that sense?

- When has a fellow believer been the cause of deep pain? Or when has a brother or sister in Christ not wanted you to speak honestly about your pain?

- I shared some snapshots from my life. What are those moments from your life that are etched into your soul and psyche and that cast their long shadows into the present?

- Hope and healing are to be found in Christ. Finding them does not happen immediately; it is a process. We begin that process by being open to healing. What, if anything, is causing you to be hesitant about starting the healing process?

- Identifying snapshots from your own life is a step toward healing. Share each of those snapshots with Jesus; bring them into His healing light.

2

GOD, DO YOU SEE MY PAIN?

*How long, O LORD? Will You forget me forever? How long will
You hide Your face from me? How long shall I take counsel in my
soul, having sorrow in my heart daily?*

—PSALM 13:1–2

*O LORD, how long shall I cry, and You will not hear? Even cry
out to You, "Violence!" and You will not save. Why do You show
me iniquity, and cause me to see trouble? For plundering and
violence are before me; there is strife, and contention arises.*

—HABAKKUK 1:2–3

*I*f I am going to be willing to open up the most painful parts of
my life to God, I need to know two things.

First, does God see what is going on in my life? Does He see the pain
and how it colors everything that is me?

Second, does He care? How can I open up to Someone who is unaware
or ambivalent about the details of my life? So these are our questions here.

Do You see me, God?

Were You there when I was being hurt?

Do You care?

If You care, then how could You let these things happen?

AN EMPTY GRAVE

On the evening before Easter Sunday, Christian and I make resurrection
cookies. Someone gave me the recipe a couple of years ago, and it is
becoming a family tradition. The ingredients are simple. We take two tea-

spoons of vinegar to represent the liquid that Christ was offered to relieve His thirst on the cross, three egg whites to symbolize His purity, one cup of sugar denoting the sweetness that His life brings to our bitter existence, and a cup of crushed pecans, a reminder of how His body was bruised and broken for us. The oven is heated to 300 degrees, and we spoon the mixture onto grease-proof paper. Once they are positioned in the oven, I turn it off, and Christian takes tape and seals up our oven "tomb." In the morning when we break the seal, the cookies have risen and cracked open, revealing a hollow center.

On Easter Sunday 2003 as Christian was devouring his third cookie, he asked me, "What would have happened if when Mary went to the tomb, Jesus was still in there? Would I still get an Easter basket?"

I smiled at his childlike focus, then asked him, "Do you remember last Easter when we took our dyed eggs into the yard and rolled them down the hill?"

"I sure do!" he replied. "That was cool!"

"Well, when we roll our eggs, Darling, it's to remind us of the stone being rolled away that first Easter morning when Jesus' friends found that the tomb was empty. Without an empty tomb a full Easter basket wouldn't be enough. We would be lost. The whole point of our lives is not just that Jesus died on the cross, but that He rose again."

That is the foundation of all we believe as Christians. If Jesus had remained in the tomb, we would be lost. But we believe that our God raised Jesus from the dead. We believe that Jesus will return one day and take us to be with Him forever. That is, of course, the big, final picture. What about now? We know that heaven is our heritage and destiny, but how does the resurrection of Christ affect the pain we carry on a daily basis? What does a risen Christ have to say to our broken hearts? We know that we will spend all eternity with our Father, but is He paying attention to our lives now? I have received hundreds of letters from women who wanted to know where God was when their lives were falling apart.

- Was God watching when my dad hit my mom, or was He busy trying to handle the situation in the Middle East?

- Did God see when my husband walked out on my children and me, or was He enjoying the praise concert down at the church?

- Did God hear the phone call I received telling me I had breast cancer, or was He at the bedside of someone with more faith than I have?

- Was getting me saved all that mattered to God, and now He's off converting others and I'm on my own?

These questions address the same concern: we believe that God is in control of the world and the universe and Billy Graham's schedule, but what about the very personal circumstances of life today?

Does God see my sick child?

Has God checked my bank balance, and does He remember when the bills have to be paid?

Can God hear the inner cries of despair that hide behind this very "together" smile?

Many women express the same heart cry to me. Perhaps you have been there too. You believe that God is good, but life does not seem to be working right now. You want to be willing to expose your wounds and brokenness to God, but is He too busy to see you? Or could it be that He sees you, but He is too busy with other crises to stop everything else, turn around, and help you? Do you wonder whether the pain that God has allowed into your life is some kind of test to see if you will be faithful to Him when you are suffering? I asked Christian once if he thought that God was kind. He replied, "Well, He made my cat, Lily, so that was nice of Him, but He also made wasps. What was the point of them?"

Does God ever seem cruel or indifferent to you?

IF YOU HAD ONLY BEEN HERE

Two of Jesus' closest friends carried that pain and asked that very question. You may remember the story of Mary, Martha, and their brother, Lazarus. It is clear from the gospel accounts that this family was close to Jesus. One of the accounts in Luke's gospel shows something of the relationship the sisters had with Him.

Now it happened as they went that He entered a certain village; and a certain woman named Martha welcomed Him into her house.

And she had a sister called Mary, who also sat at Jesus' feet and heard His word. But Martha was distracted with much serving, and she approached Him and said, "Lord, do You not care that my sister has left me to serve alone? Therefore tell her to help me." And Jesus answered and said to her, "Martha, Martha, you are worried and troubled about many things. But one thing is needed, and Mary has chosen that good part, which will not be taken away from her." (Luke 10:38–42)

Martha was obviously comfortable enough with Jesus to be able to complain to Him about her sister. There was an ease, a familiarity. Although Mary and Martha are mentioned in Luke's gospel, John's gospel is the only place where we encounter Lazarus. I find the omission of Lazarus's story from the other gospel accounts strange. Surely it was the greatest miracle of all. In calling Lazarus from the tomb back to life we see Christ's power over our most potent enemy, death. In John's gospel, however, we have a clear account of what happened that day: It began with a call for help.

Now a certain man was sick, Lazarus of Bethany, the town of Mary and her sister Martha. It was that Mary who anointed the Lord with fragrant oil and wiped His feet with her hair, whose brother Lazarus was sick. Therefore the sisters sent to Him, saying, "Lord, behold, he whom You love is sick." (John 11:1–3)

The fact that John referred to Mary's anointing Jesus' feet with costly perfume has led some people to confuse her with the woman who anointed Jesus' feet while He was dining at the house of Simon the Pharisee. That woman was described as someone who had lived a sinful life in that town. They were not the same woman. Jesus' feet were anointed twice that we know of: once by the woman whose shame brought her to the feet of Jesus and once by Mary of Bethany. But Mary of Bethany anointed Jesus' feet after her brother Lazarus had been raised from the dead.

Six days before the Passover, Jesus came to Bethany, where Lazarus was who had been dead, whom He had raised from the dead. There they made Him a supper; and Martha served, but Lazarus was one of those who sat at the table with Him. Then Mary took a pound of very costly oil of spikenard, anointed the feet of Jesus, and wiped His feet with her hair. And the house was filled with the fragrance of the oil. (John 12:1–3)

When John was retelling the story of the miracle of Lazarus being raised from the dead, he included the reference to what Mary did for Jesus, even though that part of the story occurred later. The story begins with the sisters' concern for the severity of their brother's sickness.

Mary and Martha must have been very worried about Lazarus to send for Jesus. They knew that many demands were made of Him, that the crowds asked so much from Him. But when Lazarus became deathly ill, naturally they sent word to Jesus, believing that He would come and heal their brother: "Lord, behold, he whom You love is sick" (John 11:3).

THE DISAPPOINTMENT

They waited and waited. Jesus didn't come. After He received the news, He stayed where He was two more days, and Lazarus died. When Jesus finally made it to their house, Lazarus had been dead four days.

As Jesus approached the village, Martha, always a woman of action, ran out to meet Jesus. Standing face-to-face, she said to Him, "Lord, if You had been here, my brother would not have died" (John 11:21). Martha sounded confused and hurt.

Mary stayed in the house until she heard that Jesus had asked for her. She went out to meet Him and fell on her face at Jesus' feet: "When Mary came where Jesus was, and saw Him, she fell down at His feet, saying to Him, 'Lord, if You had been here, my brother would not have died'" (John 11:32). Mary sounded wounded and broken. When she got up and looked in his eyes her question was, "Do you see my pain?"

Martha wanted to know why Jesus hadn't hurried. Mary just wanted to know why He didn't come. She knew if He had been there, the outcome would have been different. The heartache was wondering why Christ did not come when they called Him.

Do you hear your own voice there? "If You love me, Lord, why didn't You come when I called? Do you see the pain I am in?"

WHERE WERE YOU, GOD?

A friend of mine lost her child before her first birthday. As we have talked and walked through the pain and grief together, her honest questions have challenged me.

"I found it very hard to be comforted by God at first," she said. "I could accept comfort from others because they were powerless to prevent her death, but God could have done something and He didn't."

Surely that is one of the greatest obstacles in bringing everything to God. *We are invited to bring our heartache to the One who could have prevented it.*

One of the most painful privileges that I am ever given is to sing at a funeral. In the spring of 2003 I was asked to sing at the service of a woman I had never met. I knew her daughter. She and Christian are about the same age and attend the same school, but by the time Christian started kindergarten, "Sara" (the name has been changed to protect the family's privacy) was already undergoing chemotherapy for a virulent form of cancer. I knew her name well because when the kindergarten moms would gather together once a month to pray for our children and their teachers, we would pray for her, for her husband, and for their three children. Wonderful friends prayed faithfully for her, wept with her, laughed with her—they even wrote out Scripture verses on large sheets of paper and literally wrapped her up in them.

Then the day before I was to leave for a conference, I heard that she had died. One of Sara's friends called from the funeral home and asked if I would sing at her service the next day. I was initially a little reluctant because I felt I would be an intruder at such an agonizingly intimate time for the family.

"I never actually met Sara," I said. "I've talked to her darling daughter when I've taken Christian to school, but I don't know Sara or her husband. Do you think he will be comfortable with my involvement?"

The friend told me that he would welcome it. Sara had one of my worship CDs by her hospital bed, and when the pain became too intense or when she felt afraid, she would put the headphones on, turn on the CD, and lift her hands in worship.

The next day as I stood behind the casket and looked out at those gathered to say good-bye to a beautiful wife, devoted mom, and loyal friend, I experienced one of those moments when I feel as if I am holding two truths in my spirit that seem from a human perspective to be incompatible: A young mom is gone, and God is good.

I sang a song that I had written a few years ago when a dear friend of mine died.

> There is an ache within my soul
> A longing deep as rivers roll
> An ancient song, a song of praise
> To hear Your voice and see Your face.
>
> And I believe that every man
> Is restless till he takes his stand
> Beneath the cross he finds his place
> To hear Your voice and see Your face.
>
> And I will walk upon this earth
> Until my journey finds its end
> Then I will stand by amazing grace
> And hear Your voice and see Your face.

As I mingled with Sara's friends and family before the service began, I heard the same things again and again:

> "She was a wonderful mother."
> "She had such faith right up until the end."
> "She was such a worshiper, even in her pain."

I looked at her youngest child crawling under the sealed casket, blissfully unaware of the fact that her mommy's body lay inside. Sara was a woman who loved God, her family, and her friends. She was young and full of life until this brutal invader destroyed her body, cell by cell. As a church, we prayed for a miracle. We asked God to remove this curse from His child.

The truth is that on the day Sara died, her cancer did completely disappear along with everything else that is broken about us as human beings. Sara was finally free from the pain and disappointment of this life.

Even before she died, God was healing Sara's heart and preparing her for her grand arrival home at last.

BUT WHAT ABOUT THOSE LEFT BEHIND?

They can't hear the sounds of heaven or experience the joy of being in God's presence, free from all pain. There are now empty places at the dinner table and a broken place in every heart. My son said to me one day, "When we die, Mom, let's all do it together." That's not how life works though. There are always those left behind to process the pain and the questions.

My prayer for the children as they grow is that they will know that they can be completely honest with God. They can be angry and sad and confused, and God will not dismiss them.

I heard the children at the funeral sing with those of us who gathered, "You are awesome in this place, mighty God." I have sung that chorus many times, but it has never had the impact on me that it did that day, in that place. It is easy to sing, "You are awesome in this place," when the place in question is a wedding or a heart filled with joy at the goodness of God. But when the place is near the casket of a young mother, then the song comes from the deepest recesses of our souls. By faith it is the marrying of those two seemingly incompatible truths:

1. God is awesome.

2. He allows devastating pain into our lives.

Jesus invites us to come, as we are when we are tired of life and burdened down by the things that make no sense. He calls us to come when we are angry and confused. Jesus calls us to come to Him as a child would to a parent without wondering if he would be welcomed.

COME AS YOU ARE

My mom told me about an incident that happened when she and my dad were dating. They were visiting a new church, and during the service, a young woman got up to tell her story. She said, "You all know that I was pregnant and last week gave birth to a stillborn child, but I want you to know that we are rejoicing, no tears, no sorrow, for God is in control." Mom thought it very strange that this woman was doing well with such a recent loss. After the service she went into the ladies' rest room, and this poor woman was sitting alone in a stall crying her eyes out. *The message she had picked up from this congregation was clear: If you've got good news, we'll rejoice with you; if not, cry alone!*

That was a mandate I had lived by. I assumed that people who watched me daily on television wanted to hear only good news, and so I cried alone. No wonder the woman who joined me for coffee in the mall was surprised to hear that I had just been released from a psychiatric hospital that day. When she had tuned in to our broadcast, she saw a smiling face with a bag full of answers for life's problems, not a woman in pain.

Do you think that's what God wants from you?

Then who would want to come to a God like that?

Who would want to be in relationship with a God who demanded that we cover up all that is true about our hearts?

God is not interested in our cover-ups. In Psalm 145:18 we read:

The LORD is near to all who call upon him, to all who call upon Him in truth.

Isn't it interesting that though God is not like that, we live as if He is? We think that to be a good Christian means to look victorious all the time, ignoring the heartache. Remember, Jesus wept as He stood outside the tomb of Lazarus. He wept for Mary and Martha, and I believe He wept for the mess that this planet had become. It was never supposed to be like that, where sisters would weep at the devastating loss of their brother. Relationships were never supposed to have been broken; children were never supposed to die; mothers were never supposed to be torn away from their sons and daughters. The question is, will you come to God when you believe He could have changed things?

One of the most precious gifts that my son gives me is his trust in the midst of his pain. That comes easily to him when someone else has hurt him, but it is much more difficult when he is angry with me, perceiving me as the one who has inflicted the wound.

On one occasion I told him that if he continued with a certain behavior, I would take his two favorite robots, and it would be up to me to determine when he would get them back. Needless to say, he pushed the envelope to see what he could get away with. I sat down with him and explained that because of his choice, the robots were mine for the day. He was very upset and rude. I informed him that now the robots were mine for two days.

He went to his room, got into his bed, and pulled the covers over his head. After some time he reappeared with a very penitent look on his face.

"Mom, if I am very, very sorry, can I have my robots back?"

"I am glad that you are sorry, Christian, but you can't have them back yet," I replied.

"Pretty please with frosting on," he said.

"No, Darling."

"Then I'm not one bit sorry!" he said as he marched out of the room.

That night was the first night of his life when he went to bed without saying good night to me. I went into his room as he lay with his back to me in the darkness, and I said, "I know that you are angry, Christian, but I want you to know that I love you. I didn't take your robots away to make you miserable, but to help you see that obedience and respect matter. It matters how we treat one another, Sweet Boy."

He said nothing. Sometime later I heard him call for his dad. Barry went to his room, and when he reappeared, he told me that Christian wanted to see me. He was sitting up in bed with big tears in his eyes. He held out his arms. I went over to him and gathered him up in a big hug. He cried and cried.

"I'm sorry, Mommy. I don't want to be naughty. It just keeps happening."

"I understand, Darling, I struggle with that too," I assured him.

Christian was upset with me and yet he longed to be comforted by me.

We are the same with our heavenly Father. Even when we question Him, we long to be comforted by Him. You don't have to wait until your emotions are in check before you come to Him. Jesus wants us to come as we are, broken and bruised with tear-stained faces. We bring together all that is true about us and all that is true about God. Sara's family wept that day as they said good-bye to her, but they stood surrounded by friends and sang, "You are awesome in this place, mighty God."

We are invited to come right now as we are, ragged at the edges, splattered by the mud of life, invited into the very heart of heaven, and called to move close and approach the throne of grace. You don't have to tidy yourself up, clean up your own mess, or wait till you feel holy. Just come now into His presence. Jesus sees your pain and longs to comfort you. As my friend, Barbara Johnson says, "Let God wrap you in his comfort blanket of love."

> Oh come, let us sing to the LORD!
> Let us shout joyfully to the Rock of our salvation.
> Let us come before His presence with thanksgiving;
> Let us shout joyfully to Him with psalms.
> For the LORD is the great God,
> And the great King above all gods.
> In His hand are the deep places of the earth;
> The heights of the hills are His also.
> The sea is His, for He made it;
> And His hands formed the dry land.
> Oh come, let us worship and bow down;
> Let us kneel before the LORD our Maker.
> For He is our God,
> And we are the people of His pasture,
> And the sheep of His hand. (Ps. 95:1–7)

Father,

I praise You today that You welcome me to worship You in spirit and in truth. I don't understand why You allow things to happen that are so painful, but I ask You to teach me to trust You. Thank You that You love me. Amen.

APPLICATION POINTS

- What personal circumstances, past or present, make you wonder if God is in control of the very personal circumstances of your life? If He sees you? If He cares about you?

- "A young mom is gone, and God is good." What difficult, painful, or tragic events in your life have you had to juxtapose next to God's goodness?

- God is awesome—yet He allows devastating pain in our lives. What evidence of God's awesomeness do you see around you? Ask God to open your eyes.

- Jesus wants us to come as we are to Him. We bring together all that is true about us and all that is true about God. List truths about yourself as well as truths about God. To what truths about yourself do the truths about God speak?

3

THE TRUTH ABOUT OUR SHAME

You have severely broken us in the place of jackals,
And covered us with the shadow of death.

—PSALM 44:19

The preacher pulls the little cord that turns on the lectern light
and deals out his note cards like a riverboat gambler. The stakes
have never been higher.

—FREDERICK BUECHNER

Jesus sees our pain, and He invites us to come as we are, so why do we stay away? Why don't we run into His presence and allow Him to love us? Perhaps we stay away because of a deep sense of shame. Shame is different from guilt. Guilt tells us that we have *done* something wrong, but shame tells us that we *are* something wrong. If you feel deep inside that you are unacceptable and unlovable, it is very hard to come out of hiding. The door to God's presence is wide open, but like my son, we hide with the blankets pulled up over our heads. You can hide in a bed or on national television, in a church or in your home. Our cover can be a blanket or a smile. Why do we hide? Perhaps we are ashamed of who we are. So let's look at the weight of shame.

AN OVERCOAT OF SHAME

For years I stayed away from coming to God with an open heart because of the image of myself that I carried with me; it was carved deep into my soul.

Tapes that played over and over in my head told me,

You're not thin enough.
You're not pretty enough.
You're not good enough.
You will never be enough!

I was so used to them that I didn't hear them anymore; they had been there since I was a child. I had the memories of moments that seemed to define who I was, and their voices were powerful and convincing.

THE BEGINNING OF MY STORY

I was born in Cumnock, a small town on the west coast of Scotland. I am the middle child born to Francis and Elizabeth Walsh. My sister, Frances, is two years older; my brother, Stephen, three years younger. Coal mining was the heart and soul of our community, and it claimed the years and lungs of many of the men. They would come home from the Killoch pit encrusted in the pitch-black dust that clung to them, inside and out. Leaving their heavy black boots on the back door step, they would sink into a chair by the fire, waiting for the evening meal, warmed by the flaming black diamonds that they spent their lives excavating from deep inside the Scottish hillside.

As a tomboy child, I was fascinated by the world of the miners. No one in our town at that time had central heating, so everyone depended on coal fires to take the chill off winter mornings and evenings. I remember on school days hugging the covers up to my neck on bitterly cold winter mornings, watching my breath dance in the air like puffy clouds. My mom would call upstairs, "Sheila, are you up yet?" I would put one leg out of bed and stretch until my foot touched the floor so that it would be technically true when I yelled back, "Yes, I am." Finally as I heard her at the bottom of the stairs to my room, I would summon all my mettle and dash out of bed and down the stairs to the warmth of the fire.

Once a week the coal man appeared in our backyard, bent over by the large sack on his back that he would dump into our outside coal cellar. It would be brought in as needed in a small coal scuttle. I was intrigued by the coal man. Even the whites of his eyes were flecked with black dust. It was only when he smiled that a trace of white brought his face to life like a poorly paid minstrel. I determined as a child that there could be nothing more terrifying than spending most of your life under the earth, crawling through small spaces, knees wet, coughing your way to one more meager paycheck. Many of the young men in our town were resolute in their commitment to find a better way to live, but times were hard and jobs were few. One by one, virgin miners were claimed and plunged into the inky darkness.

My father wasn't a miner. He was a traveling salesman. We were not a wealthy family, but there was a lot of love in our home mixed with faith in God and fragile human hopes and dreams. My sister, Frances, was a quiet child, content to sit with one project for hours. I was not. My mom declares that she never sat down until I was five! I was very much a daddy's girl. I loved the adventure of having a father, one who would say yes to things that a mother felt obliged to say no to.

My father and mother were faithful believers, committed to Christ. That was rare when I was a child; less than 5 percent of our population attended church, much less enjoyed a friendship with God. But despite their firm belief in the goodness of God, they were about to face something that would challenge that belief to the core. Like Job, my parents had no warning that their well-lit path was about to suddenly plunge them into a dark ravine. One evening my dad was fine; by the next morning he would never be fine again. A cerebral thrombosis exploded in his brain as he slept, robbing him initially of speech and the ability to use his right side, but ultimately seizing his life. He spent some time in intensive care, fighting for every breath. Then he was moved to a regular ward and began therapy to learn to walk and talk again. When Dad came home, it was clear to us that he was different, but he was still my dad because his eyes had not changed. Then he began to experience storms like the one that bombarded Job's children. Only his storms were in his brain. The damage was huge. It changed the landscape of his personality. He went from being a safe, fun dad to a frightening stranger. The devastation that the storms wreaked was seen in his eyes. The last time that my father looked at me, it was with a look of pure hatred.

When it became apparent to my mom that it was no longer safe to have my dad in the house, he was taken to a psychiatric hospital just outside our town. He never came home again. He died there. If someone had taken a knife and carved his or her initials on my face, it would not have been as devastating as what was carved into my heart and soul.

THE PAIN THAT
FOLLOWS US THROUGH LIFE

Now I am forty-seven years old. It has been twenty years since I left Scotland and moved to America. I live in Nashville, Tennessee, with my husband, Barry, and our seven-year-old son, Christian. The world of coal dust and the icy dread of a pit cave-in are miles away, but I discovered that there are other ways of being thrust into darkness with cold fear as a daily companion. The events of childhood can plunge us into shadowy places because, even though our bodies grow, our spirits still live there, stuck in time. To those around us, it may seem as if we are living in the light of God's grace and love, but we know that deep inside—where no one can see and no X-ray can expose the truth—there is another story, another life we live. *It's the story of the unhappy ghosts, people stuck somewhere between really living and finally dying.*

The path that led me to the front doors of a psychiatric unit began all the way back in that small house in Shankston Crescent in Cumnock, Scotland. I kept a journal during my stay in the psychiatric unit. It was the first time I faced the truth about how my father's illness and death affected everything about me. I wrote, "When I was just a child I learned that love could strip you bare. Can take a bright and hopeful heart and in a moment tear your world apart. No warning bells or neon sign prepares you for the pain of having loved and having lost, and dare we love again?"

I'll never know what went on in my father's heart and mind during the short time he had left to live. He never recovered the ability to speak. But in my mother's life, the tragedy that could have consumed her spirit, by God's grace, only made her faith stronger. She was able to process that this stranger with violent outbursts was not her beloved Frank. She understood the progress of his illness. As a child, however, even though my mother did all she knew to do to heal those wounds, I was left with a well of confusion and unanswered questions.

When devastation meets with childhood, everything changes. Internally it is as if someone takes the canvas of that young life and throws a bag of coal dust over the original artwork. Although my father couldn't talk, he could roar like an animal when he was angry, and he seemed to have the strength of three men when such a rage possessed him. Unlike my mother, I was unable to accurately process the events in our home. I had a few threads of what I believed to be true, and I wove the next twenty-five years of my life out of them. My thoughts were bleak and defensive: *Better behave—even your dad can turn against you. Life is unpredictable—never let your guard down. Don't get angry—anger is dangerous. Nothing is forever. Protect and guard your heart—the less you need others, the better. Make yourself useful to God and His people.*

FACING THE FEAR

In 1992 when I spent a month in a psychiatric unit, I slowly began to understand my own life and why I responded the way I did to God, to others, and to myself. I have always been terrified of anger, beyond what would be reasonable. If I was faced with an angry person, I felt as if my life was in danger. In my mind I knew that was irrational, but in my gut I experienced the terror of a child acquainted with violence.

I remember as a teenager spending the day in Glasgow, Scotland, with my brother. We were walking along the street when a man gave Stephen a pen. Stephen took it and thanked him. The man then told him that he owed him money. My brother, recognizing the scam, refused. The man demanded that he return the pen. Stephen again refused, saying that it was a gift. The man was furious and grabbed Stephen's arm. I screamed. I screamed not as a person trying to get help but as a child terrified for her very life. Stephen returned the pen. I sat on the side of the road and wept. I felt devastated by the experience while my brother thanked God one more time that he was a boy! But I wasn't responding out of a feminine fainting spell. I was recalling the look of hatred that was etched into my heart, and it was life threatening. I thought that I would never be free of this internal terror.

I remember as a nineteen-year-old standing on a bridge in London, England, where I was attending seminary, looking down at the railway tracks, feeling the urge to throw myself off the bridge. I didn't want to die, but I wanted the pain to stop. I was tired of being afraid all the time. I felt a pull toward ending it all, a pull fueled by the belief that I would never find healing on this earth. I couldn't voice those fears to anyone, not even to God. To those around me, I'm sure I seemed like a fairly together person, but in the cellar of my soul another story was going on. The questions that rumbled around the cellar haunted me.

Will I ever be free?
What is wrong with me?
Am I losing my mind?

FACING THE SHAME

For the first time during that month in 1992 I allowed myself to feel what was going on inside and to say out loud what I felt I would not survive. I had built a wall around my emotions, for I believed if I started to cry, I would never stop. The thought of actually dealing with all my questions was overwhelming to me.

One morning my therapist asked me, "What are you so afraid of, Sheila?"

"Right now I'm afraid of what others would think of me if they knew where I am. I'm afraid of what might happen," I said.

"What could happen?" he asked.

"I don't know," I replied. "But I know that it wouldn't be good."

"What's the worst that could happen?" he asked.

His question shocked me. I had no desire to imagine what the worst thing might be. It seemed to me that I had spent much of my life in a committed effort to stay several steps ahead of the worst thing. I didn't answer his question.

"Are you afraid of even thinking about that?" he asked.

I stared at my hands for several moments before I answered: "All my life I have had this horrible feeling that I've done something wrong. When the phone rings, I think it's for me, and I'm in trouble. If someone asks to see me, I have this feeling of dread in the pit of my stomach about what he might want. It's not a rational thing. It's not related to anything I can think of that I might have done. It's not as if I have a secret life and I'm just waiting to be exposed, but that's what it feels like." Sobs began to rack my body. I wrapped my arms around myself. I felt as if I was unraveling.

"Sheila, do you believe that God loves you?" he asked.

"Of course I do," I said.

"Do you believe that God knows everything about you?"

"Yes."

"Then do you think we could ask God to help you face the worst that might happen?" he asked.

"I don't know," I whispered.

"I want to explain something to you," he began. "When tragedy intersects with childhood, there is a lot of damage done. Your father's death when you were just a child has left an imprint on your heart and soul, but it has crushed your spirit."

"I don't know what you mean," I said.

"Think of yourself divided into body, soul, and spirit. After the tragedy of your father's death, your body continued to grow. You are now thirty-six years old. You are a grown woman. You don't have the body of a four-year-old girl. Your soul and your personality continued to grow and develop over the years. What you liked as a child has changed. You've developed your own style. You know the kind of movies you like, the kind of books you like to read, etc. But your spirit, that tender part of you that loves and trusts, that is made to worship God and embrace all the joys and sorrows of life, has been crushed. It is as if there is a rock on top of it."

"That doesn't make any sense," I said. "If that's true, I'm in worse trouble than I think I'm in. Plus, my spirit has grown. I gave my life to Christ when I was eleven. I felt God calling me to seminary when I was nineteen. Did He crawl under the rock to talk to me?"

He smiled at my sarcasm, my weapon of defense.

I continued, "This is just what I expected here, a whole bunch of psycho mumbo jumbo. Why don't you just give me a happy pill, and we can all get back to life as normal? I won't have to rock anyone's boat. I can carry on smiling my way through the next thirty-five years until I get to heaven and this life is finally over!" I buried my face in my hands and wept.

"Do you remember the verse where Jesus said, 'I have come to give you life'?" he asked.

"Yes," I whispered. "I love that verse."

"Do you think the way that you are living is what He meant?"

"I don't know," I replied. "I couldn't work any harder for Him than I have been. I'm at the studio by seven o'clock every morning, and I often don't get home till eight or nine in the evening."

"Jesus said *life*, not a schedule," he stated. "I understand that you have responded to God's call on your life at many points, but often from a place of fear or duty, not from love."

"Are you saying that I don't love God?" I asked.

"Not at all," he said. "I'm saying that there is a place in your heart, a room of pain, where you closed the door a long time ago and threw away the key. It's hard for you to let God love you. It's hard for you to love yourself or let anyone get close to you."

"So what can I do?" I asked.

"We can start by asking God to give you the grace and courage to bring the heartache that no one sees into His light. We can start there."

Even as I am writing about that conversation that took place more than eleven years ago, I remember the terror I experienced as I thought about bringing all that was true about me into the open. We didn't uncover any great secrets. There was no hidden childhood sexual abuse or events that I had completely buried, but what I did discover was that for years I had been in hiding, even though I was a very public person. I was able to identify words that described my inner life: *fear, shame, anger,* and *dread.*

Is that a familiar thought to you? Are you terrified of facing all that's true from your past, convinced it would consume you?

Has the truth about your life dressed you in shame?

Did you experience abuse at the hands of someone you should have been able to trust, and that betrayal has changed the landscape of your life?

Do you overreact in your marriage because of events that occurred long before you were married?

I understand how past pain can crop up years later and intrude in present relationships. I met Barry about a year after my stay in the hospital. When we had been dating for a few months, I broke off our relationship while he was out of town. We spoke on the phone several times. He was upset because the reasons I gave made no sense to him. He suggested that we talk face-to-face when he got back.

On the evening that I knew he was flying in, I suddenly panicked at the thought of a confrontation. I turned off all the lights in my apartment and hid in the bathroom. I heard him ring the doorbell a few times, and I cowered in the bathroom until he left. Barry is not a violent person. He is kind and caring, but something in me, a reaction to the very thought that someone close to me was upset with me, sent me flying back through the years to a terrified little girl who was afraid of her father's anger. I was amazed that a distant memory could still have such power in my life. The trouble is that these childhood wounds are not just memories; they are stamps, imprints on our souls.

In the hospital I faced my fear that my past might consume me, but

I had forgotten that Christ has promised to be with us in the valley of the shadow of death. As I read and reread Psalm 23 I was struck by the promise of the Lord's companionship even in the darkness—*"Yea, though I walk through the valley of the shadow of death, I will fear no evil; for You are with me; Your rod and Your staff, they comfort me"* (v. 4).

FACING THE TRUTH

When Jesus was addressing a group of Jews who had professed a level of belief in Him, He said to them, "You shall know the truth, and the truth shall make you free" (John 8:32).

Free from *what* they asked. They didn't understand what Jesus was talking about. They protested that they had never been slaves, conveniently ignoring their present position being ruled over by a Roman government. Jesus was not talking, however, about political freedom; He was talking about freedom from sin, from fear, from the dark cellars of our lives, freedom from the dictates of our inner events.

Part of my healing was facing everything that was true about my life: why I behaved the way I did when I felt unloved, where the barely repressed anger came from, how I used sarcasm as a shield around my soul, why I felt so alone even in a crowd of friends. In facing these ugly parts of my soul I was able to bring them into the light of God's grace. *I saw that I couldn't be free if I wouldn't face what was true.*

The freedom that Christ offers is the fruit of facing the truth, no matter how ugly we feel it is or how ashamed we feel.

WHAT HAVE YOU BEEN SHAMED BY?

I receive many letters from pastors' wives talking about how difficult it is to be honest about their struggles or the struggles of their husbands or children because of the expectation from their congregations that they should be perfect.

"As I write to you today my husband is on anxiety medication." The woman who wrote this was dealing with the fact that her husband's apparently serene disposition before they came to the church in question now required chemical support; she was also dealing with the humiliation of what she believed that fact said about them as Christians. You may understand that. I do. I take medication for clinical depression. I have since 1992. I made a decision several years ago to be open and honest about that whenever I speak at conferences and churches. I do it not because I'm excited about it but because I want others who struggle under the weight of shame to know that I understand how that feels.

I will never forget an encounter with a woman who was about the age of my mother. She showed me a picture of her daughter.

"She would have been thirty-five this week," she began. "She worked full-time in a large church but had been struggling with depression for some time. She asked the pastor for a short leave of absence to get some help. He told her they didn't believe that a Christian should seek help from a psychiatrist. My daughter killed herself. She loved God but she killed herself."

Too many people do not understand the nature of depression, equating it with a "bad day." Those who speak not always out of a lack of compassion but out of a lack of understanding have inflicted much cruelty.

I know how hard it is to see the look of disapproval, disappointment, and dismissal in the eyes of others. People have told me that I shouldn't be in public ministry until I'm "fixed." People have questioned my very faith in God. Some comments are intentionally cruel; others are spoken out of misunderstanding about the nature of brain chemistry. Every single time that I speak—whether it's in a church in the poorest area of town, an arena at a Women of Faith Conference, or the ritziest country club in California—I hear the same things: "Thank you for saying that you can love God and still take medication." "Thank you for bringing my private shame into God's light."

What have you been shamed by?

Perhaps you struggle with depression.

Perhaps you are divorced.

Perhaps you still can't get over abuse that happened years ago.

Perhaps you are overweight and you feel dismissed by what people see and how they respond to you, which only reflects what you already feel about yourself inside.

It doesn't matter what your story is; the pain and the shame are the same. When we accept that shame and live in it, we join the ranks of the unhappy ghosts who may be in a large crowd but feel totally alone.

My loneliness was based on my belief that if you knew what was really true about me, you wouldn't like me. I knew that because I didn't like me. At my core I was ashamed of my sadness. Jesus had died for me, so what was wrong with me? Why couldn't I just live in the joy of that?

GOD MEETS US IN OUR MESS

The best dog I've ever had was a West Highland white terrier called Charlie. I got him in 1990. When he was just a few weeks old, I took him with me to the Christian Broadcasting Network studios to show him to our viewers on that day's show. On the way home I stopped by the supermarket to pick up a couple of things. I decided that it would be easier to leave Charlie in the car by himself for ten minutes than try and wrestle with bananas, milk, and a wiggly puppy.

When I got back to the car, I couldn't believe what I saw. I realized that day that when this little dog got nervous, his bowels surrendered all they held. Unfortunately they held a lot. He had then proceeded to dance around in his mess, distributing it equally over all four leather seats. It's one of the worst things I have ever seen. I looked at his little face, bright eyed, longing for love and companionship, his tail wagging back and forth, back and forth, further distributing his gruesome gift to every window.

It took me quite some time to clean up everything, but that night as I sat by the fire with a freshly bathed puppy fast asleep in doggy dreamland, I was participating in what was about to happen to me. It was a foreshadowing of a date I had with God just two years later. It wasn't on my calendar, but it was on His. When everything in my life fell apart, God met me in the midst of the mess and lovingly held me, cleaned me up, restored my soul, and lay me down to rest. I am amazed by His grace.

What is your story?

Have you ever taken time to write down the inner events of your life and face them, staring up at you in black and white?

Are you afraid to acknowledge how you feel inside because as a Christian, you shouldn't feel that way?

Do you feel shamed by the truth of your story?

Do you believe God is big enough and loving enough to handle whatever you might put down on paper?

Do you think you're the only one who has felt those feelings or thought those thoughts?

Remember Christ's liberating invitation: "Come to Me, all you who labor and are heavy laden, and I will give you rest."

That's where I was, laboring, heavy laden, and needing rest.

I was amazed to discover the identities of some of my fellow patients who were in the psychiatric unit at the same time I was; they were traveling companions who were learning to walk in truth. More than that, they were people who were tired of pretending. They were weary.

They were tired of pretending that they were fine when they were not fine. They were tired of grabbing on to healing that left as quickly as it arrived.

We were all at the end of the road. This time we wanted God to do something permanent in our hearts or nothing at all.

There was a pastor who was exhausted from trying to persuade his congregation how much God loves them, perhaps because he was unable to believe it.

A beautiful girl who daily cut into her flesh, hoping that the physical pain would distract her from the unbearable reality that her father, who was an elder in their church, had sexually abused her as a child.

A missionary who was embittered from years of service to a God she did not like.

A mother who was worn out, not from raising her three children but from carrying the one hundred extra pounds on her frame as a wall between her and the world.

A teacher who was loved and respected but couldn't believe any of the kind things said to him because he had never heard a kind word from his own father.

We were an odd bunch—religious television host, pastor, daughter, missionary, mother, and teacher. The common thread was this: we all loved God, had a relationship with Him, but were prisoners of past events and inner darkness.

Is that your story?

You've tried to put it all behind you. You reason with yourself, "I have a good life now. There is no need to keep dragging this old baggage around." But no matter what you try to do, the baggage remains yours. So, are you stuck forever? Will this remain your story and nothing can change it?

As I said earlier, I used to believe that was true, but I don't believe that anymore. I believe that we can invite Christ into dark rooms and secret places and pull back the drapes to let the light of His love burst into our prisons and set us free.

I wouldn't even pretend to understand your particular pain. The deep wounds that you carry inside are very personal. But this book is not about what I believe simply based on my life experiences. This book is about what you and I can stake our lives on, revealed through the person of Christ and the depths of God's Word.

> You, who have shown me great and severe troubles,
> Shall revive me again,
> And bring me up again from the depths of the earth. (Ps. 71:20)

In his book *Telling the Truth*, Frederick Buechner described Sunday morning as one of the least honest times in the Christian community. Often it begins in the pulpit as we read at the beginning of this chapter:

> The preacher pulls the little cord that turns on the lectern light
> and deals out his note cards like a riverboat gambler. The stakes
> have never been higher.

Will he dare to tell the truth or only what he believes his people want to hear? Will he speak the truth, the questions we wrestle with, the shame we carry or just present the answer? That's the temptation, isn't it? We ignore the nagging questions and pretend to be living in the answers. We tidy ourselves up for each other and for God, but inside we feel as if we are dying.

That is why I am so grateful to be part of the Women of Faith team. We tell the truth to our audience about our lives, the pain, the doubt, and the fear. We don't tell everything, of course. Some things infringe on the privacy of those we love and there are those in our families who don't want to share their lives publicly; but where we feel that our own story can help and encourage another, we gladly share it. Barbara Johnson has buried two sons, and Marilyn Meberg has lost a daughter. Thelma Wells has experienced incredible racial hatred and prejudice, and Patsy Clairmont spent years housebound due to agoraphobia, chain-smoking cigarettes and downing pots of coffee. Luci Swindoll has seventy years of life experience under her belt with all the joys and disappointments those years have held.

We believe that Christ invites pastor, teacher, mother, worker, student, child, drug addict, alcoholic, adulterer, and us to come as we are and experience His forgiveness and His grace. Facing the truth means that we bring the sins for which we are responsible to the Cross and live in the light of confession and forgiveness, for we have been told, "If we confess our sins, He is faithful and just to forgive us our sins and to cleanse us from all unrighteousness" (1 John 1:9).

Whatever your story is, whatever you have done or whatever has been done to you, healing begins by bringing everything that's true out of the darkness into the cleansing embrace of the grace of God.

Are you willing to face the truth?

You will not face it alone. God's grace will enable you, His strength will keep you, and His love will hold you.

"What then shall we say to these things? If God is for us, who can be against us? He who did not spare His own Son, but delivered Him up for us all, how shall He not with Him also freely give us all things? Who shall bring a charge against God's elect? It is God who justifies. Who is he who condemns? It is Christ who died, and furthermore is also risen, who is even at the right hand of God, who also makes intercession for us." (Rom. 8:31–34)

Come as you are; you are loved by God.
Face what is true.

"Behold, You desire truth in the inward parts,
And in the hidden part You will make me to know wisdom." (Ps. 51:6)

✦

Father,

Thank you for your love that calls me to face the truth about my life without the fear of being turned away. I bring my shame to you in Jesus' name. Amen.

APPLICATION POINTS

- What events from your childhood have cast your spirit into a shadowy place where it's stuck in the darkness? What tragedy, if any, intersected with your childhood and did great damage? What person(s) and/or event(s) shamed you and taught you not that you *did* something wrong, but that you *are* something wrong, someone unacceptable and unlovable?

- If you're a believer, you may have responded to God's call on your life—as I did—from a place of fear or duty, not out of love for your heavenly Father. If that's the case, give an example or two. Also, consider whether it's hard for you to let God love you and whether it's hard for you to love yourself or let anyone get close to you. What may be behind those fears?

- Are you terrified of facing all that's true from your past, convinced that it would consume you? Do you think that if you started to cry, you might never stop? Stating these fears—and sharing them with God—can lessen their power. Take some time to pray.

- Think about—and even write down—your life's key events, internal as well as external. Do you believe that you have to clean yourself up before you can go to God? (You don't!) Do you believe that God is big enough and loving enough to handle whatever is on your list? (He is!)

- What, if anything, is keeping you from inviting Christ into the dark rooms and secret places of your life and heart and letting the light of His love burst into your prison and set you free?

4

THE LIES WE HAVE BELIEVED

Do not be conformed to this world, but be transformed by the renewing of your mind, that you may prove what is that good and acceptable and perfect will of God.

—ROMANS 12:2

When he [the devil] speaks a lie, he speaks from his own resources, for he is a liar and the father of it.

—JOHN 8:44

*J*esus invites us to bring our shame to Him and be healed. We have a Savior who loves us even as we bring the worst that is true about us into His light. Not only do we have a wonderful, redeeming Savior, but we have an enemy who wants to keep us shackled to our shame and living in darkness. God's Word tells us that he is a liar, but too often the things he whispers to us sound so familiar, we believe them to be the truth. Being healed and free to live in Christ calls us to be aware and awake, so let's examine our enemy and how he operates.

NEVER ENOUGH

I remember my first professional photo shoot for an album cover. (Yes, it was an album back then!) They brought in a makeup artist, a hair stylist, and a wardrobe person. They descended upon my poor Scottish frame, and when I emerged several hours later, I didn't recognize myself. I looked very glamorous; I just didn't look like me! When the photos came back to the record company, the cover designer fixed any remaining imperfections by computer with software called Photoshop. The designer got rid of any little wrinkles, gave me false nails, and made my rear end look smaller! If only life was that easy!

When I toured across America with that album, I know people must have looked at the front cover, looked at me, looked at the front cover again, and gone into immediate prayer and fasting that God would deliver me from whatever tragedy had decimated my once-perfect physique! Ironically all this attention to making sure my image was perfect made me feel even more insecure about my physical appearance. The message I picked up was loud and clear: in my true form I was not acceptable; I needed repackaging.

WHO IS THAT GIRL IN THE MIRROR?

As a teenager, I was not attractive. I struggled with my weight. Scottish schoolgirls are a hardy bunch. It is very windy on the west coast where I grew up, and I think we ate more for ballast than pleasure! I remember when I was fourteen; I picked up an American magazine in a store because one of the headlines read, "Do You Know Your Ideal Weight?" I looked to see what I should weigh at five feet four inches tall, and the discrepancy between the ideal and the reality was quite a vast cavern. I was horrified. I went to a local drugstore, Boots the Chemist, and bought a pack of unappetizing-looking-meal replacement cookies. I had them for dinner that night, much to the alarm of my mother, who thought I looked just lovely the way I was. The flavor was abysmal. It was like eating two old dry sponges. I weighed myself the next morning, assuming that during the night, the sponges would have done their work and soaked up all excess fat. But I had actually gained a pound!

My skin was a problem as well. My face produced enough grease to fry a hearty breakfast for a family of four. I had lovely dark hair—yes, I said dark—but because my mother didn't have much discretionary income, when I got my hair cut she wanted her money's worth, so my bangs were cut so short I had brain freeze on a regular basis. All in all when I looked in the mirror, I didn't like what I saw. No one ever actually said to me, "You don't fit in—you're not attractive enough to be one of the cool girls," but I watched the way life works in our world, and the silent messages were loud and clear. I bought into the belief system of our popular culture because it made sense to me. I looked at the magazines and I looked in the mirror and I didn't look like those girls. They were thin with wind-blown hair, perfect skin, perfect smiles, and perfect boyfriends.

And I bought into the not-so-subtle lies behind the pictures.

> *Being thin will make me happy.*
> *Clothes are an effective anesthetic against internal pain.*
> *If I wear something new, I'll feel more acceptable.*
> *If I can just find the right man to marry, then I will be happy.*
> *If others approve of me, I'll feel better about myself.*

I didn't want to look better just to fit in more; I thought that having the outside of my life look good would heal the insecurity that I carried inside.

MASKING THE PAIN

When I was a student at university in London I ran up quite an amount of store-credit-card debt trying to make myself feel of some worth. I was sure that if I looked better on the outside, then I would feel better on the inside. It didn't work, but I felt compelled to keep trying. It was a punishing cycle of effort and disappointment because no matter what I looked like on the outside, I still felt the same about myself on the inside.

The last time my father looked at me, it was with rage and raw hatred, and that image burned itself into my soul. The one man that I looked to as a child to receive unconditional love and approval was unable to give that. What I read into his look was that I was disappointing and unacceptable. More than that, it seemed as if he hated me. The confusion and damage in his brain caused by a thrombosis caused him to strike out in a myriad of ways, and I was the only one of his three children that he struck out at.

The brain is fascinating and complex. My father's doctor explained to my mom that at times when there is damage to a particular part of the brain, emotions are reversed and the one you are closest to is the one you hit out at. I was a tomboy and had a great affinity with my dad. The thrombosis left him paralyzed down the right side of his body, so he had no use of his right arm. He dragged his right leg, and the right side of his face was twisted. After he came home from the hospital, he had good days and bad days, which for a child was confusing. Some days he would smile at me, a strange, lopsided smile but with the same twinkle in his eyes. On bad days he would pull my hair or spit at me and growl like an animal. I hate writing this about my dad. I feel as if at a gut level I am betraying him. But I know that was not my real dad. That was a man trapped inside a broken body with fierce storms blowing through his mind. When the storm passed, he would sit with his head in his hands and weep.

I know enough about my dad from my mom and others who loved him and were close to him before his illness to recognize that if his nightmare could in any way be used to help another person make sense of the heartache of childhood, he would want that to happen. My father had a heart for God and a heart for those who are broken. I look forward to the day when I can tell him face to face how God took the pain of our lives as a family and brought healing to so many. Children take two and two and make twenty. We take what happened to us and reach dire conclusions about what that says about us.

When I looked in the mirror as a young woman, I saw damaged goods.

When you look in the mirror, what do you see?

Do you see a woman who is worthless because of how someone else used you?

Do you see someone who disgusts you because of your lack of self-control over habits that torment you?

Do you think, *If only this was different or that could change,* you would feel better about yourself?

I discovered that all the things I thought would make a difference in my life didn't help at all.

I got thinner. I let my hair grow, and my skin cleared up. I had a job with a generous clothing allowance, but inside I still felt like the same ugly little girl who didn't fit in. I realized I had spent years believing a world of lies.

As women, we live in a culture that exalts glamour over character. Young women starve themselves in an attempt to be as stick thin as the models they see in magazines and on television. Much of the allure is a myth. The models have a posse of stylists and make-up artists retouching their look between every shot and then correcting anything that appears to be less than perfect by computer. Many stay thin by smoking or using drugs. The marketing message behind this billion-dollar industry is, if you look like this you will be happy, fulfilled, successful, the envy of every other woman in the room and the desire of every man. The implication is that you are worth something; you have value. If you don't look like this, you have little value or voice in our society.

We are tormented by these lies, and Satan uses them to twist his knife into our souls. Behind every lie on Madison Avenue is a lie from the pit of hell. Remember the text we read at the beginning of this chapter? "When he [the devil] speaks a lie, he speaks from his own resources, for he is a liar and the father of it." Our world, internal and external, is filled with the lies of the enemy of our souls who does not want our broken hearts to be healed by the One who is truth.

A BIGGER LIE

But behind the lies of our culture, I had bought into a much more damaging well of deception. I bought into the lies that would keep me from the only One who can heal me—the greater lies that tell us that God's love for us is based on our performance.

Within the church we have our own peculiar list of damaging lies:

If I read my Bible regularly, God will love me more.
If I can stop these bad behavior patterns, God will love me more.
If I feel close to God, He is close to me.
If I feel far away from God, He is far away from me.
If I live in a way that makes God happy, He will answer my prayers.
If God doesn't answer my prayers, there is something wrong with my faith.

Those lies have kept many of us in lonely bondage for years.

YOU ARE NOT WORTHY OF GOD'S LOVE

I received an e-mail from a woman who was obviously in terrible pain. She had been sexually abused by a family member as a child and had recently married. Her husband is training to be a pastor. She wrote that no matter how things seem on the surface, she feels disconnected from God, lost, alone, as if her prayers go no higher than the bedroom ceiling. She told me that she feels like a hypocrite.

I ached for her as I read her words. I heard the cry to be at peace, but the thunderous voice of condemnation in her head told her that things will never change, that she isn't worth God's time because she'll just mess up again.

Do you hear that voice in your head too?

I listened to that voice for years and thought that I would never be free of its convincing clamor.

THE BEGINNING

To understand how we can be free from some of the lies we believe about ourselves, we must understand where our bondage began. Before we can rest in the truth, we have to recognize the lie and where it started.

God Speaks

> Then the LORD God took the man and put him in the garden of Eden to tend and keep it. And the LORD God commanded the man, saying, "Of every tree of the garden you may freely eat; but of the tree of the knowledge of good and evil you shall not eat, for in the day that you eat of it you shall surely die." (Gen. 2:15–17)

The Liar Speaks

> Then the serpent said to the woman, "You will not surely die. For God knows that in the day you eat of it your eyes will be opened, and you will be like God, knowing good and evil." (Gen. 3:4–5)

This text illustrates the hellish audacity of the enemy of God as he directly contradicts God's words to his beloved Adam and Eve. They are the only two human beings in all of history who knew what it was like to live life as God intended it to be lived. Only these two people have experienced a world where there is no shame, no anger, no anxiety, no pain, physical or spiritual, no self-doubt, no fear, and no darkness. They lived in a perfect world. They walked and talked openly with God. They were naked and pure. They loved each other perfectly. They slept the innocent sleep of newborn babes. Then one thing changed all of that. In one moment they lost everything, and the cost was felt not only in Eden but also in heaven and in hell.

They surrendered to a lie. God told them not to eat from the Tree of Knowledge of Good and Evil, "for in the day that you eat of it you shall surely die." Those were clear instructions from a loving Father passionately concerned with His children. Into the perfection of the Garden of Eden, Satan appeared, approaching Eve as a serpent. Today we think of serpents as threatening creatures, but there would have been nothing intrinsically alarming to Eve about the approach of a serpent, no negative connotation then, because all of the animals lived in harmony. The danger was not in his form but in the lie he brought with him.

"You will not surely die," the serpent said to the woman. He contradicted God, and he offered Eve power: "You will be like God."

There is something in us that wants to see what else is out there for us. The pull to sin is so strong that Eve would ignore the mandate of her Father to investigate the claims of a serpent.

The very temptation that caused a riot in heaven caused chaos on earth. Eve believed the lie. She reached out and took the apple, and in that moment she chose to accept the words of the serpent over the word of God. Scripture says that she was "deceived." We refer to what happened as the Fall. What an understatement! It was the greatest crash that this world will ever know. We get caught up in the events of our world, the stock market, house prices, interest rates, homeland security, but they are whispers compared to the wail that must have gone up from the Garden when Adam and Eve realized what they had done. Satan had pulled them into his own story, and they saw themselves as naked and lost.

The Fallen One

How you are fallen from heaven,
O Lucifer, son of the morning!
How you are cut down to the ground,
You who weakened the nations!
For you have said in your heart:
"I will ascend into heaven,
I will exalt my throne above the stars of God;

I will also sit on the mount of the congregation
On the farthest sides of the north;
I will ascend above the heights of the clouds,
I will be like the Most High." (Isa. 14:12–14)

Isaiah actually wrote those words about the king of Babylon, who had set himself up against God, for he recognized the power behind this king's blasphemy. He heard the voice of Satan. Jesus revisited them in Luke's gospel, referring to Satan: "I saw Satan fall like lightning from heaven" (10:18).

The spirit is the same, and it comes from only one place, from the pit of hell.

That is the root of all of our heartache and trouble. Satan is a liar, and we have believed his lies. His corrupt passion is that we would fall for his sweet words, which seem to offer freedom, rebel against God as he did, and then suffer the eternal damnation and separation from God that he will suffer. He hates us. He hates anyone and anything that God loves.

Have you said any of these things to yourself?

I'm not worth God's love.
I've failed too many times.
I'll talk to God when I've cleaned up my act.
God would love me more if I could be like her.
I'm not enough.

Let me suggest something to you: These aren't your thoughts. They are the enemy's lies. Each one of these beliefs that has disabled so many women is contradicted again and again in Scripture:

[Jesus said,] "As the Father loved Me, I also have loved you; abide in My love." (John 15:9)

The LORD has appeared of old to me, saying:
"Yes, I have loved you with an everlasting love;
Therefore with lovingkindness I have drawn you." (Jer. 31:3)

The LORD is near to those who have a broken heart,
And saves such as have a contrite spirit. (Ps. 34:18)

Now this is the confidence that we have in Him, that if we ask anything according to His will, He hears us. (1 John 5:14)

There is a world of comfort and truth in just these four verses. Think about what we are given here!

We read that *Jesus loves us as the Father loves Him.* Think about that! Jesus loves us with the same eternal passion and commitment, the same perfect love, that God the Father has for Him.

God's love and kindness are everlasting, not temporary "rewards" He gives us for our good behavior or our ability to keep all the rules.

God does not despise us when we are down and broken; rather, He draws close to us.

We can have the absolute assurance that *when we draw close to God, longing for His will in our lives, He hears us.*

We can read these words again and again, but it's hard to let their truth penetrate our hurt or climb over our defensive walls.

GOD'S DRAMATIC SHOW-AND-TELL

Into our brokenness stepped the Lamb of God. God knew that we wanted to know what perfect love looks like, but where on earth could we find that love? God decided to show us. So unto us a Child was born:

For unto us a Child is born,
Unto us a Son is given;
And the government will be upon His shoulder.
And His name will be called Wonderful, Counselor, Mighty God,
Everlasting Father, Prince of Peace.
Of the increase of His government and peace
There will be no end,
Upon the throne of David and over His kingdom,
To order it and establish it with judgment and justice
From that time forward, even forever.
The zeal of the LORD of hosts will perform this. (Isa. 9:6–7)

GOD REPAINTS THE PICTURE OF LOVE

Everything about the Christ child opposed the spirit of Satan. Do you remember what Paul wrote to the church in Philippi?

> Let this mind be in you which was also in Christ Jesus, who, being in the form of God, did not consider it robbery to be equal with God, but made Himself of no reputation, taking the form of a bondservant, and coming in the likeness of men. And being found in appearance as a man, He humbled Himself and became obedient to the point of death, even the death of the cross. Therefore God also has highly exalted Him and given Him the name which is above every name, that at the name of Jesus every knee should bow, of those in heaven, and of those on earth, and of those under the earth, and that every tongue should confess that Jesus Christ is Lord, to the glory of God the Father. Therefore, my beloved, as you have always obeyed, not as in my presence only, but now much more in my absence, work out your own salvation with fear and trembling. (Philippians 2:5–12)

I think that is one of the most glorious passages in Scripture. Don't rush over it. Consider Him!

> He made Himself nothing.
> He humbled Himself.
> The One who had the right to stand on this earth and demand that every creature should worship Him got down on His knees and washed His friends' feet.

In Satan we see all that is wrong with the world, and in Christ we see how God will put it all right. This may seem eons away from your world right now, but it is the heart of all that is wrong in us. It's only when we see how much trouble we are really in without Christ that we can celebrate His restoration. It's my passion that we won't live one more day under Satan's lies, but that in Jesus' name we will be free.

> Satan tells us: "You are weak!"
> Jesus tells us: "In Me you are strong!"

Satan tells us: "You are lost!"
Jesus tells us: "In Me you are found!"

Satan tells us: "You are a victim!"
Jesus tells us: "In Me you are a victor!"

Satan tells us: "You are ugly, inside and out!"
Jesus tells us: "You are beautiful."

Satan tells us: "You will never be healed!"

Isaiah tells us of Jesus: "He was wounded for our transgressions, He was bruised for our iniquities; The chastisement for our peace was upon Him, And by His stripes we are healed" (Isa. 53:5).

What are our wounds? Our wounds are the aching void that existed between God and man. Our wounds are the devastating lies we have believed that even after a bridge had been built between God and us, we should stay on our side because of the brokenness that exists in us. Our wounds are the lies that we can never be healed and we can never be loved.

Surely it is time to answer the age-old question,

WHO ARE WE GOING TO BELIEVE?

Satan is a liar; he is by nature an accuser. Let's take a look at a passage from Zechariah and see how he has always positioned himself in the place of the accuser. We are not alone in our feelings of condemnation. Many have been there before us.

Then he showed me Joshua the high priest standing before the angel of the LORD, and Satan standing at his right hand to accuse him. The LORD said to Satan, "The LORD rebuke you, Satan! The LORD, who has chosen Jerusalem, rebuke you! Is not this man a burning stick snatched from the fire? (Zech. 3:1–2 NIV)

In this vision from the prophet Zechariah, Joshua the man stood as a figure representing all of Israel, God's chosen people, who messed up time after time. Satan stood at Joshua's right hand, which was the side where an accuser would stand in a court of law ("Set a wicked man over him, and let an accuser stand at his right hand" [Ps. 109:6]).

Satan knew God's plan for Israel, and his intent was to thwart it. But notice who sprang to Israel's defense—the Lord! A traditional defense lawyer would attempt to prove that his client did not commit the crime in question—or at least create reasonable doubt about it. Christ did not do that. He knew we were guilty and deserved the worst that God could mete out to us. What Christ did was far more spectacular; He took our place. He took our punishment..

Israel as a nation could not save itself. The people continuously failed to keep God's law; they blew it again and again. Using the symbol of the man Joshua, the angel of the Lord described him as a stick (NIV) snatched from the fire, a sure foreshadowing of what is true for you and me today. We stand before God as those who cannot save ourselves. Satan would stand at our right side as our accuser, but look at who stands as our defender. Remember?

Who shall bring a charge against God's elect? It is God who justifies. Who is he who condemns? It is Christ who died, and furthermore is also risen, who is even at the right hand of God, who also makes intercession for us. (Rom. 8:33–34)

While Satan would stand at our right side and condemn us, Christ stands at the right hand of God and intercedes for us. What a miracle! What a gift of grace! Can you get a picture of this in your mind's eye? It is a picture worth carrying with you at all times because it is the truth of what is happening in the spiritual realm.

See yourself standing with all your faults and failures, and Satan is whispering into your right ear:

> "You did it again!"
> "You'll never change."
> "You're a hypocrite!"
> "God couldn't love you!"

Then picture Christ, standing beside His Father, praying for you:

> "I love her, Father."
> "She is my heart."
> "I paid for her sin."

Never forget that Jesus Himself stands beside His Father calling out your name. You might want to write out that passage or commit it to memory so that the next time waves of condemnation wash over you, you can deflect the lies with the Word of God.

You can say, "Be quiet, Satan! Listen, do you hear who is praying for me?" That will send him fleeing from you.

That is the reality of the situation in heaven: Jesus is interceding for us. The reality of the situation here on earth is that Satan is constantly standing at our right hand, lying to us and about us, spitting the ice-cold venom of hatred at those God loves. Recognize the source. Remember who he is and resist him in Jesus' name.

Let's go back to the desperate words from the woman who wrote to me and stand them side by side with God's answer to her cry, to our cry. She feels lost, separated from God, but we read that nothing can separate us from His love. She feels condemned by her lack of faith but Paul reminds us that Christ Himself is interceding for us!

When we hear that voice of condemnation, one thing is absolutely clear: it is not from our Father; it is from our accuser. It's easier to grasp that in our minds than to let it take root in our hearts. We are so used to the voice of condemnation, and it never sounds like the enemy; it just sounds familiar. It sounds like us. That's why we have to make a conscious choice when we hear that voice to stop and remind ourselves, "This is not God's voice; this is the voice of the one who deals in the big lie. Satan says we are not worth healing, but the Lamb of God gave His life because we are."

LIFE IN THE FUN HOUSE

Twice a year a carnival comes to the parking lot of a mall in our area of Nashville. Christian loves the rides, Barry loves the greasy food, and I love trying to win one more goldfish that will live for twenty minutes and then be declared "a floater" by our matter-of-fact son. In the spring of 2003 we saw the garish lights of the carnival as we drove past the mall one evening. We pulled into a parking spot, bought a book of tickets for the rides, and began our usual pursuits. Christian wanted to try out the fun house so we surrendered nine tickets and went in. The first thing I encountered was a mirror that made me look twelve feet tall and three inches wide, then one that reduced me to the size and shape of a pregnant toad. Moving on, we tried to walk on the path in front of us, but it was in constant motion, making it very difficult to balance.

That is the world that you and I live in. Things that should be straight are crooked, and when we look in the mirror, we see a caricature of God's perfect plan. What we need to remember is that for now, we are in this terrestrial fun house, this land of distortion. We need to keep before us a vision of what is true.

When Adam and Eve looked in the mirror of their world, the picture was clear. They looked exactly as God intended that men and women should look, but the mirror has been broken and broken glass cannot give a true reflection. There will be a day when all is put right again. Until that day we are called to be wise and aware.

We will look in more depth at the need to be alert against the assaults of Satan in Chapter 10, but for the purpose of this chapter we need to recognize that he is a liar who whispers to us that we can't be healed, that we are not worthy of being healed, that we have failed too often to be healed, and that the sin we commit is too offensive to God for us to receive mercy. None of that is true; consider the source.

THE CRY BENEATH THE LIE

Even as we recognize the lies of the enemy, we have our human longing to be loved, healed, and received. Like beggars with bowls, we sit on the corners of life holding up our emptiness, aching to be filled. As the character Edgar in Shakespeare's *King Lear* says, "The weight of this sad time we must obey; Speak what we feel, not what we ought to say."

Surely that is the dilemma of the human heart; we long to be loved. Being loved and received as we are is the most primary human need. Only when we reject the lie of the enemy that we are not worth healing and we come to God as we are, right now, can we experience healing that will last for a lifetime. Don't buy into the lies of the enemy for one more day. God invites you to come right now as you are into His presence. Because of Christ we have been made worthy, so come!

❧

Father God,
   I come to You in the name of Your Son, Jesus. Thank You that he

is truth. Thank You that even when my heart condemns me You are bigger than my heart. Help me to recognize and resist the lies of the enemy.

In Jesus' name, Amen.

APPLICATION POINTS

- Satan is a liar, but he's often very subtle in his lies. What untruths has he whispered to you so often that you accept them as true? If you're not sure, make that a focus of prayer and even of counsel from someone who knows you well.

- What lies does Satan whisper or perhaps shout to you through the media? (See page 79.)

- More tragically, what lies have you heard from within Christ's church? (See pages 82–83.)

- When we're children, we take two and two and make twenty—and Satan doesn't correct our math! What false conclusions did you reach as a child?

- When we hear the voice of condemnation, we can know it's not from our Father. Condemnation comes from Satan; conviction, from our Father's Holy Spirit. Yet we are so used to the voice of condemnation that it never sounds like the enemy. It sounds familiar; it sounds like us. What voices of condemnation have you been living with? Recognize their source and then silence them by clinging to God's Word. (See the Bible study section for Chapter 4 on page 222.)

5

LONGING TO BE LOVED

But You, O GOD the Lord, deal with me for Your name's sake;
because Your mercy is good, deliver me. For I am poor and needy,
and my heart is wounded within me.

—PSALM 109:21–22

THE TALE OF THE BOXES

*I*n a land far away, over vast oceans and through dark green forests, lived two sisters. They lived in cottages, side by side. They had lived there all their lives and knew no other life. Every morning they would sit together on the stump of an old oak tree that once offered shade but now invited conversation. They would talk about their hopes and dreams. Nothing much changed from day to day, but they enjoyed the companionship they shared. Then one morning, something changed. Both sisters found a gift box on their front doorsteps and, with the boxes in hand, hurried to meet at the oak tree.

"Look, Sister," one began. "Look at what I found on my doorstep this morning." She held up her box.

"I have one too," the other sister added. "But unfortunately my box is empty."

"Yes, my box is empty," the first sister said. "But I will treasure it."

"There is nothing to treasure," her sister replied. "I will sit mine on the doorstep each night and see if by morning it has been filled."

A year passed. The sisters' experiences with the gifts were worlds apart. One sister had used her box in the spring to gather flowers, in the summer to pick berries; in the fall she filled it with leaves of gold, umber, and scarlet; and in the winter, a single candle stood in the box and added its soft, warm light to the long, dark hours.

The other sister had a disappointing year. Each morning she looked to see if her box had been filled. It was always empty. After some time she stopped looking and never knew that the blustery winds of fall had carried the box away one night.

For one sister, the box was filled with hope and promise. For the other, the box was simply empty. She saw nothing beautiful or useful in the gift, and it never crossed her mind to put anything in it.

THE CRY OF OUR HEARTS

It seems as if the curse of our culture is loneliness. Several years ago a book resonated with women all across America. It was promoted on *The Oprah Winfrey Show,* and with that wind beneath its banner, it proudly blustered up the bestseller list and landed at the top. It was called *The Bridges of Madison County,* a romantic tale of stolen moments between a married woman, Francesca Johnson, and Robert Kincaid, a photographer from *National Geographic* magazine, whose latest assignment brought him to her door. The killer line for many who read the book was the photographer telling the woman that he *saw her.* Those were words of life spoken into the very mundane day-to-day existence she was leading as a wife and a mom. Into her black-and-white world, a knight with shining cameras arrived, and he focused on her in color. I read the book and I wept. I was glad that she chose to stay with her husband in the end rather than leave with this relative stranger, yet somewhere in my romantic soul I felt that in choosing the right thing, she had sacrificed what every woman longs for—to be seen and loved.

Then they made the book into a movie with Meryl Streep and Clint Eastwood in the starring roles, and women all across America flocked to the box office. A palpable sigh went through the movie theater the day I saw the film as Robert looked longingly into Francesca's eyes and assured her with rugged passion that he did, indeed, *see her.* As we all filed out, it seemed we determined that what was wrong with our lives was that we were not *seen.* What we were longing for was *out there* somewhere. The reason we felt lonely or dissatisfied was that the significant people in our lives didn't really see us. The feeling lasted about two hours after the movie for me, and when its opiate effect had dissipated, I felt very foolish. (I also thought it would get old very quickly to be followed everywhere by someone with a camera who *saw me!*)

The fallout of the book and the movie, in my opinion, was to blast the pit of loneliness a little deeper into every soul who absorbed its message. The implicit statement is that what is wrong inside us could be fixed if we could just find that one human being who would see all that is true about us—every unspoken cry, every ache and longing, physical or emotional—and meet those needs. This is the romantic dream of our culture that somewhere *out there* is the one person who would completely see us and love us. What lies beneath that romantic dream? Where did that desire come from? It seems to me that the longings we have as human beings that remain unfulfilled stand as evidence to the fact that we were made to be in perfect relationship with God. Adam and Eve knew that completeness and the memories of that fellowship still seem to be planted deep in our genes. One day, when we see Jesus face-to-face we will finally be whole, but until that day we will deal with longings that have no ultimate fulfillment on this earth.

THE DISAPPOINTMENT OF ROMANCE

I moved to California after I got out of the hospital to begin studies at Fuller Theological Seminary. My friends there, knowing that I was not married, determined that they would find Mr. Right for me. I was set up with some of the goofiest dates in human history. One guy—on our first (and only) date—wanted to know if I would be willing to have children with him. All I could think was that I didn't even want to have coffee with him!

I double-dated with friends who wanted to see if I would click with a friend of theirs. He seemed fairly normal, and the dinner was going well until he asked me if I had seen the movie *The Bridges of Madison County*. I told him that I had. He said that the ending devastated him, that in his opinion Francesca should have left her husband and children and catapulted herself into a life of passionate adventure with the photographer. I asked him if he was a Christian. He said that he was. I asked him how he could justify his position. I could see my friends beginning to wriggle in their seats, sorry they had set this up.

"Because love must be guarded at all costs," he said, gazing at the sunset out the window. "Such love is rare and must be cherished."

"That is the biggest load of self-serving baloney I've ever heard!" I said.

He never invited me out again. I wonder why?

Our culture is dominated by images of people having wildly passionate relationships that are fulfilling on every level, emotional, physical, and spiritual. I've never been a soap opera fan, but when my mother-in-law used to stay with us and tune in to her favorite soap, I was amazed at what was dished up in the name of "real life."

"I thought my husband was dead!" she cried. "I saw his head chopped off in the helicopter accident."

"He's been in Sweden, Veronica, undergoing experimental surgery."

On television, in magazines, and in books, the impossible in human terms becomes possible, leaving so many of us disappointed with our lives. We long to hold on to what we once felt when we first fell in love, with the same intensity, but we change, and those around us change too. This can be a wonderful growing and maturing of our relationships, or it can be heartache if our inner brokenness has not been healed. When everything gets filtered through that painful place, we repeat the same old mistakes again and again.

ALL THE LONELY PEOPLE

The truth is that life on this planet is lonely at times, and being in relationship with God and others doesn't completely erase that.

I love the story that Luci Swindoll tells of the beginnings of her thirty-year friendship with Marilyn Meberg.

She said to Marilyn one day, "Being single, I sometimes get lonely. You have Ken. It must be nice never to feel lonely."

"Being married doesn't preclude loneliness," Marilyn replied.

Luci thought about that for a moment, not wanting to admit she couldn't remember what *preclude* meant. Finally she said, "Marilyn, what does *preclude* mean?"

Marilyn replied, "I don't know, but Rachmaninoff wrote one!"

We all experience loneliness. Some might take issue with me on this point, saying that if we are in relationship with God, we should never experience loneliness. All I can say is that I have experienced loneliness and, at times, still do. Part of existence in this fun house is that life is not how it was supposed to be. Adam and Eve were the only two who have known true wholeness. They were never lonely. Their relationship with God and each other was uninterrupted, intimate. There were no harsh words between them, no bricks in a wall that would eventually, when enough bricks were put in place, block out any possibility of relationship.

They were *seen,* but seen in truth and beauty as made in God's perfect image. Their sin caused them to reach for cover and pull away from each other and from God. And so began the search for someone else to recognize that one's box is empty and the hope that the other person would fill it.

In my little tale of the boxes I presented two sisters who view life differently. The boxes represent their lives. One sees the emptiness and waits for someone to come under cover of night and fill that emptiness. She lives a disappointing life. One sees the box and accepts it as a gift. Part of the joy of her day is filling her life with good things. She always has something to share, something to give, while her sister waits alone. Both represent believers, one who is disappointed and one who receives the gift of life. At different times in my life I have been both sisters. One is an unhappy ghost, and one a resurrected child of God brought back from the dead places of her past.

As long as we are looking for someone to fill us up, we will be disenchanted and needy, and rather than cause others to want to be in relationship with us, we will push them far away, deepening our pain.

Think of the number of marriages that have failed because of disillusionment, unmet needs, and disappointment.

Think of the church shopping that goes on as we try to find a place where our wounds will be healed and our needs met.

I received a note from an old friend who had moved away from our area with the promise of a good job in a church and a place where her gifts would be seen and used. It looked like a gift from heaven. She had friends there, and it seemed that she would be able to use her gifts to a greater degree. She talked it over with friends and family. Some had concerns that there wasn't a definite offer of a job or a concrete salary, but my friend had a strong sense that God was asking her to step out in faith. So she packed up and headed off.

Doors continued to open. Someone in the church offered her a furnished home to live in, and with a part-time job she was able to volunteer some time to the ministry that she believed would grow into something more. From everything she had been told, it certainly seemed that was the long-term plan.

A few months later she wrote to me to tell me that things had not worked out as she had hoped and expected. She had uprooted her whole life, relocated, and now felt like a fool.

She is not a fool, far from it. She is not a young, impulsive believer but a godly woman whose heartfelt passion is to do the will of God. Yet one more time she finds herself in a dark night of disappointment and despair, let down, she feels, by her heart and by others. What deepens the pain for her is the sense that she has been there before. How many times have you beaten yourself up, thinking, *How can I be here again? Will I never change?*

I, too, have shed many tears as I find myself down the same old dead-end streets. At those moments I remind myself that were it not for the Lord's mercy, we would be consumed, lost, hopeless, but His mercies are new every morning.

WOUNDED BY THOSE WE TRUST

Part of the pain for my friend is that she feels that a fellow believer misled her. In her heart and mind she believed that certain things, if not exactly promised, were understood by both parties. Trust was involved, and trust is a precious gift.

In Chapter 13 we will explore this enormous subject of feeling that another Christian has deceived us. I believe that God has something to say to us that will set us free from the chains of resentment and hurt. But for now, what can we do as we sit with an empty box and long for what Hollywood and romantic novels offer, or on a deeper level the intimacy and healing that we know should be ours in Christ? Where do we take the pain?

We would love to think that some man would come along and really see all our wounds and needs and bring total healing and restoration. That's not realistic. No human being is equipped to fill the emptiness in another's life.

THIS ISN'T WORKING

When Christian was a little boy, I found him one day trying to stick a carrot in the keyhole and open the front door.

"What are you doing, Sweet Pea?" I asked.

"I'm going for a walk."

"The door's locked," I said.

"I know, Mommy, but I'm going to open it with this."

He held up the remains of a devastated carrot, half of which was stuck in the keyhole. "This is hard!" he said as he shoved in the rest.

Carrots were not made to open doors, and we are not made to meet every need of another human soul. We can walk side by side, we can enjoy intimacy and companionship, but only Christ can fill our boxes. I am very aware that my box is not full. I love God, and it is the passion of my heart to let Him love me and love others through me, but my box leaks. I can spend a weekend with twenty thousand women, worshiping God and receiving words of life from the Holy Spirit. I fly home, thinking that my box is so full, it will overflow on anyone who comes near me, but then the other side of life kicks in. There is laundry to be done, the vacuum cleaner breaks an hour before guests arrive, harsh words are spoken, frustration builds, PMS rears its ugly head, you name it, I face it, and this once-full box empties out. I have discovered that if I expect to get from one conference to the next or one church service to the next on what I received a week ago, I won't make it. I need to have my box filled daily, moment by moment.

MESSIAH HAS COME!

The psalmist David wrote:

> You will show me the path of life;
> In Your presence is fullness of joy. (Ps. 16:11)

In Acts 2:28 Peter revisited those words of David and brought them into an active relationship with Christ. As he stood before a large gathering of people, his message to them was that everything they were waiting for, longing for, hoping for, had already been given to them in Christ Jesus. That was not good news to the hearers. The people were devastated, realizing that they crucified the very One they had been waiting for:

> When they heard this, they were cut to the heart, and said to Peter and the rest of the apostles, "Men and brethren, what shall we do?" (Acts 2:37).

Peter told them to turn from the way they were living and fall in love with Jesus. About three thousand people that day heard Peter's message and turned to Christ. That should be the end of the journey, right? We are longing for love, looking for it in human flesh, and then realize that it can be found only in God. As Augustine wrote, "Our hearts are restless till they rest in thee." But when we come to Christ, we don't come empty-handed; we bring our bags. The people in the crowd that day, even as they began the most exciting adventure offered to a man or woman, would have many disappointing and disillusioning days ahead. Perhaps they thought that now that they had received Messiah, all of life's problems would be gone. You and I know that is not true. I see two separate issues here.

1. We Will Still Face Hard Times Ahead

Jesus made that clear: "These things I have spoken to you, that in Me you may have peace. In the world you will have tribulation; but be of good cheer, I have overcome the world" (John 16:33).

It's interesting that Jesus combined peace and tribulation. The offer of peace does not remove the reality of tribulation, and the presence of tribulation does not annihilate the promise of peace.

2. We Carry Our Bags from the Past

We come to Christ with baggage from the past, and that is what He wants to heal us from. It doesn't mean that we will never hurt again or escape the harsher reality of life. It means that we will invite Him to mend our broken hearts and give us a right understanding of life so that we can live in this world and process information correctly. As a child, I thought my dad hit me because he hated me. Now I know that it was because he was ill. Perhaps when you were a child, a man mistreated you, and now as an adult you accept that treatment from someone else because it is familiar and you feel that you deserve it. Christ's healing would enable you to say, "I had no control over that as a child, but I do now and this is unacceptable behavior."

Sometimes people live with abuse because they don't want to be alone. One of the most difficult callings in life is to be married. One of the most difficult callings in life is to be single. One of the most difficult callings in life is to be human. We are born with a need to belong, to find our place. Michael W. Smith found that his song "Place in This World" took him from a mostly Christian radio audience to a wider arena.

Looking for a reason,
Roaming through the night to find our place in this world.

It struck a chord. We all long to find our place in this world. In the seventies and eighties we joined Norm and the gang at a Boston bar called Cheers, "where everyone knows your name." Something about that place warmed our hearts. We loved it when Norm walked in, everyone greeted him, noticed he was there, had his favorite seat ready and waiting. We want to be wanted.

THE HUMAN CRY

I'm sitting in my favorite spot in my favorite Starbucks one morning working on this book. I know the crowd here. There are students from Vanderbilt University cramming for exams, medical students from one of the local teaching hospitals, musicians whose day doesn't really begin until evening, and moms with little ones popping in for a shot of caffeine to fuel the day ahead. I ask one of my musician friends how his writing is going.

"Okay, I guess," he says. "I just can't get off this one theme. We're all longing to find that one person who will love us as we want to be loved. But how many more songs can I write about it?"

Let's line everyone up together—the sisters with the boxes, the women who read *The Bridges of Madison County* or saw the movie, my friend who feels like an old fool, the crowd gathered at Peter's feet, the songwriter, you, me—what do we all have in common?

We want to be loved.
We want to find a perfect love.
We have been disappointed with others and ourselves.
We are waiting for others to fill us.
We want to belong.
We are stuck.

THE PROBLEM IS ME

I have made a fascinating discovery about myself. Here it is: everywhere I go, there I am! Before you write me off as sleep deprived, let me explain what I mean. I used to believe that my problems and pain revolved around other people and situations:

"If he wasn't in my life, I'd be happy."

"If I didn't have to work with her, I would be different."

"I'm only like this when I'm around them."

You can add your own convictions to my list:

"I only get mad when he talks to me like that."

"If she wasn't so difficult, I would enjoy working here."

"If they would just leave the church, we could all get on with loving God."

While there might be some truth to those passionate beliefs and they might make us feel better about ourselves, they do us no service at all if we earnestly long to live in a way that would bring honor to the name of Christ and joy to the heart of God. Either Christ died and rose again to enable us to live freely and peacefully wherever He takes us, or we have based our lives on a shaky foundation. One of the most liberating lessons I have learned is to take responsibility for my own life, actions, words, behavior, and heart. Doing that doesn't come naturally to any of us. Shame makes us want to shift the blame because we feel that if we mess up, we will be left alone, abandoned.

IT WASN'T MY FAULT

My son loves to play soccer and basketball. Whenever he comes home from school, he heads straight for the backyard and locates the muddiest spot as the center of his activities. I have very few house rules, but one that matters to me is that he takes his shoes off when he comes back inside. We have light hardwood floors and a cream carpet in the bedroom. Time after time he runs back into the house, over the hardwood floors, into the bedroom where he throws himself with boyish abandon onto the bed, muddy shoes still in place. When he realizes that he has forgotten the rules one more time, his responses are varied but similar.

"You forgot to remind me!"

"The baby-sitter told me to come in, and she never mentioned my shoes."

"I think I was being chased by a big dog!"

"Haven't you ever been six?"

The bottom line—it's not my fault. We'll then sit down and talk about taking responsibility for our own actions, but it does not come naturally. Part of it is that he doesn't want me to be angry with him; he wants everything to be sunny all the time. Our hearts are fragile and break so easily. My son thinks that if I am cross with him, it means that I don't love him. I keep repeating, "What you *did* was not good, but I love who you *are*."

A STOLEN MOMENT

When I was ten years old, I stole the British equivalent of a dollar from my mother's purse to buy peas in their pods. All the other kids on our street had agreed to meet at the park with a bag of peas. The young, freshly picked peas were delicious. The problem was that I had already spent my allowance on five gummy worms and two chocolate frogs so I had nothing left. I asked if I could have an advance on my allowance.

"You did," Mom said, "two days ago."

"Oh, right, I forgot."

When Mom went into the kitchen, I quietly opened the drawer where I knew she kept her wallet and took the money. Peas have never tasted as bad to me as they did that day. After supper I had a quick bath and went to bed. I tried to get to sleep and anesthetize my conscience, to no avail. Finally I went downstairs and told my mom what I had done. Through a well of tears, I said, "I'm so sorry that I stole from you. I know I should be punished but please still love me."

The terror of my heart was that my behavior would leave me alone in this world. I stole the money because I wanted to fit in with my friends, but I couldn't rest because I had lied to my mother. As I spilled the truth out, I expected to see in my mom's eyes the same disgust that I had once seen in my dad's. My mom reassured me that although I would be punished, there was nothing I could do to destroy her love for me.

OUR FRAGILE HEARTS

On a recent trip I saw again how fragile our hearts are and how easily we are wounded. I was speaking at a church retreat for women. A local young woman was the worship leader for our sessions. I liked her a lot and grabbed a few moments to find out more about her life. She told me that she and her husband were unable to have children, so they adopted a boy from Russia. He was a boy who had been abandoned in the gutter as a baby and taken to a local orphanage. He received so little love and nurture that even though he was six months old when they got him, he was the weight of a normal newborn baby. After they brought him back to America, he had to undergo several surgeries to correct improperly developed organs and hearing and vision deficiencies. I told her that I would love to meet him, and she suggested taking us to the airport for our flight home.

After the retreat was over, she and her son arrived at our hotel to take Barry, Christian, and me to catch our flight. Christian sat beside him in the van, and they chatted all the way to the airport. When we got out, I stooped down beside this slight child with big blue eyes.

"Thank you so much for coming with us," I said. "You're an amazing boy. I can't wait to hear about all the fantastic things you will do with your life from your mom. You are a miracle!"

We arrived at the airport, said our good-byes, checked our bags, and went through security. When we got to our gate, Christian asked me if he could sit somewhere by himself. I looked over at him sitting in a row of empty seats, head down, eyes averted from my direction. I walked over to him.

"May I sit here?" I asked.

"Sure," he replied quietly.

"Did I do something to hurt your feelings?" I asked him.

He looked at me with sadness in his big chestnutbrown eyes. "You've never called me a miracle," he whispered.

My son is a very well-loved boy. His dad and I adore him and tell him that constantly. We are a kissy, huggy family, but even so, the human ego is as fragile as a spider's web and easily torn. If Christian, with two parents who love him and shelter him as much as possible from the pain of life, feels bereft and wounded at times, it's not surprising that even as you hold this book in your hands, you hold so much pain in your heart. That's why God sent Jesus. He sent Him to show us what God is like. Where He saw people who were brokenhearted, He wept with them, touched them, and looked them in the eyes. Where He saw people who were shamed by their choices, He stood with them.

Into our weary world, our shattered dreams, and broken hearts God sent a healer. He was a healer in disguise. You would need to be desperate to find Him, but to those who are desperate, He is here!

God saw that we were stuck and gave birth to the answer: "For God so loved the world that He gave His only begotten Son, that whoever believes in Him should not perish but have everlasting life" (John 3:16).

I have known this verse since I was a child in Sunday school. It is probably the first verse I ever memorized. It's a verse full of life and meaning.

The Greek word used here for "everlasting" refers not only to how long we will live but also to the quality of life we live right now, as contrasted with a sense of hopelessness. Everlasting, or eternal, life is a deepening and growing experience every day. It can never be exhausted. It speaks of a new quality of life. *We are not saved to simply make it through this world until we are finally home free. Christ died to give us life, life right now.* Are you experiencing that? If, like me, you are longing to be in relationship with the only One who sees all our brokenness and longs to bring healing and hope, may I remind you that there is such a One? His name is Jesus.

> Looking on our brokenness
> Weeping for our emptiness
> Moved by love and tenderness
> The Lamb of God has come.
>
> Now I know that the LORD saves His anointed;
> He will answer him from His holy heaven
> With the saving strength of His right hand. (Ps. 20:6)

Father God,

I praise You for the way You have made me. You have made me to know You and love You. Teach me to bring my emptiness to You to be filled and give me the grace to live in this imperfect world. Amen.

APPLICATION POINTS

- Each of us is given the gift of life, symbolized in my parable by an empty box. Think about your perspective on your life and your response to that gift. Which sister are you more like? Are you waiting for someone to fill your box, or are you filling your life with good things? Give details to support your answer.

- The romantic dream of our culture is that somewhere out there is the one person who will completely see us and love us. In what ways, if any, has this dream tripped you up?

- To what or to whom are you looking to fill up your box? Only Christ can fill our boxes. As Augustine wrote, "Our hearts are restless till they rest in thee."

- Believers still face hard times (John 16:33), and we still have to deal with bags we carry from the past.

    What hard times have you faced since naming Jesus as your Savior and Lord? Describe your reaction to those times.

    And what baggage from the past are you lugging along with you? Ask Jesus to help you set it down—for good!

- Our fragile hearts compel us to shift the blame rather than take responsibility and to fear rejection because we aren't good enough. In our hearts we want to be wanted, and we long for the healing and hope only Jesus can bring us. Are you open to the possibility that your unhappiness with your life is due not to trouble out there, but to roots somewhere in your own heart? What will be your response to this possibility?

6

THE WOUNDED HEALER

He is despised and rejected by men, a Man of sorrows and acquainted with grief. And we hid, as it were, our faces from Him; He was despised, and we did not esteem Him. Surely He has borne our griefs and carried our sorrows; yet we esteemed Him stricken, smitten by God, and afflicted. But He was wounded for our transgressions, He was bruised for our iniquities; the chastisement for our peace was upon Him, and by His stripes we are healed.

—ISAIAH 53:3–5

Can't you talk to Him, Mary?" Phoebe asked. "Surely He will listen to His own mother."

Mary was silent.

"If He's not careful, He'll end up in terrible trouble. He's upsetting everyone."

"He is doing what He has to do," Mary replied.

"But He doesn't have to be so controversial. He's making some outrageous statements," she said.

"Since Jesus was a young boy, He has made outrageous statements," His mother replied. "He is not like other men. He will do what He has to do."

"Well, it'll be His cross to carry," Phoebe said as she picked up her belongings and left.

Mary buried her face in her hands.

"You have no idea," she whispered.

A LONG WALK IN THE SAME DIRECTION

We all know that someday we will die. Some of us are obsessed with tormenting thoughts of sickness and death; some of us give it very little thought, but we all know that someday it will be our turn. But what must it have been like for Jesus to live, knowing that every step He took was one step closer to a brutal betrayal and execution?

Jesus would have been aware of the agony that He was walking toward. Crucifixion was one of the most cruel and barbarous forms of death known to man. It was practiced, especially in times of war, by the Phoenicians, Carthaginians, Egyptians, and later by those who would crucify Christ, the Romans. Even before Christ's time on earth, the cares and troubles of life were often compared to a cross.

"She's carrying quite a cross!"

"That will be a terrible cross to carry."

The agony of the crucified victim was brought about by several elements of the long process. The painful wounds were inflicted as nails were driven into wrists and ankles. The wounds didn't kill the person, but the pain was excruciating. Then the body was suspended at such an abnormal position that every movement to try to alleviate the crushing burden of lungs and heart would add fresh waves of nauseating pain. Then there was the raging fever brought on by hanging like that for so long. It was a cruel, drawn-out death. It took many men two or three days to die.

That was what Jesus willingly chose to experience for you and for me. Jesus was born to die. He left the worship of angels, the glory of heaven, and the companionship of His Father to step into human time and treachery to answer the cry of our hearts:

"Who will help me?"

"Who can heal me?"

"Does anyone see me?"

"Does anyone really love me?"

AN UNLIKELY BEGINNING

If you should ever find yourself in a French church on Easter Sunday morning, you will hear this phrase: *L'Amour de Dieu est folie*. It means,

"The love of God is foolishness." That might seem an outrageous, even irreverent statement, but God's love is outrageous and His arrival on our human stage seems irreverent. Can you imagine if you had told the religious leaders of the day, "Messiah is coming! His mother is an unmarried teenager, and He'll be born in a shed"? Outrageous, irreverent, perhaps even blasphemous.

At times within the church we are uncomfortable with the raw reality of Jesus Christ, and we try to tidy Him up. I remember my image of Christ when I was a child in Sunday school. He was tall with long, flowing hair, a handsome, rugged man with a gentle smile. He was always carrying a very white lamb perched peacefully on His shoulders. That's not how the prophet Isaiah described the Messiah:

> He has no form or comeliness;
> And when we see Him,
> There is no beauty that we should desire Him. (Isa. 53:2)

Nothing about the arrival or appearance of Christ was expected.

Their scholars had told Jews who were waiting for the Messiah that He would appear on the pinnacle of the temple, so they were looking in the wrong place.

LOOKING IN THE WRONG PLACE

Imagine with me that it's the night of the birth of Christ and Jerusalem is crowded. You notice that the area around the temple is mobbed with people. They are standing shoulder to shoulder staring straight up into the sky.

"What are you looking at?" you ask.

"Nothing. I'm waiting," is the sharp reply.

"Waiting for what?" you want to know.

"Not what; it's who! We're waiting for the arrival of the Messiah."

You slip away from the mass of impatient men and women jockeying for a better position and head out into the countryside southwest of Jerusalem. It's quiet now, peaceful. You gaze up at the stars and are amazed that the crisp night air has made the stars seem so bright, so close. There is one in particular. It is so bright that it cuts through the darkness like a brilliant lantern. You follow. You walk for about five miles and find yourself in the small town of Bethlehem.

"Nice night!" you say to a small group of shepherds as you catch up with them. You mean to ask them if they know of a good place to stay, but they're in a hurry, so you just follow. You arrive at a small barn and reason that they must be looking for shelter for themselves.

You go in. But something outrageous is going on here. There, lying in a cattle feed box, is a baby. The shepherds get on their knees, and you join them. You can't stand. There is such a swelling in your heart, you think it just might burst. Deep inside your soul you know. You know that the crowd is standing in the wrong place. Those people have missed the miracle by five miles. They are standing looking up when Messiah has come down.

> They are calling out, "Where are You, God?"
> And God cries out in a baby's pure song, "I am here."

Obviously I am not suggesting that every night those who were expecting Messiah stood staring up at the temple. My point is this: when Jesus came, He came in a way that no one expected. He came to do what no one else could do. He came to bring healing that no one else could bring. He came to you and to me. He came to fulfill the promise of Psalm 147:3: *Christ heals the brokenhearted and binds up their wounds. That is His commitment to us.*

So many missed Jesus that night. They were so close, but so far away, like someone who has sat in church for fifty years and never gotten the point. You can be inches away from the Christ and still miss the gift. You can be a very religious person and never receive the hope and healing offered through the sacrifice that Jesus made. You can stand staring up at the sky, crying out, "Does anyone in this cold, cruel world see me?" Jesus stepped into all the horror and betrayal of our world to answer our cry for help.

AN UNLIKELY AUDIENCE

What did the shepherds understand that night? We'll never know. They knew that there was something very unusual about the child. Very few human eyes have seen the sky fit to burst with the presence of angels. Few human ears have heard singing like that or such a message directly from the throne room of heaven.

> The angel said to them, "Do not be afraid, for behold, I bring you good tidings of great joy which will be to all people. For there is born to you this day in the city of David a Savior, who is Christ the Lord. And this will be the sign to you: You will find a Babe wrapped in swaddling cloths, lying in a manger." And suddenly there was with the angel a multitude of the heavenly host praising God and saying:
> "Glory to God in the highest,
> And on earth peace, goodwill toward men!"
> So it was, when the angels had gone away from them into heaven, that the shepherds said to one another, "Let us now go to Bethlehem and see this thing that has come to pass, which the Lord has made known to us." (Luke 2:10–15)

It's interesting that every time an angel addresses a man or woman, he has to start by saying, "Don't be afraid!" Angels must be spectacular to look at. Angels are very much part of the life of the believer. I don't think we even begin to take in the power that is around us every day. We have watered down the truth of the majesty and might of God's kingdom and the mighty warriors who fight day and night in the name of God. The arrival in Bethlehem was not the mild-mannered, sanitized depiction that we see on our Christmas cards every year. It was an invasion of all that is holy and good into everything that is corrupt and evil, a divine covert operation to set us free. In the guise of an innocent child, all of heaven was waging war with the enemy of our souls to set us free.

Do you see how much you are loved?

Do you see how much you are valued?

Can you tell that God sees you?

HOLY WARRIORS

My son was very upset to discover that the movie version of *The Incredible Hulk* was given a PG-13 rating.

76

"That is so unfair, Mom! Kids never get to do cool things. We never get to see cool tough guys."

I said to him, "Don't look now, but did you know that there are always angels with us?"

"Angels!" he said in disgust. "I don't want a girl in a pink dress."

"Christian! Do I have a surprise in store for you! Let me tell you about angels," I said. "First of all, they have superhuman strength and intelligence. And they are tough!"

"Tougher than the Hulk?" he asked.

"Way tougher! Once when some bad guys were coming after a man called Lot, who was a friend of God's, the angels blinded them." (See Genesis 19:11.)

"Cool!" he said. "Tell me more."

"Do you remember a man named Paul?" I asked.

"Sure. He was in a shipwreck."

"Well, one night he and some of his friends were being held in jail, and God sent an angel to get them out." (See Acts 5:19.)

"What else?" he asked. "The Hulk can knock out ten people at once. Can they do that?"

"Piece of cake!" I replied. "There was a group of people called the Assyrians, and they had it in for God's people, so God sent out angels to take care of them. They killed 185,000 in one night." (See 2 Kings 19:35.)

For a moment he was speechless. "Do you think they'll make a movie?" he asked.

"Better than that. Movies are here one week and gone the next, but God's mighty warriors are with us all the time right up to the final battle."

The problem is that we can pay seven dollars and see the Hulk, but God's mighty warriors are usually invisible to human eyes. Our culture teaches us to pay attention to the here and now. We want instant everything. We want big bangs and flashing lights, and we miss the most amazing live theater that is going on at every moment. Do you ever stop and wonder how many times God sends His angels to intervene on your behalf? You are held up for a moment in a store and just miss a terrible wreck. You suddenly decide to turn left instead of right and are protected from a disaster that you will never know about. There is a holy war raging all around us because God passionately loves us and has given everything to save and protect us.

The people missed the miracle by five miles on that starlit evening. It's a mistake we have continued.

We reach for the cookie jar to feed a deeper hunger.

And God says, "I am here."

We lose ourselves in romantic novels and soap operas, longing for someone who will see us and love us.

And God says, "I am here."

We argue with those we love because we are disappointed that they miss our pain.

And God says, "I am right here," pressing His hand on our hearts.

Jesus came to show us what God is like, to teach us how to live and love, and to do what only He could do.

A PAINFUL GIFT

Every Christmas in churches around the world little ones don their bathrobes and reenact that first Christmas. Shepherds crowd around the manger, vying for a good camera position for their parents, and then the wise men arrive with their gifts. For purposes of a church presentation, everything happens in a matter of an hour or so. But that's not how things happened.

It's clear from Matthew's gospel that some time had passed from the birth of Christ until the visit of the Magi: "When they had come into the house, they saw the young Child with Mary His mother, and fell down and worshiped Him. And when they had opened their treasures, they presented gifts to Him: gold, frankincense, and myrrh" (Matt. 2:11).

Mary, Joseph, and Jesus were settled in a house. The Greek word used to describe Jesus on the night He was born is the word for "baby," *brephos*, but the word used during the visit of the Magi is the word for "small child," *paidion*.

Mary knew that this boy to whom she had given birth was no ordinary child. An angel had visited her, and she shared those first moments as she held her tiny boy to her breast with shepherds who told a fantastic story. But days had turned to weeks, and they had moved on with their lives. They were in their own home now. Jesus had said His first word, perhaps taken His first step. She was a young mother with all the hopes and dreams of any young mother, and then the Magi arrived.

I imagine Mary receiving the gifts. She would be moved and overwhelmed by the gift of gold from the men. Their gifts signified that they recognized a greater One than they was in the room. The frankincense was a costly perfume and would be gratefully received. But did Mary recoil as they presented the gift of myrrh? Did her face betray her shock that already this child's destiny was being prepared? Myrrh exudes from a tree found in Arabia and was a much-valued spice and perfume. Myrrh was an anesthetic and a substance used in embalming.

What a strange gift to give to a child! It was a gift that would be offered again as Jesus was about to be crucified. Merciful women would approach those about to be executed and offer myrrh, which would act as a sedative.

Jesus refused the cup offered to take the edge off His pain. He fully embraced everything that lay ahead:

> They brought Jesus to the place called Golgotha (which means The Place of the Skull). Then they offered him wine mixed with myrrh, but he did not take it. And they crucified him. (Mark 15:22-24 NIV)

By His stripes (wounds) we are healed.
Jesus embraced loneliness on the cross so that we will never be alone.
He took the punishment for our sin so that we can be forgiven.
He was broken so that we can be whole.
His death brought us forgiveness.
His resurrection brought us hope for eternal life.
His wounds heal us.

OUR DAILY BREAD

In 2003 a huge new church opened just a few miles away from our house. One Sunday morning that summer we slept through the alarm. As we were scrambling to get ready, I realized that we wouldn't make our service on time.

"Why don't we visit the church at the end of the street?" I suggested to Barry. "We could make it before the service starts."

He agreed, and we slipped in just as the service was about to begin. That morning the congregation was celebrating the Lord's Supper.

"Can I join in, Mom?" Christian asked.

"Yes, you can, Darling," I said. "This is a feast for everyone who has given his life to Jesus."

As the basket with the small pieces of bread was passed from hand to hand, Christian looked at me as if to say, "This is not much of a feast!"

As we took the bread together, the pastor encouraged us to invite this moment into our everyday lives. To remember on a daily basis that Jesus gave His body for us. *We follow a Wounded Healer who loves us more than we will ever grasp until we see Him face-to-face.* It's easy in the midst of the busyness of life to forget, so now, whenever I put rolls on the dinner table or toast out for breakfast, I take just a moment to remember that Christ gave His body for me. As a family, we take just a moment to acknowledge at mealtimes that no matter what else is going on in life, Jesus gave Himself for us so that we can find healing for our broken hearts.

> As they were eating, Jesus took bread, blessed and broke it, and gave it to them and said, "Take, eat; this is My body." Then He took the cup, and when He had given thanks He gave it to them, and they all drank from it. And He said to them, "This is My blood of the new covenant, which is shed for many." (Mark 14:22–24)

He was broken so that we can be whole.
He was poured out so that we can be filled.

FREE IF YOU'RE BROKE!

When Christian graduated from kindergarten in 2003, he was excited about how grown up he was. He said, "I'm no longer in kindergarten. I'm a grader!"

On the first day of summer vacation I asked him what he wanted to do.

"I'd like to have a lemonade stand, Mom. It's just the beginning of the summer, and I'm going to need some income."

"What for?" I asked.

"It's hard to say at the moment, but things pop up."

We agreed to have a lemonade stand for anything that might pop up.

I got the lemonade ready as Christian prepared his sign on his blackboard.

"What should I say?" he asked.

"What do you want to say?"

He thought for a moment.

"'Christian's Deluxe Lemonade—$1, Free Refills.'"

"Sounds good," I said.

We carried everything out into the backyard. Our house edges the eighth hole of a golf course, so the potential for thirsty clients was good. He set up his little table and chairs and displayed his sign where no one could miss it. The first few golfers through were very obliging and purchased some lemonade. Then two kids came through who were thirsty but had no money. Christian said, "We have to change the sign."

He changed it to "Christian's Deluxe Lemonade, $1, Free If You're Broke."

That's how we come to Christ. We are thirsty, dying of thirst, but we are broke. We can't help ourselves.

> Ho! Everyone who thirsts,
> Come to the waters;
> And you who have no money,
> Come, buy and eat.
> Yes, come, buy wine and milk
> Without money and without price. (Isa. 55:1)

OUR SONG

A song that has become one of my theme songs in 2004 sums up in a few stanzas the message of this book and the promise that Christ offers to each one of us. It tells the story of our rescue from hell and from the lies of the enemy. It celebrates our liberty from the heartache that no one but Jesus sees.

HE HOLDS THE KEYS!

> Death rides blackened clouds across the sky
> The Son of Man lays down to die
> With every pounding blow upon the nails
> Thunder rumbles all through hell
> And from death's barren womb the captives cry
> Who is there to free us should He die?

His grave becomes a door He enters in
To face the author of all sin
Defying death and the grave He takes their keys
And with them, every captive frees
And from death's barren womb the captives cry
Arise, for our redemption draweth nigh!

For He holds the keys
He holds the keys
And though we've been held captive at long last we are free
For He holds the keys

Against the gates of hell I now resist
For the shackles that had torn my wrists
Lay before me now upon the ground
To sin I am no longer bound
For from death's barren womb He heard my cry
And loosed the chains that bound me to a lie
For He holds the keys
He holds the keys
And though we've been held captive at long last we are free
For He holds the keys

And to all the things that have kept you away
That keep you defeated day after day after day
The heartache that nobody sees that eats at your soul like a cruel
    disease
He who set the captives free, it is He; it is He who holds your keys!

Lord Jesus Christ,

You are the Lamb of God who gave Yourself for me. I come to You now with all my heartache and brokenness, knowing that You are familiar with these things. Thank You for facing all that death and hell could throw at You to set me free. I bring my wounds to You. I bring my life to You. Amen.

APPLICATION POINTS

- What detail about the Crucifixion was new or especially significant to you? Why? What evidence of God's love for you do you find in that remarkable scene?

- What detail about the birth of Christ was new or especially significant to you? Why? What evidence of God's love for you do you find in that wondrous scene?

- What evidence of God's love for you do you find in the discussion of angels?

- In what ways is God saying to you, "I am here"?

- What wounds do you want—and need—to give to your Wounded Healer?

7

IF I HAVE ENOUGH FAITH, WILL GOD HEAL MY BODY TOO?

Heal me, O LORD, and I shall be healed; save me, and I shall be saved, for You are my praise.

—JEREMIAH 17:14

*My loved ones and my friends stand aloof from my plague,
And my relatives stand afar off.*

—PSALM 38:11

*D*uring my tenure as co-host of *The 700 Club* on the Christian Broadcasting Network, a radio station invited me to be part of a panel discussion on the subject of healing. We were a pretty diverse bunch, denominationally and experientially. I won't use real names, so I can tell you what I really think! Suffice it to say, there were many points of view represented.

One guest believed that if you are not healed from a physical illness, it is because of sin in your life. (I had a big problem with him!)

Another panelist believed that God no longer heals; it was a gift for the time of Christ and the apostolic age alone.

One believed that God heals if you are in the right place at the right time. The healing, therefore, is situational; if you get to the right crusade with the right evangelist, you're home free. If you miss it by a night and show up to discover that the dog show is in town, any hope for healing is replaced by a truckload of kibble.

I wasn't able to agree with anyone on the panel. I just don't have life that neatly sewn up. Anytime in the past when I thought that I finally had a handle on how God works, something happened to blow that theory out of the water.

I do believe that God still physically heals people. I believe it is our joy to pray for one another when we are sick so that we might be healed. Not just our joy, but it is a mandate from God's Word: "Confess your trespasses to one another, and pray for one another, that you may be healed. The effective, fervent prayer of a righteous man avails much" (James 5:16).

Mutual confession and prayer are linked here. The idea is that sometimes I'll need to confess my sin to you, sometimes you to me, and that we will pray for each other.

Though I believe that God still heals today, I also believe that there has been much cruelty inflicted on broken hearts and bodies by those who promise what only God can deliver. Dramatic, radical healing, the kind of spectacular intervention where God shows up and delivers someone from a death threat of cancer or some other devastating illness, doesn't happen as often as we would like it to or at times pretend it does.

AN EMPTY PROMISE

I was invited to participate in a Christian festival in Hawaii in the 1980s. We had three days of music and seminars to train young people to prepare for the mission field. One of the team members who most impressed me was a young man in a wheelchair. He was smart and handsome and a great basketball player with a wickedly wonderful sense of humor. He told me that he had been in a wheelchair since he was a child. I'll call him Sam. Sam had no use of his legs at all. They hung below his torso as a daily reminder that we are participants in the fallout of life here on a broken planet. Despite that, he showed no self-pity. I know that behind closed doors and at different points on his journey he must have faced anger and pain, but those feelings did not dominate his life or slow him down on the basketball court.

On the final evening of the festival our guest speaker was an evangelist known for his healing ministry. I was intrigued to see what God would do. I had very little exposure at that point to those who pray for the sick, and so I was excited. I sang a few songs and then handed the program to our main speaker.

His opening sentence shocked me: "God is going to heal everyone in this place tonight. Not one physical sickness will remain."

The only person I could think about was Sam. I was overjoyed. I couldn't wait to see him walk and run and slam-dunk a ball! I had no doubt that he would be healed that night. Our guest was a credible man, and he declared God's intention with such total conviction that I didn't even think to question it. The evangelist preached for about an hour, and then he began to pray for the sick. People streamed to the front of the stage. Some knelt down; others stood in silent prayer. Some wept as I did.

I couldn't see my friend because there were so many people in the tent. I knew he was somewhere near the back, but I didn't worry about it because of what our speaker said about everyone being healed. I determined that it didn't matter where you sat or whether you could make it to the front or not; God could see you.

At the end of the service the evangelist was quickly escorted out of the tent, into a waiting car, and back to his hotel. As the crowd began to disperse, I looked for Sam. I didn't see him until the tent was almost empty. Our eyes met. I waited until we were the only two left. I walked to the back of the tent and sat on the grass beside his wheelchair.

"You feel a lot worse about this than I do, you know," he said.

"How can you say that?" I asked. "You're the one still in a wheelchair."

"Sheila, I know that God could heal me in a moment. He is God! He can do anything. So far, He has said no."

"But he said everyone! He said everyone would be healed. We should have stopped his car and not let him leave until you were healed or at least until he said sorry, or that he was wrong!"

I was angry and grieved and confused.

My friend continued, "I am used to being everyone's guinea pig. Anyone who wants to practice healing has a go on me." He said it with a wry smile.

"Doesn't that make you angry?" I asked.

"It did at first, and sad, but not anymore. My faith is in God, not in a man or a woman. If I did challenge him on the discrepancy between what he said and the fact that I was not healed, I'm pretty sure what his answer would be," he said.

"What possible answer could he have for that?" I asked. "Basically he lied or at best misled us."

"He would say that there is sin or unforgiveness in my heart that was hindering my healing. The problem would not be his; the problem would be mine. What he wouldn't know is that I've already forgiven him."

(On a side note, I saw the evangelist the next day at the airport. He came over to me, laid his hands on my stomach, and prayed loudly that God would bless the child presently in my womb. Should the child ever come out, he or she would now be about twenty years old!)

The memories of that experience have stayed with me through the years that followed. Sam's story was on my mind that night as I sat with the other panelists addressing a radio audience. We discussed the various issues surrounding healing, and the host opened up the phone line for callers to ask questions. I found the questions heartbreaking.

"My child died of leukemia, and I know that it's because my husband drinks, so I'm going to leave him. Do you think that's the right thing to do?"

"I'm having chemotherapy at the moment, and it doesn't seem to be working. I've tried to think of the sin I might be harboring, but I can't think clearly. I'm tired and sick all the time. What should I do?"

"I sent money to a ministry, and they sent me a prayer cloth to place over my wallet so that God would bless my finances, but it's not working. What am I doing wrong?"

"My pastor told me that I couldn't come back to church because I left my husband. But he was beating the children and me. Why is God angry with me?"

"I have bone cancer, and I've prayed and prayed to be healed, but there is no change in my tests. Then I thought perhaps God isn't listening because I'm not on my knees. I got onto my knees and I broke a hip. I don't know what else to do."

The calls went on and on. The sad note that rang out from all of them was the conviction that they must be doing something wrong. What a peculiar pain to think that your child, husband, or loved one is sick and you're to blame. If you could just get it right, find the magic password, then God would hear and answer. *It became really clear to me that night that it is possible to love God and totally miss the point of the gospel.*

We can miss the great, liberating news that God looked down on His broken, lost people and had compassion on us. He saw that we couldn't help ourselves so He sent Christ to take our place in every way. Jesus faced

Satan in the wilderness so that we never have to be left with such an unguarded encounter. He knelt down in broken agony in the Garden so that we can stand up, even in our pain, knowing that He is with us. He embraced total isolation on the cross so that you and I are never alone.

God's love is a gift, not a reward for good behavior.

You may wonder why does God physically heal some people and not others? It is a mystery. I don't understand why God heals some people and not others, but to lay the blame on the shoulders of an already broken heart is obscene. I'm not negating the fact that when we do harbor resentment, bitterness, and unforgiveness, we can pay a physical and spiritual price: "Whenever you stand praying, if you have anything against anyone, forgive him, that your Father in heaven may also forgive you your trespasses" (Mark 11:25).

It's clear, too, that the body and the mind form a tightly woven garment; what goes on in the mind affects the body, and what goes on in the body affects the mind. I saw that in the life of a woman with whom I used to work. For years she had taken care of her sick mother. She didn't want to do it, but because she was the only daughter, it was left to her. It was a burden that she picked up bitterly. I never experienced a kind word from this woman. She was critical of everything and everyone around her. By the time she died, her body was twisted into knots with arthritis. It was as if there was a picture on the outside to show what was going on inside.

Now, I don't mean to imply that everyone with arthritis is bitter! But it seemed that for every poisonous word that spilled out of this woman's mouth, her body twisted in agreement. I understand that unforgiveness and bitterness take their toll on us, but to suggest to people who are sick that these things must be present in their lives or God wouldn't be punishing them is cruel.

Have you faced this in your life?

Do you wonder why it seems as if God answers other people's prayers, but yours never seem to go beyond the ceiling?

Have you doubted your faith and wondered what's wrong with you?

Have you tried every avenue you know, every voice that offers instant hope, only to be left more disappointed than before?

Have you given up praying because you think, *What is the point? God's going to do what God's going to do anyway?*

MY CRY FOR HEALING BECOMES PERSONAL

When Eleanor, my mother-in-law, was diagnosed with liver cancer, she was horrified, as we all were. She was only in her sixties; she loved being a grandmother to Christian.

I went with her to a cancer specialist in Nashville to receive her prognosis. William, her husband, didn't want to know, and it was too painful for Barry to deal with. Eleanor and I were escorted into the doctor's office. He had the results of all her tests in front of him.

"I'd like to know the truth," she said.

"We can give you more chemo. That will buy you a little more time, but as you know, it will make you sick," he said.

"Is there a chance that it will cure me?" she asked.

"No," he replied quietly but kindly. "At best you have two years."

Barry and I tried everything we knew. I used up every contact I had ever made in Christian broadcasting to get Eleanor to the right people at the right time, but she died almost two years to the day of that appointment.

Perhaps you have faced that in your own life or family. You have prayed and prayed, believing that God will hear and answer. In 2003 I lost a dear friend who believed up until her last breath that God was going to step in and heal her. Her husband believed it too. My friend woke up in the arms of Jesus, but what about her husband? He wakes up alone every morning, and in the middle of the night when he reaches for her, there is nothing but space as vacant as his heart. How does such an experience affect how he prays in the future?

In my own life if Barry or I had cancer, would I do the same as we did with Eleanor? Have I given up hope or faith that God heals? No, I would probably do the same thing again. It's not that I think that now I have refined the magic formula—far from it—but we do everything we can, knowing that God is the One who says yes or no. It doesn't mean that He heals because we got to the right church in Chicago at the right time or because we suddenly remembered that when we were six, we kicked the neighbor's cat and confessed that last little block in the road to healing.

God is sovereign. He is in control. He is good and loving and awesome in every way. We come to God as children, asking that in His mercy He will hear our prayers, and we worship, awaiting His answer, whether it's what we asked for or not. I don't say that lightly. It is devastating to lose a loved one, but at those moments we have to lean on God and let Him love us.

I've been a Christian since I was eleven years old, and in 2004 I'll turn forty-eight. I have held the hands of friends and family as they died, I have walked in some really dark places when God did not answer my prayers as I asked Him to, but I have to tell you, I love Him more today than I ever have.

Even when nothing makes sense, He is here.
Even when hearts are broken, He is here.
Even when prayers seek to lie in pools of tears at our feet, He is here.
He hears every prayer you pray, and He loves you. Jesus loves you.

What I've learned is to lean on Him. I can't even begin to express how huge this is in my life, but since this is a book and I am supposed to be an author, I'll give it a shot!

One of my dearest friends is Joni Eareckson Tada. If you know her story, you know that she has been in a wheelchair since she was a teenager. A diving accident rendered Joni quadriplegic. She is one of the most amazing women you could ever hope to meet. Our friendship is marked by music. Every time we are together, whether in person or on the phone, we sing. We met in Holland at a Christian festival when we were in our twenties. Joni was beautifully dressed in a smart, feminine suit. I, however, had spiky hair and was dressed in leather pants, and my music gave my mother a headache. Our looks were different, but our hearts were the same.

Several years (and wardrobe changes) later, Joni asked me to speak at her donors' conference in Chicago. Among other things, she raises money to send disabled children to camp and to buy wheelchairs for those around the world who can't afford one. This conference was a way of saying thank you to those who share her passion to help those who cannot help themselves.

At the end of the conference we grabbed a few moments to talk in private and catch up on family news. She said something to me that night that I will never forget: "Sheila, in some ways you are more disabled than I am."

"What do you mean?" I asked, knowing that since it was Joni speaking, the answer would be profound.

"I can never forget that I am disabled," she said. "It is with me every moment of every day. I can't brush my hair or blow my own nose. I am completely dependent on the Lord and on others. At times you are aware of your brokenness, but it must be easy to forget and carry on as if you can do everything by yourself now."

I knew exactly what she meant. There are moments in my life when I clearly understand that apart from Christ, I can do nothing. There are moments when things are going well, and I think, *I've really got my act together now. I'm just growing by leaps and bounds!*

During the writing of this book, God gave me a gift. I want to share it with you.

THE LESSON OF THE CAMEL

I was in my coffee spot, battering away on my laptop. At the far end of the table where I was working, two guys were talking. I'm pretty intense when I write, so I don't hear much around me, but every now and then I picked up a word or two and I could tell that they were Christians.

After a while one left, and the other gentleman, looking at the pile of books beside me, said, "I see you like Brennan Manning's books."

"I love them. He is a wonderful writer."

We introduced ourselves and talked for a moment about some mutual friends that we discovered. Then he got up to leave. As he reached the door, he stopped and turned back.

He said, "God gave me a verse to share with you. This verse has been with me over and over for a week, and the Lord asked me to share it with you: 'Commit your works to the LORD, and your thoughts will be established' [Prov. 16:3]."

I had such a sense that this was indeed a special word from God to my heart that I began a word study of the verse. The word *commit* in the context of this verse is very interesting. The Hebrew word is *galal.* It means, "To roll; roll away."

It is also used in this passage:

Commit your way to the LORD,
Trust also in Him,
And He shall bring it to pass.
He shall bring forth your righteousness as the light,
And your justice as the noonday. (Ps. 37:5–6, emphasis added)

The word *galal* is used often to describe the way a camel gets rid of its burden. It is a two-step process. First, it kneels down, and then it rolls to the left and the load falls off the camel's back. The picture for us is a beautiful one. We are invited to kneel before God but encouraged not to stop there. We are called to roll over and let the burden fall off our backs. We are called to roll every burden, every concern for the future, onto the Lord, sure that He will accept that responsibility and will bless us. *Whatever you are facing right now, kneel before God and roll into His grace.*

He wants to carry your burden. You don't have to carry it anymore.

Is your husband sick? Kneel down and roll the burden onto your Father.

Are you worried about your child? Kneel down and roll the burden onto your Father.

Are you anxious about anything? Kneel down in worship of the God who is in control of every detail of your life, and let your burdens roll away.

My friend Chuck Girard wrote a song that I used to sing:

Lay your burden down,
Lay your burden down
Take your weary heart, your tired mind and lay your burden down

There are many things on this side of eternity that we simply don't know. What we do know is that God will be with us at the moments that make sense and the moments that make no sense at all.

LONGING FOR SIGNS OR LONGING FOR JESUS?

It seems as if every decade in the church gives birth to new trends. The nineties were no exception in regard to healing. Stories of all sorts of physical manifestations of God's presence were rampant. At some churches gold dust would apparently appear when they prayed for you.

I had a somewhat unfortunate encounter with a man at a Christian Booksellers Association Convention in that regard. When I was getting ready in the morning for the interviews that were scheduled for that day, I realized that I left my regular body cream at home. The only thing I had was a sun cream with a little sparkle to it that I use on my legs in the summer. I put it on anyway, deciding that since I was wearing a suit, no one would notice my sparkly arms and legs. As I was walking through the booths on the convention floor, a man stopped me to remind me that I had interviewed him several years before on *The 700 Club*. We talked a bit, and then he asked if he could pray for me. I said yes.

Then he said, "I have an unusual gift."

"What's that?" I inquired.

"When I pray for people, gold dust sometimes appears on them."

"Wow!" I said. "Carry on."

After he prayed for me, he asked me if I would take off my jacket and roll up my sleeves. As I did, the light from the booth showed the cream on my arms. I had forgotten all about it.

"See! I told you," he said.

I didn't have the heart to tell him my sparkle came from a tube.

LONGING FOR GOD

Whether we are looking for signs and wonders, physical healing, or a balm for our wounded souls, underneath it all we are longing for God. We might not recognize that, but we are made to be in intimate relationship with Him. When we are not, we try to fill that void with whatever we perceive to be our greatest felt need. Underneath it all we want God to be real to us, to touch us.

God moves in many different ways, and who am I to say what God will do for anyone or how He might choose to manifest His presence? I have learned enough to know that God's ways and thoughts are outside my human capacity for reason. What troubles me, though, is that we seek what God might *do* instead of seeking God Himself. What troubles me is that we are more after God's hand than God's face.

You could have every tooth in your head turn to gold, but what would it profit you in the long run? What we need is heart surgery. We need God to heal our broken hearts. God could heal your body, but if your heart is still full of pain, bitterness, and disappointment, the healing is limited to what would show up in an X-ray.

God asks that we be hungry for Him, seek Him, kneel down and roll our burdens onto Him. The greatest gift that you and I can give ourselves is to fall in love with Jesus. Everything else in this life is temporary; only life with Him has any lasting meaning. *Let's not occupy our lives chasing after the latest craze; let's chase after the God who is crazy about us.*

☙

Father God,
    Teach me to long for You more than for what You might do for me. Help me to lay my burdens down and rest in You. Amen.

APPLICATION POINTS

- God's love is a gift, not a reward for good behavior. What guilt are you carrying around, thinking—wrongly—that your child, husband, or loved one is sick and you're to blame? *Optional:* Where do you think you got this idea? What biblical truth(s) correct this idea?

- It is a mystery that God physically heals some people and not others. What questions for God does this raise in your mind? (See some examples on page 87.) What peace, if any, have you made with this issue?

- As I said earlier, I have walked in some very dark places when God did not answer my prayers as I asked Him to, but I love Him more today than I ever have. Even when nothing makes sense, He is here. Even when hearts are broken, He is here. I'm sure that God hasn't always answered your prayers as you've asked Him to. In what ways, if any, have those disappointing answers increased your love for God and even your faith in Him?

- My friend Joni can never forget that she is disabled, but I can. As she wisely pointed out, at times I am aware of my brokenness, but it is all too easy to forget and to carry on as if I can do everything by myself. What are the advantages of always being aware of our need for the Lord? What keeps you from that constant awareness? What might you do to be more aware that you are dependent on God's grace for everything?

- There are many things on this side of eternity that we simply don't know or understand. What we do know is that God will be with us in the moments that make sense and in the moments that make no sense at all. When has the presence of a family member or friend made all the difference for you even when circumstances didn't change? What blessings come from God's presence with you even when circumstances don't change in the way or at the speed you want them to?

8

HOW CAN YOU MEND A BROKEN HEART?

I am forgotten like a dead man, out of mind;
I am like a broken vessel.

—PSALM 31:12

Heal me, O LORD, and I shall be healed;
Save me, and I shall be saved, For you are My praise.

—JEREMIAH 17:14

The heart cry of this book can be summed up in the words of the prophet Jeremiah cited at the beginning of this chapter.

I hear his cry as a wail from deep inside a desperate soul. He was a man who knew that if God didn't do something, then he was lost.

I understand that.

Is that where you are now? "God, if You don't do something, I am lost. I'm at the end of myself. I have nowhere else to go."

Let me introduce you to a woman who knew that place well. You might have met her briefly before, but as with lots of stories that get passed from person to person, the details of her life have become confused over time. I'd like to try and set the record straight because, as our sister, she has a lot to say to us.

HER NAME WAS MARY

The root meaning of her name in Greek is "bitter and sorrow." She was well named, for she experienced all of those places in her life. The New

Testament refers to her as Mary Magdalene. Magdala was the town she was from, just as Christ, from Nazareth, was sometimes known as the Nazarene. Magdala was a wealthy community on the coast of the Sea of Galilee. The wealth came from the textile and dye industry. It is thought that Mary was well placed financially, and that enabled her to serve and follow Christ freely. It's also considered that with other wealthy women, she might have made it possible for Christ and the disciples to do what they did without concern for finances.

Mary was a woman with a world of trouble inside her. She was a tormented woman before her encounter with Christ.

> Now it came to pass, afterward, that He went through every city and village, preaching and bringing the glad tidings of the kingdom of God. And the twelve were with Him, and certain women who had been healed of evil spirits and infirmities—Mary called Magdalene, out of whom had come seven demons. (Luke 8:1–2)

Many have assumed that Mary Magdalene was a prostitute. The town of Magdala, according to the Jewish Talmud, had a terrible reputation for immorality and was in fact destroyed because of that, and some put two and two together and labeled Mary a prostitute.

There is little evidence to suggest that was true and a lot of evidence to suggest it was not true. When the early church fathers wrote about the Christian community, they wrote about Mary, and there was nothing to suggest that she had an immoral reputation. She was held in the highest esteem.

Mary had been set free from seven demons: "When He [Jesus] rose early on the first day of the week, He appeared first to Mary Magdalene, out of whom He had cast seven demons" (Mark 16:9).

She was a woman tormented and tortured in her mind. *Seven* in biblical terms is seen as the number of perfection. The point seems clear; she was tormented absolutely. When Christ encountered Mary, she must have been a frightening sight to look at, eyes wide with demonic rage, hair disheveled, twisted in body and mind. I find it amazing that when Jesus looked at her, He didn't see the kind of woman that you and I would cross the street to avoid; instead He saw a woman in trouble. How could Christ bring peace to this tormented woman? How could

He even get close to one who would hit out at any attempt to be helped?

We don't know what happened to her in her life that brought her to such a place of despair. Was she abused as a child? Had she walked through some heartache that had torn her heart in two? How had she come to be so plagued by Satan? Do you identify with her plight at all? I do. I know what it feels like to be crying out for help and yet keeping everyone at a distance because I'm sure no one can help me.

MAN OF THE TOMBS

She was like the man who lived wild among the tombs, cutting into his flesh with rocks, perhaps to see if he still bled, if there was anything left in him that was still alive. My friend Bob Bennett wrote the song "Man of the Tombs" that captures the torture of a mind out of control. I first heard it ten years ago. To this day, I can't listen to it without weeping.

> Underneath this thing that I've become
> A fading memory of flesh and blood
> I curse the womb, I bless the grave
> I've lost my heart, I cannot be saved
> Like those who fear me, I'm afraid
> Like those I hurt, I can feel pain

That must have been how Mary felt. I'm sure that those who loved her wanted to help, but how do you help someone who strikes out at your every attempt to reach her?

Have you been there?

Are you crying out for help, but you lash out at anyone who tries to reach you?

Has your heart been broken for so long that you are tired of people offering help that does so little?

Mary must have been that way until that day when she came face-to-face with Jesus.

> Down at the shoreline,
> Two sets of footprints meet
> One voice is screaming,

Other voice begins to speak
In only a moment and only a word
The evil departs like thundering herd
Man of the tombs, he hears this cry out loud . . .

I give you life beyond the grave
I heal your heart, I come to save
No need to fear, be not afraid
This man of sorrows knows your name
I come to take your sin
And bear its marks upon my skin
When no one can touch you, still I can
For Son of God I am

After she had been delivered of the demons that tormented her, Mary became the most devoted follower of Christ. When the women who traveled with Jesus were listed, Mary Magdalene always came first, unless Jesus' mother or his aunt was present, and then out of respect she was listed after them. Her placement shows that she was regarded as a leader among the women who followed Jesus.

Christ lived an itinerant life, going from place to place. Mary and the other women who served Him followed Him. She was there on Jesus' last journey from Galilee to Jerusalem. She stood in the hall as Pilate announced Christ's death sentence, and she was there at the foot of the cross. What must she have thought? Before she met Christ, she was an aberration to herself and to others, a terrifying woman who would suddenly be gripped with uncontrollable outbursts. Into her private hell walked the Lamb of God and set her free. Now as she watched, the Lamb's very life-blood was dripping away. She knew, as few did, who He really was.

Mary stood as close to the cross as she could. She heard Christ's cries, saw the day turn as black as night, and as she watched, a soldier thrust his sword into Jesus' side and declared Him dead. In Rubens's masterpiece, the *Descent of the Cross*, you see four figures handling the broken body of Jesus: Joseph of Arimathea; Nicodemus; Mary, wife of Clopas; and Mary Magdalene. Joseph, a wealthy man, had given Christ his garden tomb as a place to be buried. After the body was removed from the cross and placed on a sheet, they carried Him to the garden tomb. The men laid His body on a shelf inside the cave, and Mary watched as they hurried to get the heavy stone in place before the Sabbath began. She sat grief stricken as the stone was rolled across the entrance, closing Christ's body into the dank darkness of a tomb.

> When Joseph had taken the body, he wrapped it in a clean linen cloth, and laid it in his new tomb which he had hewn out of the rock; and he rolled a large stone against the door of the tomb, and departed. And Mary Magdalene was there, and the other Mary, sitting opposite the tomb. (Matt. 27:59–61)

I wonder how she felt that night. The very One who had stepped into her darkness and set her free was now entombed in darkness. I see her sitting alone in the dark, rocking back and forth, back and forth, like a baby with no one to comfort her.

DON'T LEAVE HIM IN THE DARK

Death is such an unseemly part of our human existence.

I remember the night that my father-in-law died. I had never had to cope with making arrangements for a body before, but because Barry was in Florida, there was no one else to do it. Christian and I followed the ambulance. The doctor on duty at the emergency room told me that William had died. He took me to the room where they had his body. He was still warm. It seemed to me that an unfinished conversation hung between us. We had been talking about what to get Barry for Christmas, and he wanted to go in on a joint gift. As I left the room, the nurse in charge asked me what arrangements I had made.

"What do you mean?" I asked, uninitiated in the practicalities of death.

"Have you made arrangements for the body?" she clarified.

"No!" I said, a little shocked. "What do I do?"

"Do you have a funeral home of choice?" she asked.

"No," I said. "I don't think my husband will want him buried here. He'll want him with his mom in Charleston."

"That's fine," she said. "We just need a funeral home here to collect the body and prepare it to be transported to Charleston."

I stood there unable to think what to do.

She seemed to understand. "Why don't you take your son home? It's after midnight. You can call us with the details in the morning."

I thanked her and turned to leave. A sick feeling gripped me in my stomach.

"What are you going to do with him tonight?" I asked.

"We'll take care of him," she said.

"But where are you going to put him? He doesn't like the dark, and he hates to be alone."

Even as the words spilled out of my mouth, I realized how ridiculous they were, but there is just something harsh about those first few moments and hours that separate the living and the dead. They have crossed a river, and they can't look back.

HE'S ALIVE!

How must it have been for Mary? She had watched the cruel torture and ridicule inflicted on the greatest Man who ever walked this earth. She saw them strip the life from the One who gave her life back to her. She was last at the cross and first at the garden tomb when Passover was over. Mary was the first to see that the tomb was empty. She rushed to tell the others what had happened. The disciples ran to the garden and looked inside. Christ was gone. The grave clothes were still there, but the body was gone. The bandage that had been around Jesus' head was separate from the other wraps. It sat alone, wrapped neatly.

There is great significance in that. If in those days you hired a carpenter to come to your home and make a table and chairs, he would work on it for as many days as it took. When he was finished, he would take the cloth he used to clean it off and fold it neatly, letting you know he was finished. It was finished. Christ's work was done!

The disciples eventually left the garden tomb, wondering what on earth had happened, but once more Mary was the one who stayed. Weeping bitter tears, she looked into the tomb again and saw two angels sitting where Christ's body had been, one at the head and one at the feet. Then she heard a voice outside the tomb. She thought it was the gardener and said, "Sir, if You have carried Him away, tell me where You have laid Him, and I will take Him away (John 20:15). I love that about her! She was just one woman, but in her passionate love for Christ she would have carried Him by herself. Then He said her name, "Mary!" Mary Magdalene, a woman with a tortured past, was given the joy of being the first one to see Jesus alive. Mary, whose heart was broken, was the first to receive the healing that is offered to all who recognize the risen Christ. We are going to experience pain and sorrow on this earth. We all know that, but the fact that we follow a risen Jesus changes everything.

"That's great, Sheila!" you say. "I love the story and I'm happy for Mary, but what does her story have to do with me?"

I'm so glad you asked—it has everything to do with you and with me! *Jesus sees you not only as you are but also as you can be.*

I don't know what caused your broken heart. I don't know if you feel there is a twist in your soul that makes you spit out venom and then hate yourself because it's not who you want to be. But Jesus knows. When He looked at Mary, He did not see just a woman out of control, in trouble, desperate and ugly. He saw Mary, and He saw how Mary could live if she was healed and filled with His love. And He was committed to doing just that. It's why He came.

When Jesus looked at me, He didn't see just a woman who was shut off emotionally, afraid, angry, sarcastic, and deeply sad. He saw me. He saw Sheila Walsh, the real me. Jesus loved me back to life. I was a woman afraid of everything, and He met me in the graveyard of my mind and set me free. He took me from someone who was afraid of everything and showed me that because He is always with me, I don't have to be afraid. He took me from someone who was afraid of being rejected and told me that He would never reject me. He took me from someone fighting for control to someone who believes that God is in control and He is good, so I can rest in Him.

He wants to do the same for you. Jesus didn't come just to rescue us from hell; He came to rescue us from a life of hell on earth too.

Do you remember Paul's greeting to the church in Philippi?

Grace to you and peace from God our Father and the Lord Jesus Christ. I thank my God upon every remembrance of you, always in every prayer of mine making request for you all with joy, for your fellowship in the gospel from the first day until now, being confident of this very thing, that He who has begun a good work in you will complete it until the day of Jesus Christ. (Phil. 1:2–6)

Paul reminded the believers in Philippi, and through that letter to us, that it is God who began the good work, and He is the One committed to finishing it. The Greek word for "save" is *sozo;* it means "to save and to heal." Jesus didn't come just to get us out of hell, but to get hell out of us while we live on earth.

When Jesus looks at you, He doesn't see the things that make others turn away or the things that make you turn away from others. He sees you! He sees you and He loves you and He wants to heal you. Jesus wants to set you free to be the woman He created you to be. Do you believe it is possible?

I know that it is!

On October 21, 1992, someone sent me a letter. He had been watching *The 700 Club,* and Pat Robertson said that I was taking time off because I was exhausted. This man did not know that as he wrote to me, I was in the locked ward of a psychiatric institution. In his letter he said that he was an amateur haiku writer. I had no idea what that was. I now know that it is a form of Japanese poetry with seventeen syllables in three unrhymed lines of five, seven, and five syllables.

He wrote that as he prayed for me, he had the sense of a stray animal suddenly finding herself free. There was the beginning of some autumn sunshine.

> A three-legged stray
> Downstream . . . returned to herself
> Stands wet in the leaves

That strange little poem means the world to me, for that is how I felt. It was as if I had just gone over a waterfall and not expected to survive, but there I was, battered, bruised but still standing.

That's what God wants to do for you.

"You don't know what happened to me," you say. "I can never recover from my wounds. There are moments, moments in my past that I can't even talk about."

JESUS IN YOUR DEFINING MOMENTS

I've heard them described in various fashions:

- defining moments

- crisis points

- trigger events

No matter what label you give them, they are the moments that change our lives forever. They are the moments that cause us to think that things will never be any different.

I had the television on in my room one day as I was getting ready for a conference. I wasn't paying much attention to the subject at hand until the tone in a woman's voice made me put down my hairbrush and listen.

The host had apparently asked her what her defining moment was.

She said, "It was the day my father looked at me as I picked up a cookie, and he blew his cheeks out to look like a fat pig. He never said a word, but I got it. I got the message loud and clear." She then went on to describe her lifetime struggle with bulimia.

"Every time I picked up something to eat I saw my father's face, but I couldn't stop myself. So I would eat and eat and then make myself sick. I was eight years old when it happened, but it has ruined my life."

Then a male guest spoke: "All my life, all I have wanted was for my father to say, 'Well done!' All through grade school and high school, no matter how well I did, it was never enough. Finally I graduated from college at the top of my class. After the ceremony, I went over to my dad, and he told me that I should have had my hair cut, I looked a mess. I looked in his eyes, and at that moment I just gave up. I thought, *What's the point?*"

He sat with his head in his hands and wept. His wife sat beside him.

"He's a wonderful husband and a great dad," she said. "But he doesn't believe it. He's still waiting to hear it from his own dad. He never will. His father died last year."

Another female guest said, "It was the first time my father struck me. I was so shocked. I was shocked that he would hit me, but I was more shocked by the look in his eyes. I've been married twice. Both husbands have hit me. I stayed because I thought it was what I deserved."

What are your defining moments?

Some defining moments are wonderful. Some looks are what great choices are birthed from, but for our purposes here I refer to those painful moments that cut a deep trench through our hearts.

I have no conscious memory of one of my most acute defining moments. I know the details only through my mother who was there and told me what happened. I was only four years old, but the impact that it had on my life was huge. It was the last day I ever saw my dad alive. The look he gave me was full of hate and rage, and then he was gone. In those days, particularly in my Scottish culture, there was no thought of counseling for children to help them process traumatic events. Those resources were simply not available. As long as the child appeared to be functioning fairly normally, it was assumed that she was coping.

I didn't act up at school or cause trouble at home, but I had terrible nightmares and I walked in my sleep. I went up to my room when there was a male visitor, even though it would be an uncle or someone from our church just popping in to see how we were doing.

Each defining moment can have a lifetime of repercussions if we are not able to bring those fresh wounds into the light of God's grace and be healed. Over time the wounds become calloused, protected by the layering of years.

If I compare the way Christian, my son, copes with loss to the way I coped at age four, we are worlds apart. After the death of my father, I was not convinced that he was dead. I never saw him again after that terrible day when he was taken away. I never went to a funeral or a grave site. I never talked about him again, but he was with me in my head. I heard his words; I saw his expression and felt the threat of unfinished business. That's why I walked in my sleep and had nightmares where I was condemned to death for something that I didn't do, but no one would believe me. I wanted no photos of my dad around. It was too disturbing to revisit his image.

On that night when my father-in-law, William, died, Christian and I were with him. As I said earlier, Barry was in Florida. We had a few moments alone with William when he was still conscious before the paramedics arrived. Christian asked me if he could help. I told him to get a wet rag and sit beside his papa, holding it to his head. When the paramedics arrived, I asked Christian to fix a few things to take to the hospital for Papa. He filled his backpack with toys and books—a child's first aid kit.

We followed the ambulance, but William was dead when we arrived. Over the next few days and weeks Christian wept bitterly. William had lived with us for two years and was dearly loved. Then Christian began to experience deep anger, at God, at life, at anyone who got in his way. We talked about it, and I bought him a punching bag and boxing gloves so that he would have a safe place to take his understandable rage.

We have photos of William around the house. We talk about him. We cry and laugh at how William, Christian, and I used to embarrass Barry in restaurants by doing the "butt dance" around the table. (Don't ask!)

We are learning so much now about how to help our children deal with pain and loss, how to protect them from abuse, what is acceptable and unacceptable behavior. But perhaps, like me, you had no path out of your pain, and the wounds of childhood have stayed with you. I hear about them every weekend as I listen to women pour out the details of the events that sabotaged their sanity.

A TIME FOR HEALING

It's time to invite Christ into these broken places and let Him make us whole. Let's consider what the psalmist David said as he cried out to God:

> Have mercy on me, O LORD, for I am weak;
> O LORD, heal me, for my bones are troubled.
> My soul also is greatly troubled;
> But You, O LORD—how long?
> Return, O LORD, deliver me!
> Oh, save me for Your mercies' sake! (Ps. 6:2–4)

> The sacrifices of God are a broken spirit,
> A broken and a contrite heart—
> These, O God, You will not despise. (Ps. 51:17)

You might find it helpful to get a journal or a notebook and write down what the Spirit of God brings to mind. Beside each entry of pain or sadness, covering each wound you can write:

> He was wounded for our transgressions,
> He was bruised for our iniquities;
> The chastisement for our peace was upon Him,
> And by His stripes we are healed. (Isa. 53:5)

His punishment is meant to bring us peace; His wounds bring us healing.

Some of your wounds may be so great and so painful that it would be wise to find a godly counselor to help you deal with them. Your pastor may be available to help or refer you to someone who can walk with you. There are counselors who deal specifically with sexual abuse, with eating disorders, with rape trauma. Don't be ashamed to ask for help, and don't be put off until you find the right person to help you. Jesus gave His life for you. You are worth saving!

If you struggle with depression, situational or genetic, there is great help available. I have been on the drug Zoloft for more than ten years and have found it to be a gift from God. The church is divided on the use of psychiatric medicine and even psychiatric counseling. We'll look at that more in depth in Chapter 15. Let me just say here, though, *if you need help, get help.* Don't be ashamed to reach out and take the help that is available. *God wants you restored, strong, and full of His life and love.*

That might be a little scary at first. We can become used to having a broken heart. Whether our broken hearts are a result of things that have been done to us, such as abuse or tragic loss, or whether we struggle with depression and anxiety that can be genetically inherited, the effect on the heart is the same. Only Christ can heal us.

ARE YOU WILLING?

Jesus once asked a man, "Do you want to get well?" The man in question had been sick for a long time. He was identified by it; people recognized him as the one who could do nothing to help himself. Jesus' question required a lot of him. Healing in this case happened in a moment, but he would have to live out the rest of his life making different choices. When he lay by the pool, those who passed him might have thrown some coins toward his plight or a kind word, a moment of sympathy and human connection. If he was healed, he must become part of the healing of others.

Being healed by Christ teaches you one thing for sure: we are healed to come to others in Jesus' name, offering the same healing. We are no longer at liberty to be part of the problem; we are given the joy of being part of the solution. Do you want to get well? Those who have been broken and restored by Christ have a God-given ability to connect with others in pain and offer hope and healing. It is one of the greatest privileges of my life to watch the way God uses what was a nightmare to me at the time as a candle in the darkness to others.

When Christ heals us, when we get up and walk again, we discover there is work to be done. We have begun to live again!

As we move on in the book, we will study the issue of spiritual warfare. Christ longs to heal us, but what part do we play in defending the territory that He has restored? As we begin to retrain our minds to listen to God's truth and not the enemy's lies, Satan will try to bring them back to us every day in a million ways. As we start to rest in the knowledge that just as we are right now God loves us, our enemy will try to hold up an old mirror and convince us that nothing has changed; we are fooling ourselves.

How do we protect ourselves from the enemy who is out to destroy all that God loves? Is it possible to live in this world with all the pain and uncertainty and be at peace? We will look at these questions and then how we are called to live in community with one another. We have been left with a map of the steps on the road that leads us home to God. Let's not miss one of them.

❧

Father God,

I come to You in the name of Your Son and my Savior, Jesus. I confess to You that my heart has become calloused. Help me, Father. Give me eyes to see, ears to hear, and a heart to understand that You love me and want to heal me. You say in Your Word that if I understand with my heart and turn to You, then You will heal me. I turn to You now in Jesus' name and accept healing for my broken heart. As You give me grace, I will bring every wound to You as the Holy Spirit brings it to my mind so that I might leave each of them at the cross. Thank You, Father.

In Jesus' name, amen.

APPLICATION POINTS

- Like Mary Magdalene before Jesus delivered her from seven demons, in what ways—if any—are you crying out for help, but lashing out at anyone who tries to reach you?

- We are going to experience pain and sorrow on this earth. But the fact that we follow a risen Jesus changes everything. Give an example or two (ideally but not necessarily from your own life) of Jesus' presence in someone's life and heart, changing his or her experience of pain and sorrow. Jesus sees you not only as you are, but also as you can be. He saw me not as a woman who was shut off emotionally, afraid, angry, sarcastic, and deeply sad. Jesus loved me back to life. He took me from being someone who was afraid of everything and showed me that because He is always with me, I don't have to be afraid. He took me from being someone who feared rejection and told me that He would never reject me. He took me from being someone fighting for control to someone who believes that God is in control and that He is good, so I can rest in Him. Jesus wants to do these same things for you. What encouragement and reason(s) for hope do you find in this truth?

- Jesus didn't just come to rescue us from hell; He came to rescue us from a life of hell on earth too. What aspects of hell, if any, has Jesus already rescued you from? What kind of hell do you still need Him to deliver you from? Be specific.

- As I wrote in the chapter, it's time to invite Christ into your broken places and to let Him make you whole. I also mentioned that you might find it very helpful to write down in a journal or notebook what the Spirit of God brings to your mind as you ask Him to help you recall every wound so that you can leave each one at the cross. Beside each entry of pain or sadness, write Isaiah 53:5. Jesus suffered the punishment for our sins on the cross so that we might know peace with God and healing for our wounded souls.

Warfare

9

IT'S A MINEFIELD OUT THERE!

Put on the full armor of God so that you can take your stand against the devil's schemes.

—EPHESIANS 6:11 NIV

Be self-controlled and alert. Your enemy the devil prowls around like a roaring lion looking for someone to devour.

—1 PETER 5:8 NIV

In the last chapter we discussed that we have a very real enemy who would love to undo the healing work of Christ in our hearts. We know that he is a liar who hates all that God loves. A year after I left the hospital, I began to experience another downward spiral. I recognized the dark night of depression coming on again. I had been taking my medication and had been in counseling, and yet I felt that I was losing much of the ground that I had gained. That scared me.

Dark thoughts plagued my mind. I was lonely and sad and felt the familiar pull to get in bed and pull the covers over my head. At my next session with my counselor I talked about this, and she asked me how I was doing battle with the enemy. I wasn't sure what she meant. I knew that the enemy tries to tempt us to sin or to stay away from God's presence, but what did he have to do with depression? For the next few sessions we talked about all that we can do as God's people to resist the enemy in all the ways he attacks us. I believed that God could heal me instantly from depression, but at that moment He had not done that. I gratefully took my medication, exercised, and tried to eat well.

Yet there was more that I was called to do. I was and am called to daily put on the whole armor of God to protect myself, mind, body, and spirit. Even though I have been a believer since I was eleven years old, I had underestimated the spiritual battles that rage around us every day. I knew that Satan was real, but I assumed he was occupied in Washington, D.C., or Jerusalem, where decisions were being made that affected world peace, not in my little home and heart. But God began to open my eyes.

AN AWAKENING

I mark my awakening twelve years ago to warfare in the spiritual realm by the first time I read Frank Peretti's book *This Present Darkness*. The story had quite an impact on me. The action takes place in a small, sleepy town somewhere in a "nothing strange happens here" part of America. Through the vehicle of fiction, we are given access to two realities that are going on at the same time in the same lives. The first story centers on the residents of the town, the newspaper reporter, the local pastor, and others. The second story, woven in with the first, is what is happening in the unseen realm, the spiritual realm with angels and demons. I had never read such a pairing of realities in a novel before.

In his book, Frank Peretti puts flesh and shoe size, moment-by-moment tension, into the spiritual battle that we know to be a reality from God's Word. As the story develops, the reader is made privy to the tricks of the demons and how they impact the lives of the people in the town, believer and unbeliever alike. We see the strength and awesome power of God's angelic beings as they fight to hold back the darkness that threatens to overtake the town. My response to the book seemed to have been shared by many because it shot to the top of the bestseller list in very little time.

I wasn't sure how to react to the message of the book after I finished reading. Part of me felt guilty for all the times I had let God down, suddenly imagining the demons high-fiving one another and the angels grieving over my careless attitude toward my walk with God. Part of me felt a renewed commitment to live a godly life in an ungodly world, knowing that in Jesus' name we have been given weapons to combat the attacks of the enemy.

Since childhood, I have been aware that we have an enemy who prowls around like a roaring lion seeking to peel off any unsuspecting, unguarded Christian. My experience, however, was of two extremes.

On one extreme, I encountered people who discounted the presence of a real devil and real demonic powers as nothing more than the invention of Hollywood or narrow-minded fundamentalists: "Surely if there is a loving God, He would never allow a place like hell to exist. How could a good God permit people to be tortured? The very idea is barbaric."

The other extreme was from those who saw demons jumping out of every bush. The last time that I toured the United Kingdom we traveled in buses. The person responsible for selling T-shirts and CDs was on my bus. He was a very fervent, intense young man whose relationship with supposed demons occupied a significant amount of his time. If he fell over a box, which he frequently did because he was clumsy, he would say that a demon tripped him up. If his burger wasn't cooked thoroughly, he would declare it a hellish plot to poison him. By the end of the tour I was so tired of his assumed entourage that I was coming up with a few plots of my own!

I fell somewhere in the middle. It was clear to me that there is a real devil, but as far as I was concerned, he was occupied menacing far bigger fish than I.

Between those two positions stands the truth that most believers embrace. There is a real enemy who has his followers, a house of fallen angels, and they have set themselves against God and all He loves. But we have not been left unprepared in this battle. *It is God's desire to heal our hearts and to show us how to guard that territory against a further onslaught of evil.* I think every believer should begin her journey of understanding spiritual warfare by looking at Christ's confrontation with Satan in the wilderness. There is much to learn from that encounter.

THE SON AND THE FALLEN ANGEL

We read that Satan made his entrance into the ministry years of Christ right after Jesus was baptized:

> Immediately the Spirit drove Him into the wilderness. And He was there in the wilderness forty days, tempted by Satan, and was with the wild beasts; and the angels ministered to Him. (Mark 1:12–13) [The children of Israel spent forty years wandering in the desert, getting it all wrong. Jesus spent forty days in the desert and showed us how to live and choose rightly.]

With each temptation that the devil offered, Jesus resisted by using the Word of God: "It is written . . . it is written . . . it is written . . ." Satan offered three things:

1. Relief from Jesus' hunger: turn these stones into bread.
2. A spectacular launch into the public eye: throw Yourself off the temple (remember that is where many thought Messiah was supposed to appear).
3. A way to avoid the Cross: if You will bow down and worship me, I'll give You everything.

I find it fascinating that Christ's responses were so low key. There was no great wielding of swords or summoning up of angelic beings—just a simple, direct proclamation of the living Word of God. It is clear from this that the power is in God's Word, not in our raised voices or dramatic stances. I would imagine that if I were face-to-face with the author of all evil, it would be a cataclysmic event. Jesus rested not in displays of power but in the truth of the Word of God.

There are no new tricks, just a reassertion of what has always been true—only God is worthy of our worship. Satan came after Jesus three times and then left Him, but we read, "When the devil had ended every temptation, he departed from Him *until an opportune time*" (Luke 4:13, emphasis added).

He would be back. He always comes back. He was just waiting for the right moment.

He was there that day as Jesus met with His friends for His last meal before the Cross: "Supper being ended, the devil having already put it into the heart of Judas Iscariot, Simon's son, to betray Him . . ." (John 13:2).

He was there that day in the crowd, crying out, "Crucify Him! Crucify Him!"

I imagine him there at the foot of the cross, lying back on the grass, feet up on a stone, soaking in the scent of hatred and betrayal that hung heavy in the air. What did he think when the sky turned inky black? Did he think that God was in mourning for His Son? As the thunder ripped the sky in two, did his laughter challenge the decibel level of the heavens?

Then Christ cried out, "It is finished!" and bowed His head and died.

Did Satan fall into an arrogant, self-satisfied sleep?

But things were happening. Matthew's gospel gives us the most detailed account:

The veil of the temple was torn in two from top to bottom; and the earth quaked, and the rocks were split, and the graves were opened; and many bodies of the saints who had fallen asleep were raised; and coming out of the graves after His resurrection, they went into the holy city and appeared to many. So when the centurion and those with him, who were guarding Jesus, saw the earthquake and the things that had happened, they feared greatly, saying, "Truly this was the Son of God!" (27:51–54)

Where was Satan during all of this?

Did he think he was home free?

If he stopped by the tomb on that first Easter Sunday morning, he was in for the surprise of his life. There was no more "business as usual."

Since the dawn of man, we have messed up. God gave us opportunity after opportunity to choose to live differently, and we failed. Satan and his demons were witness to our frailty and sinful nature. There was no hope. There was no hope until that morning. Even those heroes of the faith who had died before the birth of Christ had to wait for the resurrection of Christ. Without the resurrection of the perfect Lamb of God there is no celebration. But Jesus did rise again, and He holds the keys of death and hell.

Do you live in fear of death? Do you wonder who holds your destiny? It is God and God alone. Everything has changed, and Satan knows it. His time is very limited. His destiny is assured. But should we be afraid since he has nothing left to lose?

ONLY WHAT GOD ALLOWS

There is no doubt that Satan's rage is intense, but we can take heart, for he can do only what God will allow: "Simon, Simon! Indeed, Satan has *asked* for you, that he may sift you as wheat" (Luke 22:31, emphasis added).

It must have been hard for Peter to be singled out like that. Christ's statement to him came after a commendation of the disciples as a group: "You are those who have continued with Me in My trials. And I bestow upon you a kingdom, just as my Father bestowed one upon Me" (Luke 22:28–29).

Then He singled out Peter and went on to predict Peter's defection, which He attributed to the direct activity of Satan. The picture of sifting implies separating what is desirable from what is undesirable. Here the thought is that Satan wanted to prove that at least some of the disciples would fail when things got tough. God allowed this testing, but it didn't mean that it was all over for Peter. After the test, when Peter bitterly realized that he was not as strong as he thought he was, Jesus called him the Rock, the one on whom Jesus would build His church. Satan may be allowed to mess with us for a time, but it will work for our good in the end. Satan has to ask permission before he can touch us, and there is only so much that God will allow.

Do you feel as if you are a random pawn and the enemy can torment you at will? No! You are a daughter of heaven, and God will not allow anything to happen to you that He will not give you the grace to endure.

God wants us to be wise in this age in which we live, to be aware, informed, and ready. We are instructed to watch for the enemy's attacks, to be vigilant at all times:

> Be sober, be vigilant; because your adversary the devil walks about like a roaring lion, seeking whom he may devour. *Resist him*, steadfast in the faith, knowing that the same sufferings are experienced by your brotherhood in the world. (1 Peter 5:8–9, emphasis added)

> Submit to God. *Resist the devil* and he will flee from you. (James 4:7, emphasis added)

How do we resist? That seems to be the common theme. Christ resisted Satan by the power of the Word of God. It was engraved on His heart. It is so important to commit God's Word to heart so that we are not struggling to come up with something clever on our own. *The power to resist the enemy's lies is in the Word of God, not in our strength. Jesus rested in that, and we can too.*

Satan's authority is limited to what God will allow, but even the angels recognize his force and never attack him in their own strength. We see that in a letter from Jude, who is thought to be the half brother of Christ and brother to James, leader of the church in Jerusalem. He wrote, "Yet Michael the archangel, in contending with the devil, when he disputed about the body of Moses, dared not bring against him a reviling accusation, but said, 'The Lord rebuke you!'" (Jude 9).

We know this story from Jewish literature. One text refers to the devil claiming the right to Moses' body because he had committed murder in Egypt. Since Satan considers himself to be the lord of the earth, he reasoned that the body belonged to him. Yet in spite of Michael's power and dignity as the premier archangel, he would not bring a "reviling accusation" against the devil but referred the dispute to the Lord. Our authority is in Christ. Our deliverance is in Christ. Our healing is in Christ. Everything we have ever longed for and sought is in Christ.

THE SPIRITUAL JOY AND RESPONSIBILITY OF PARENTING

Becoming pregnant for the first time at forty was a shock! It took me a full week and four test kits to believe it. As the truth began to sink in, Barry and I were very excited. We were sure it was a girl and decided to call her Alexandra.

One day I was sitting in the food court of our local mall after my doctor's appointment. My plate was piled high with everything on the "what to eat for a healthy baby" list. I'm sure I had a silly grin on my face. I felt so motherly and warm. A young couple sat down at the table next to me. I smiled at them. They ignored me. I could tell that she was upset.

"I can't believe you," she said. "I thought you liked children!"

"I do like kids," he replied. "But who would want to bring one more child into this world? It's getting crazier and crazier out there."

As my smile dissipated, it seemed as if a lead weight had been dropped in my barely protruding stomach. I felt sick. I found the nearest rest room and sat with my head between my knees. I started to cry. I was suddenly overwhelmed with fear. I thought of this little one growing inside me and wondered what kind of world I was birthing a child into. After a little while I grabbed hold of myself and my dancing hormones and got out my Bible.

I read those familiar, comforting words from Psalm 139:

> I will praise You, for I am fearfully and wonderfully made;
> Marvelous are Your works,

And that my soul knows very well.
My frame was not hidden from You,
When I was made in secret,
And skillfully wrought in the lowest parts of the earth.
Your eyes saw my substance, being yet unformed.
And in Your book they all were written,
The days fashioned for me,
When as yet there were none of them. (vv. 14–16)

I read them again and again. I read them to my baby (who turned out be no more an Alexandra than Barry is).

I felt a new sense of commitment to the spiritual well-being of this little one who was growing inside me. Having a child caused me to do a reality check in my life.

Do I believe that God is in control, or do I believe that we are at the mercy of a bitter enemy? The harsh reality, as we discussed earlier, is that God's people are not immune from Satan's attacks. Just ask Job. But we have not been left defenseless either. As Martin Luther wrote in that great hymn of the Reformation of the sixteenth century,

And though this world with devils filled,
Should threaten to undo us,
We will not fear, for God hath willed
His truth to triumph through us.
The prince of darkness grim, we tremble not for him—
His rage we can endure,
For lo, his doom is sure:
One little word shall fell him.

"A Mighty Fortress Is Our God" became known as the hymn of the Reformation. Even as Martin Luther was waging war against the spiritual powers that came against him, his comfort was that one little word from the mouth of God silenced all that Satan had to say. That is our comfort too.

We need to look at what God's Word tells us about spiritual battle, how to resist the enemy, and how to guard the healing that Christ has brought to us.

A LOVE THAT WON'T LET GO

God has placed inside us women a gentle, but fierce strength that would cause us to do battle for our children and those we love. Nothing within us, though, can even begin to compare with the fierce love that God has for us. God sent His Son, Jesus, into the very jaws of hell for us. He will not let go of you. Even when it seems as if you are being pulled in a million directions, there is only so much that God will allow. God's love knows no limits on your behalf. No matter what Satan may throw at you, God will never let you go.

Father God,
Thank you for Your fierce love that will never let me go. Amen.

APPLICATION POINTS

- Reflect on teachings about Satan you've received along the way. Think, too, about what you've seen modeled by people who take Satan too seriously or not seriously enough. Where have you settled on that continuum?

- What encouragement and/or practical tips for standing against the enemy do you find in the Matthew 4 account of Jesus' temptation?

- As the examples of Job and Simon Peter illustrate, Satan can do only what God will allow. Why is this good news? (See also 1 Corinthians 10:13.)

- Do you believe that God is in control of history as well as the details of your life, or do you believe that we are at the mercy of a bitter enemy? Let the words from Martin Luther's "A Mighty Fortress Is Our God" (one stanza appears on the previous page) become your theme song!

10

DRESSED TO KILL

Put on the full armor of God so that you can take your stand against the devil's schemes. For our struggle is not against flesh and blood, but against the rulers, against the authorities, against the powers of this dark world and against the spiritual forces of evil in the heavenly realms. Therefore put on the full armor of God, so that when the day of evil comes, you may be able to stand your ground, and after you have done everything, to stand.

—EPHESIANS 6:11–13 NIV

In the 1980s I traveled as a Christian recording artist to the Philippines to work on a project with Compassion International. Compassion International is a Christian relief agency whose main vehicle of aid is child sponsorship. For a few dollars a month from a family, the child sponsorship program matches up the family in the U.S. with a child who needs financial support to be able to go to school and receive medical help. One of the programs involved taking Christian artists to various projects around the world and filming their interaction with the people there. The artists would then use part of that documentary in future concerts to let their audiences know of opportunities to change the lives of children for just a small financial commitment every month.

On this particular trip I was traveling with another artist and his new bride. We spent a couple of days in the capital city of Manila. It is a city bursting at the seams with people. It's as if they pour out of every crack in the sidewalk. The Filipino people are warm and kind with the biggest smiles I've ever seen. The children in particular are affectionate and engaging and love to follow you wherever you go. If you try to suggest they might stay where they are and quit following you, they laugh a deep belly laugh and keep right on walking, assuming you are not serious.

After two days of sightseeing, it was time to get to work. One of the local Compassion relief workers told us to be in the hotel lobby at six the next morning to be ready to visit a project village. She suggested we dress comfortably because it would be hot and we would be gone for several hours. I had visited this area before and knew a little of the terrain. I told my friend's wife that to get to the homes of the people we would be visiting, we would need to navigate a maze of wooden planks across a vast swamp area. She thanked me for my input and we said good night.

The next morning I was up early and excited to be off. I sprayed myself with bug spray, then pulled on my khakis, a short-sleeved shirt, and boots. I was the first one down in the lobby, and I wandered outside to enjoy the morning air and watch the bustle of Manila as it came to life. I turned when I heard someone call my name.

"Hi, Sheila! What a beautiful morning," she said.

As I looked at my friend's wife, I nearly choked. Before I describe how she was dressed, let me say that she is a doll; we are good friends to this day and often laugh about that particular outfit.

She had on tight pink capri pants, a pink leather jacket, and stiletto sandals with three-inch heels!

"You look really cute," I said honestly. "But do you think you'll be comfortable?"

"Sure!" she said.

To this day I still double over laughing when I think of her trying to walk over narrow, rotting wooden planks with those heels. The expressions on the faces of the local women were priceless. I don't speak Filipino, but I got what they were saying! We had to dig her out more than once. High-heeled pink sandals might work in a mall in Chicago, but they leave you ill prepared for the bug-infested mud of a Filipino village. Even as I smile at the memory of my friend, I think how often I launch into a day without giving a second thought to being dressed to protect myself from the enemy.

In the spiritual realm we have been told how to dress. Paul repeated the dress code twice: "Put on the whole armor of God . . . Take up the whole armor of God."

We are told clearly that each day we are to dress for battle, but how often do we show up in the lobby of our lives in high-heeled pumps and pink capris? Now, if you know me at all, you know that I am not a woman to attack heels! Even my tennis shoes have heels. But why would we think that we can ignore God's clear instructions for life in the spirit? Let's take a closer look at this very specific dress code.

THE BELT OF TRUTH

"Stand therefore, having girded your waist with truth . . ."
(Eph. 6:14)

Paul was writing to an audience very familiar with the armor of a Roman soldier. As he described our spiritual armor, he did so in the order that a soldier would put his armor on to prepare for battle.

First, the belt was tied tightly around the waist, indicating that the soldier was ready for battle. A soldier kept his belt tight and loosened it only when he was off duty. He would hang the scabbard, in which his sword was sheathed, from this belt. The belt of truth is one of our primary weapons of defense. Remember, our adversary is the father of all lies. So you can see why truth is so important.

There is an epidemic of lying in our world. It ranges from the ridiculous: "Take this pill before you go to sleep, and you will be ten pounds lighter in the morning," to the even more ridiculous: "If you vote for me, there will be peace in our nation." It no longer seems to mean much to place your hand on the Word of God and swear to tell the truth, the whole truth, and nothing but the truth. In our culture we separate lies into white lies and black lies, little lies and big lies.

God challenged me as a child in this area. I used to lie about stupid things. Someone would ask me if I had seen a movie, and I would say yes, even though I hadn't. It made no sense. I just wanted to feel that I was included, that I knew what to see and what to listen to.

In the movie *Notting Hill,* Hugh Grant plays the role of a bookstore owner enamored with Julia Roberts, who plays the part of a movie star. (What a stretch!) She invites him to have tea with her at her hotel one afternoon, forgetting that she also has a press junket scheduled for the same time. When he arrives, he is met at the door by her press agent, who asks him what magazine he is writing for. Instead of telling her that he is there for afternoon tea, he panics and says he is from the British publication *Horse and Hound.* He is loaded onto the conveyer belt of journalists, each given five minutes to interview the star. Her agent stays in the room with her during most of the interview, so Hugh Grant's character is obliged to follow through with the deception.

"Are there many horses in your movie?" he asks.

"No," she responds. "It is set in space."

"Right! Any . . . hounds?"

He gets deeper and deeper entrenched in his own mess. I remember thinking how funny that was when I saw the film, but the Holy Spirit pierced my heart and showed me that I did the same thing. I tended to trivialize it, thinking that it didn't hurt anyone, but God would have none of it.

We lie in lots of ways, whether it's about the weight on a driver's license or a friend's new dress. We lie about what's going on inside our hearts. Sunday morning can be one of the most dishonest times of our week.

"How are you this morning?" the pastor asks.

"Just wonderful. If I was any more victorious, I'd be flying!" we say, even though we've just had the most cutting argument with our husbands on the way to church.

Sometimes we lie because we think the person asking about us isn't really that interested. That may be true, but it still sets up a pattern in our lives that is unhealthy and ungodly.

A lie is a lie. Truth is our first line of defense against the enemy. If we adopt lies, no matter how small and insignificant they seem, we are abandoning the belt of truth, which is part of our spiritual defense, and taking up a weapon that is part of the arsenal of the enemy of God. *That is his armory. It must not be ours.* I can't stress too strongly how important I believe it is that we consciously renounce even the appearance of a lie and hold fast to the truth.

When Christ prayed for His friends in John 17, He prayed that we would be sanctified *in* the truth: "I do not pray that You should take them out of the world, but that You should keep them from the evil one. They are not of the world, just as I am not of the world. Sanctify them by Your truth. Your word is truth" (vv. 15–17).

When we deal in lies or half-truths, which are lies, we live as those who are of this world. Christ says we must live as those who are *not* of this world. Would you pray with me?

Father God,

I pause here to confess my sin to You. Holy Spirit, I ask that You would reveal to me any area in my life where I am dealing in lies. I renounce all lies as tools of the enemy and in Jesus' name I put on the belt of truth. Amen.

THE BREASTPLATE OF RIGHTEOUSNESS

". . . having put on the breastplate of righteousness . . ."
(Eph. 6:14)

On a soldier the breastplate covered the body from the neck to the thighs. Usually it was made of bronze, or at times with more senior officers, it could be made of chain mail. It offered great protection and covered the heart, just as the righteousness of Christ covers us and protects our very lives.

When God engages in warfare to bring justice, Isaiah (59:17) describes Him as wearing "righteousness as [His] breastplate." We must do likewise. Of course, we have no righteousness of our own. We are clothed in the righteousness of Christ. One of the names of God is *Jehovah-tsidkenu* (the God who is our righteousness in all things). The first time we encounter the word *righteousness* in Scripture is in Genesis 15:6: "[Abram] believed in the LORD, and He accounted it to him for righteousness."

God was about to make a covenant with Abram that would be the basis of all God's future dealings with him and his children, and through his faith, Abram was reckoned righteous. He believed God, and that was a precious gift to our Father.

When we move to the New Testament, we read in the first three chapters of Romans that we have no righteousness of our own. Having stated the case that all are unrighteous (1:18–3:20), Paul showed that God has provided the righteousness for mankind: "But now the righteousness of God apart from the law is revealed, being witnessed by the Law and the Prophets, even the righteousness of God, through faith in Jesus Christ, to all and on all who believe" (Rom. 3:21–22).

That is how we stand before God through faith in Jesus. We spend so much time trying to be "good enough" as believers, but the fact is that on our good days and on our bad days, we come to our Father the same way, dressed in the righteousness of Christ. When Satan whispers to you that you are not worthy of God's love, that you have made too many mistakes to come into God's presence, remember that you don't come in your own name. You come in the name of the Lamb of God.

AN ALL-ACCESS PASS

Since that devastating terrorist attack on U.S. soil on September 11, 2001, our world has changed in many ways. Security has been stepped up at airports and train stations; tours of the White House are limited to school groups alone. There have been changes on many levels. At Women of Faith we see beefed-up security at the arenas where we hold our events. All our staff wear laminated passes, and if you forget your pass, you have to wait until someone from the team can verify that you do indeed belong. Sometimes my son, Christian, will come over to the arena on a Friday night because he likes to listen to the worship. He and his nanny have passes, but on one particular evening he forgot to wear his pass. I was watching for him, and I saw the guard stop Christian and Sarah and ask where Christian's pass was. He looked up, saw me, and yelled, "I'm with her!"

That is our defense. We have no right to be in this holy fight, but we wear the breastplate of the righteousness of Christ. Don't show up to face the enemy without your pass! It is your defense against his primary weapon—lies.

As you hear the accuser, remember he stands at your right side whispering lies to you. You may hear him say, "You don't belong; you're a failure; you'll never change."

Your response is simple: "I'm with Jesus!"

We resist Satan as Christ did, with the Word of God. Putting on the breastplate of righteousness is a two-part process. We accept that all our righteousness is in Christ, but our part is to own and confess our sin.

When I was a teenager, my young cousins from the north of Scotland came to stay for the week. They were given my brother's room with very clear instructions from him about what they could touch and what they could not touch. His bedside lamp fascinated one of the little girls. On their first morning when my mom went in to see if they were awake, Jackie had the lamp on her lap in bed with her. Mom put it back and asked her not to play with it. The next morning when she went in, Jackie was caught red-handed once more with the lamp in her lap. She looked up at Mom and said, "This thing is in my bed again!" My mom laughed at her feigned horror but the bottom line was that she wanted to take no responsibility for the lamp being in the bed.

It's very important to own our sin. The Greek word is *homologeo,* and it means "to agree, to acknowledge, to walk cleanly in the light with God."

One Friday evening in the summer of 2003 I was sitting in the artists' catering suite at the MCI Arena in Washington, D.C., talking to Mary Graham, president of Women of Faith.

"Luci and I were in Starbucks today," Mary began, referring to Luci Swindoll, one of our teammates. "We were watching a little boy playing with the tag on the side of a newspaper stand. His mom kept telling him to be careful, but suddenly the tag snapped off. He looked to see if his mom had noticed, but since she was busy talking to the girl at the counter, he hid the broken tag in the pile of newspapers. He was about four years old."

Isn't it amazing that we learn to hide at such a young age? He's a picture of all of us. It is our tendency to hide our sin. Part of our armor is to acknowledge our sin, repent of it, and stand protected by the breastplate of the righteousness of Christ.

Father God,

Thank You that I can stand in the righteousness of Christ. Thank You for this defense against the lies of the enemy. Help me to keep short accounts with You, to be quick to see and confess my sin. In Jesus' name, amen.

THE SHOES OF PEACE

"And having shod your feet with the preparation of the gospel of peace . . ." (Eph. 6:15)

Once the breastplate was fitted into position, a soldier would put on his strong army boots. When they were off duty, the soldiers wore sandals, but for battle, especially in winter, they wore strong, thick boots that ensured a solid footing. Historians have attributed the military successes of Alexander the Great and of Julius Caesar to the fact that their armies were equipped with such heavy boots; therefore, they could march day after day over rough territory.

Our shoes, however, are called the "preparation of the gospel of peace." Here the message of the gospel is connected with the protective and supportive footgear of the Roman soldier. We have peace with God through Christ, and that gives us a sure foothold in the spiritual campaign in which we are engaged.

The weapons of our warfare are the antithesis of Satan's arsenal.

He lies; we speak the truth.

He is consumed with pride; we have no righteousness apart from Christ.

He brings discord and dissent; we are called to receive and live in the peace that Christ offers by His presence with us in every situation.

Father God,
I thank You that through Christ, I have peace with You. You have said that beautiful are the feet of the peacemaker. May I be beautiful in Your sight as I run to do Your will. Amen.

THE SHIELD OF FAITH

". . . above all, taking the shield of faith with which you will be able to quench all the fiery darts of the wicked one . . ."
(Eph. 6:16)

A Roman soldier's shield was an imposing sight. It was a large, oblong or oval piece called a *scutum,* which he held in front of him for protection. It was made of two layers of wood glued together, covered with fabric and leather, and bound with iron. Soldiers often fought side by side with shields in front of them, providing a solid wall of protection. But even a lone soldier was well protected by his shield. In ancient warfare cane darts, like small arrows, were sometimes dipped in tar and then ignited. Roman soldiers would soak their shields in water, letting the leather absorb as much water as possible so that when the fiery arrow hit, it would be immediately extinguished.

Our faith in God is our protection against the fiery darts that Satan would throw at us. When he lies to us, accuses us, tempts us—whatever he throws—we hold up the shield of faith not only to deflect his darts but also to put them out. Faith is seen as a two-sided weapon here. It is our faith in action when we step out to do something, believing God has called us to do it and He will equip us. Faith here is also the content of what we believe.

For example, we believe God is good and loving, so when Satan throws the dart, "God doesn't love you," we hold up the shield of our faith that tells us that is a lie.

It seems to me that we get to help build our shield, customize it, if you will. As we commit God's Word to heart, learn to worship, grow in our prayer life, we have a strong shield to counter Satan's attacks. I know that when I spend more time in God's presence, I have more deposited in my spirit, a strong shield to hold up against whatever is thrown in my direction.

Dear Father,

Thank You that I have not been left exposed and alone before this enemy. Thank You for Your Word and Your life. Teach me to deposit Your truth in my heart so that I can extinguish his fiery attacks. Amen.

THE HELMET OF SALVATION

"And take the helmet of salvation . . ."
(Eph. 6:17)

That again reflects the routine of a soldier. His armor bearer usually handed the helmet and sword to a soldier as the last pieces to be put on. A soldier's helmet was made of bronze with leather attachments. It was a crucial piece of armor because it protected the head.

For us, the helmet of salvation is God's protection of our minds. When Paul wrote to the church in Thessalonica, he reminded them of the assurance that their salvation was secure in Christ, no matter how they felt. He wrote, "Let us not sleep, as others do, but let us watch and be sober. For those who sleep, sleep at night, and those who get drunk are drunk at night. But let us who are of the day be sober, putting on the breastplate of faith and love, and as a helmet the hope of salvation" (1 Thess. 5:6–8).

We are often attacked in our minds and betrayed by our emotions. We don't *feel* that God loves us. We don't *feel* worthy. We don't *feel* forgiven. We put on our salvation, which is God's promise to us, no matter what we feel. Even when our minds condemn us, we are assured that we belong to God through Christ, and nothing, absolutely nothing, can separate us from His love.

Paul declared, "I am persuaded that neither death nor life, nor angels nor principalities nor powers, nor things present nor things to come, nor height nor depth, nor any other created thing, shall be able to separate us from the love of God which is in Christ Jesus our Lord" (Rom. 8:38–39).

THE SWORD OF THE SPIRIT

". . . and [take] the sword of the Spirit, which is the word of God."
(Eph. 6:17)

The final weapon is the sword. The Roman soldier's sword was a short two-edged, lethal device. The "sword of the Spirit" is the only weapon of *offense* in our arsenal; all the rest of the armor is for our protection. The "sword of the Spirit" is, as the verse says, the Word of God. Many times when writing of the Word of God, Paul used the Greek word *logos*. In this verse he used the word *rhema*. The implication is different. There is only one Word of God, but here Paul emphasized proclamation, the spoken, declarative word of God as opposed to the written word. That is how we attack the enemy.

I love to sit in the morning in my favorite chair and read God's Word, meditating on everything I am reading, but there are times when I speak God's Word out loud as a declaration to the enemy that he has no place in my life, my home, or my family. We are told that it is sharper than a two-edged sword. It cuts through the lies of the enemy with the first strike forward and with the return back strike. The picture is that it shreds the enemy's attacks.

Do you feel as if he is coming at your family, your faith, your health, or your hope?

Respond to the attack by declaring out loud the written Word of God. We stand with Jesus and say, "It is written . . . it is written . . . it is written . . . !"

Father God,

I praise You for the gift of salvation that is placed on my head as surely as a soldier wears his helmet. Thank You that nothing can snatch me from Your love. Thank You for Your Word. In Jesus' name, Amen.

MY PRAYER FOR YOU

When Christian was a baby, I prayed the armor of God over him as I put his clothes on him in the morning. As I secured that diaper snugly round his little tummy, I prayed that truth would be a treasure and refuge in his life. As I buttoned up his little shirt, I prayed that he would come to know that in his good days and bad days, his standing before God would be based on the righteousness of Christ, not on his performance on any given day. Tucking tiny toes into socks, I prayed that he would rest in the peace that comes from knowing Jesus. As I tried to plaster that rebel curl in place, I prayed that when he was still a child, he would come to know Christ as his Savior, and as he slept, I scattered the living word of God over him, praying that as he grew, he would commit those words to memory as a weapon against our enemy.

I pray that for you this day.

In Jesus' name I pray that you will learn to put on each piece of the whole armor of God, dear sister, so that you will be able to stand.

In the next couple of chapters we will consider the place of faith and trust, grace and truth in the midst of this warfare. We live in troubling times in the world, in our nation, in our schools and churches. In the midst of the battle that is being waged around us every day God calls us to be women of faith who stand for truth. Yet we are also called to be those whose hearts are like Christ, who offers grace and mercy to those who have been wounded in battle.

This is a holy war.

❧

Father God,

Thank You that You have provided this armor for me to wear in battle. Teach me the discipline of a soldier to be prepared at all times. In Jesus' name, Amen.

APPLICATION POINTS

- How often do you launch into a day without even thinking about what's appropriate to wear in order to protect yourself from the enemy? What might you do to remind yourself to put on the armor of God?

- God tells us how to dress for the spiritual battle that rages around us. Summarize what you remember—or what you've memorized!—from Ephesians 6.

- Truth is our first line of defense against the enemy. If we adopt lies, no matter how small and insignificant they seem, we are abandoning the belt of truth, which is part of our spiritual defense. To what degree is failure to tell the truth, even about unimportant things, a problem for you? What will you do to become a person of truth, a person living in sharp contrast to our lying culture?

- Just as Christian gained entry into the arena when he nodded my way and said, "I'm with her!" we gain access to God when we say, "I'm with Jesus!" Have you accepted the righteousness available to you in Christ by first owning and confessing your sin, then repenting of it, and humbly receiving Jesus as your Savior and Lord? If not, do so now—and then tell another believer about your decision.

- One aspect of faith is the content of what we believe. What truths from God's Word would help you deflect the lie(s) Satan commonly throws your way? What are you doing and/or will you do to strengthen your shield? Be specific.

- What assurance do you have that your salvation is secure in Christ, no matter how you feel? (See, for instance, 2 Thessalonians 2:13–15.) That kind of assurance is your helmet of salvation.

- In what current situation or ongoing torment from the enemy would you do well to follow Jesus' example and declare aloud, "It is written . . ."?

11

WALKING BY FAITH

Without faith it is impossible to please Him, for he who comes to God must believe that He is, and that He is a rewarder of those who diligently seek Him.

—HEBREWS 11:6

Let not your heart be troubled; you believe in God, believe also in Me.

—JOHN 14:1

Each year at our conferences, Nicole Johnson, our dramatist, prepares several short pieces that she presents throughout the course of the weekend. One of her dramas in 2003 was called *Raising the Sail.* It portrayed a single mother struggling in her relationship with her daughter, Amy. The internal war was demonstrated on stage as the difference between getting in the boat of faith and trusting God or remaining fear-bound on the dock. In an attempt to find out what Amy might be getting into at school, the mother decided to search her daughter's backpack. She was horrified to discover some pills and questioned Amy about them. Amy in turn was appalled that her mother would invade her privacy but declared that the pills didn't belong to her. The mother didn't believe her and became obsessed with tracking her daughter's life until the girl ran away from home. The crux of the piece is how often love is snuffed out by control when we choose fear instead of faith. Finally the mother in desperation threw herself on God's mercy and chose to believe that He is big enough to care for her daughter. At last she was ready to raise the sail.

Every mother in the arena identified with the drama. As Nicole says,

"What is fear before you become a parent?" When you bring a child into the world, you bring a world to that child and a world of possibilities into your own heart.

We've looked at the wounds we have carried from the past and at the One who bears the wounds for us. We've examined the nature of our enemy and how God would equip us to fight so that when everything is done, we will still be standing. In the next two chapters we will discuss moving beyond our broken hearts and charting a course toward faith and trust.

Then we will sit for a while with the overwhelming story of grace. It is much easier to remain safe on the dockside watching others out on the open seas, but we were made for more.

Perhaps as you look at all the possibilities of things that can go wrong in this life, your heart is anxious and afraid. Perhaps you have always been afraid. It's not too late to learn to live a different way. As long as there is one breath left in your body, it is not too late to choose faith over fear.

I saw that in my father-in-law, William. He was eighty years old when he moved in with us. He was a kind, funny man who had lived a timid life. He saw danger at every turn. He heard disaster with every ring of the telephone and assumed that if you went to see the doctor, you would discover that you had some disease that you would not have had if you hadn't gone! Whew! It was learned behavior. He watched his father live like that. It's amazing how much we pick up as children just by watching those around us. No one has to say anything; we get the message.

In the late Gilda Radner's book, *It's Always Something*, she told a story about a dog that was involved in a road accident. The car that struck her severed both her back legs. The dog was due to deliver puppies in a few weeks. The vet told the owner that the puppies seemed to be fine. They decided to stitch the poor mom back together as best they could and see what would happen. With great female resilience (no, I'm not a feminist; I just admire women's inner strength—even when they have four legs!) she taught herself to walk. She pulled herself along with her front legs and then swung her rear end into step. A few weeks later the puppies were born, and the owner was amazed to see that as they began to find their feet and follow their mom around, they all walked like her. They had four legs, but they acted as if they had only two.

When William moved in with us after Eleanor's death, he asked me, "What are the house rules?"

I wasn't quite sure what he meant, so I said to him, "We have very few house rules, Pop. All we try to do is to be kind to each other and lovingly speak the truth. You can make mistakes, mess up, drop the best crystal vase, or adopt a stray cat, but as long as we forgive each other, I think we'll be fine."

I watched William observe Christian, who is a fearless little boy. I watched him cringe as he saw him start toward the tallest slide in the park, then laugh at the joy in Christian's face as he came flying down. I saw him look at me when Christian fell off his bike, as if to say, "You should have known he's too little," and then smile and shake his head when Christian got right back on again. Learned behavior can go two ways. It's a lovely thing to watch a child teach an old man not to be afraid.

A few weeks before his death in November 2000, William and I were sitting by the fireplace after dinner. He said to me, "Who would have thought that God would have saved the best days of my life for the end?"

I want to suggest that to you. *Do you think it's possible that God has saved your best days for the days that lie ahead?*

I believe with all my heart that is what God would do for us. Life changes and loss is a reality. Some people are granted the gift of physical healing while others are not. But if God by His grace would plant faith, trust, and peace deep into every recess of our hearts and minds, we will be rich and blessed indeed. That would be a healing far greater than anything a doctor could offer. To move beyond fear requires faith. At some point the mother in the drama had to get in the boat, or she was going nowhere. That's the hardest part—committing oneself to a particular course of action.

BORN FREE

One night I was putting the milk carton back in the refrigerator when I felt something on my foot. I looked down and a little gray mouse was running over my foot and across the kitchen. I'm not afraid of mice, but I knew that now I was aware of its presence I had to catch it. Barry does not do mice. He will deal with wasps or spiders, but anything with four legs and a travel agenda, he will graciously pass on. He was in my downstairs office just off our bedroom.

"There was a mouse in the kitchen," I said. "I've chased it under the sofa in the den. I know you don't like mice, but I need your help to catch it. You just have to be my decoy."

"Decoy!" he replied. "Decoy! Dream on."

"Okay, then you just have to be the one with the flashlight."

"Flashlight's good," he said. "I can be the one with the flashlight."

We chased this poor beast all over the house. Finally it ran under the drapes in the sitting room. They're long and puddle on the floor, and the mouse was hiding underneath.

"Here's the deal," I said to Barry. "When I say go, lift up the drapes and I'll put this jar over it."

"When you say go? What about one, two, three?" he asked.

"One, two, three is fine," I replied.

"Do I do it on three or after three?"

"One, two, three, go!" I said. "Do it on *go!*"

We must have sat there for ten minutes debating the logistics of this not-so-covert operation. Part of our reticence was committing to the actual moment. What if I didn't get the jar over it in time? What if it ran up my leg? I think the mouse was so fed up with the whole thing, it was ready to come out and jump in the jar by itself. Finally Barry lifted the drape, and I dropped the jar over the mouse. We put it in a box, and Barry and Christian took it down to the lake to let it go.

"How did it go?" I asked Christian when they got back.

"Fine, Mom. At first he didn't want to come out. We put the box on its side on the grass, but he just stayed in there. He could see the way out, but he just stayed in."

"I bet he was afraid," I said. "Or exhausted. Dad and I chased him all over the house. How did you get him to come out?"

"Well, I tapped on the side of the box and sang 'Born Free.' I think that's what did it."

I have been like that little mouse sometimes. The box becomes familiar, if cramped. The world outside the box is scary and endless. God has provided a way out for me, but I stay in my box, afraid of committing to my freedom. Do you feel stuck? You see another way to live, to choose faith over fear, but just the thought of taking that first step terrifies you. We have one up on the mouse. Remember, you are not alone; Jesus is with you. Can you see Him tap lovingly on the side of the box and sing "Born Free"?

I love this verse from Isaiah. It makes it clear that at times we will walk through difficult places that we would never have chosen for ourselves, but we will not be alone.

> When you pass through the waters, I will be with you;
> And through the rivers, they shall not overflow you.
> When you walk through the fire, you shall not be burned,
> Nor shall the flame scorch you. (Isa. 43:2)

That is quite a promise. It doesn't say that we won't pass through the waters; it says that Christ will be with us. It doesn't tell us that rivers won't roar at our feet; it says that they will not overwhelm us. There will be fiery places, but because of God's great love, we will not be consumed. Hold on to that promise when your feet are wet and the smell of smoke is in your hair. Hold on to Christ, for He is holding on to you.

HIS LOVE COVERS US

I grew up in Ayr, a small town on the west coast of Scotland surrounded on one side by green hills and on the other by the rugged coastline. The west coast is rich farmland with acres given over to sheep and the beautiful black-and-white Ayrshire cattle. My mother worked with a firm that handled the accounts for many of the gentlemen farmers in the area. Farming is a hard, demanding life—getting up before sunrise on bitterly cold days and falling into bed at the end of a long day, back aching, either praying that rain would fall or that God would hold it back long enough to get the crops in safely. If a farmer had a bad year, it could wipe out his whole way of life. One of the stories that I heard as a child stuck with me more than any other. It was about one of our local farmers who lost everything in a fire that consumed his livelihood.

It had been a long, dry summer with little rain. The air seemed to crackle with parched tension. It might have been a spark from a bonfire on the beach, the remnants of a tourist's day, no one ever knew, but the farmer woke up to a flame-red sky. He heard the snap of the dry bales of hay as they were consumed in seconds. Running down the stairs to see what he could save, he called to his wife to get help, but as soon as he saw the barns ablaze, he knew it was too late. Everything was gone.

The next morning he walked sadly across the yard, surveying the piles of charred wood and carcasses that had once been his life. He stopped for a moment as he saw that he was about to step on the burned body of a hen. He moved it gently with his boot, and there underneath were her chicks. All of them were still alive. She had gathered them under her wings and placed her body between them and the flames.

"When you walk through the fire, you shall not be burned, nor shall the flame scorch you." To receive the truth of this verse requires that we move from living out of fear and live instead out of faith. But what exactly is faith?

Faith has received a bad rap in our contemporary Christian culture. At times it has been used as a weapon of cruelty: "If you had more faith, your daughter would not have died." It has been used as an excuse for poor judgment: "I know that I'm supposed to take this chemo, but I just have faith that I don't need it." I know there are times when someone is given a gift of faith to be able to stand on a promise that can be experienced only in the spiritual realm, an absolute "I know that I know." But so often what we call faith is just wishful thinking.

The Hebrew word for *faith* or *believe* occurs only thirty times in the Old Testament. The Greek word occurs almost five hundred times in the New Testament. The fascinating thing, however, is that most of the references to faith in the New Testament are reflections of something that happened in the Old Testament.

We are familiar with the teaching of the great apostle Paul, "The just shall live by faith" (Rom. 1:17), but he was actually quoting the Old Testament prophet Habakkuk, who wrote,

> Behold the proud,
> His soul is not upright in him;
> But the just shall live by his faith. (Hab. 2:4)

The great faith chapter of Hebrews 11 parades the ancients before our eyes, those who believed, yet never saw Messiah's birth. They spent their whole lives believing what they could not see.

So was it easier for those who saw to believe? I'm not sure it was, because Jesus didn't look like the Messiah they were expecting. Belief in God has always required a jumping-off place. It is not easy. From our vantage point in history we might assume that if we had been on earth when

Jesus walked, we would have found faith easier to access. But think about it and put yourself there.

He was the boy your son grew up with, the kid who borrowed milk for His mother, Mary. He was just Joseph's son, a nice boy, well mannered, but the Son of God? That's quite a stretch.

It is in Paul's letters that the meaning of faith is most clearly unpacked. Faith is absolute trust in Jesus, in His teaching, and in the finished work of the Cross. Faith demands a fundamental and complete commitment to Christ that He alone is our hope. For those who say that faith demands putting aside our desire for reasonable proof, I say we express that kind of faith every day. I sit down on a chair without checking to see if it can support my weight. I order a meal at a restaurant without examining the kitchen to see if everything is being properly prepared. (Sometimes I think I should!) The fact is that I have a history of sitting in chairs, and so far they have held me up. Magnify that a thousand times, and the truth is that God has a track record with me. He has proved Himself to be trustworthy again and again in my life.

Do you remember when God asked Abraham to sacrifice his son, Isaac? He said, "'Take now your son, your only son Isaac, whom you love, and go to the land of Moriah, and offer him there as a burnt offering on one of the mountains of which I shall tell you.' So Abraham rose early in the morning and saddled his donkey" (Gen. 22:2–3).

As I read that passage, the most amazing words to me are, "Abraham rose." Abraham was a hundred years old when Isaac was born. God had promised him that through this boy, He would establish an everlasting covenant. Now Abraham was being told to kill him and offer him back to God. When I try to put myself in his shoes, I realize I would have left town quietly the night before or pulled the sheets over my head the next morning.

Not Abraham. He got up. Why? Was he a careless father, immune to the terror to which he was about to subject his son? Not at all.

God had a track record with Abraham. God had always shown up at the right time; He had always been true to His word. Abraham's faith was based on what he knew of God's character and ways. So they set out, and when they arrived at the bottom of the mountain, Abraham left the servants behind. Abraham said to his servants, "Stay here with the donkey; the lad and I will go yonder and worship, and we will come back to you" (Gen. 22:5).

Do you see what he was saying? *We* will worship, and *we* will come back. God had told him that through Isaac, an everlasting covenant would be established. God had told him to take Isaac up to the top of the mountain and sacrifice him. He fully intended to do what God asked, but he told his servants, *we* will be back. Abraham knew that even if he had to plunge that knife into Isaac's heart, God could raise him from the dead.

Abraham knew that God is not a liar. "Contrary to hope, in hope [Abraham] believed" (Rom. 4:18). God is not a liar. Everything He has promised in His Word, He will do. Someone said that courage is just fear that has said its prayers.

Does all this seem like a big leap? Well, good news. On top of everything else that God has done for us, He is the One who gives us the grace to want to take that first step. That's what's so amazing about grace!

Father God,

Thank You for all the ways you have been faithful to me. Today I choose to place my trust completely in You. I choose faith over fear because You are my God and I love You. Amen.

APPLICATION POINTS

- In what ways—big and small, constantly or in certain situations—does fear affect your faith in God? Be specific.

- Look back at God's track record with you. When has He been faithful to you despite or in the midst of your fear?

- Think about that little gray mouse. It saw the freedom of the lakeside, but it didn't want to leave its box. Just how comfortable is your box? What other way to live, one that involves choosing faith over fear, do you see? Why are you terrified about taking that first step? What might you do to overcome that terror? (Hint: see Matthew 28:20.)

- Faith demands a fundamental and complete commitment to Christ and to the truth that He alone is our hope. Some say that such faith demands putting aside our desire for reasonable proof. I say that we express that kind of faith every day. What kinds of things have you done even today, acting in faith without doing thorough research and documenting hard evidence? Think, for starters, about the chairs you've sat in or the food you've eaten. Does your faith in Christ rest on less or greater evidence? Explain.

- Do you think it's possible that God has saved your best days for the days that lie ahead? Let me believe that for you!

12

GRACE AND TRUTH

He came to Nazareth, where He had been brought up. And
as His custom was, He went into the synagogue on the
Sabbath day, and stood up to read. And He was handed the
book of the prophet Isaiah. And when He had opened the
book, He found the place where it was written:

"The Spirit of the LORD is upon Me; because He has anointed Me to
preach the gospel to the poor; He has sent Me to heal the brokenhearted,
to proclaim liberty to the captives and recovery of sight to the blind, to
set at liberty those who are oppressed; to proclaim the acceptable year of
the LORD."

—LUKE 4:16–19

It was a familiar text to those in the temple—the good news about the coming Messiah, the Servant King. It was good news to the poor, both those who were poor in the eyes of the world and those who were poor in spirit, hungry for more of God. It was good news for those whose hearts were broken. They, too, were waiting. They were waiting for the One who would come and bind up their wounds. At the funerals of children, in the dust of the decimation of taxes and poverty, under the harsh rule of Roman law, God's people would look at one another and say, "Messiah is coming. Just hold on. Messiah is coming."

He would proclaim freedom for the captives and the opening of prisons for those who were bound. They were longing for freedom, liberty, and their own land! Messiah would proclaim the acceptable year of the

Lord and the day of vengeance of God. That promise brought comfort and satisfaction to those who had been kept down and abused, those who cast their eyes downward as the Roman guards moved through town.

"Our day is coming," they would say. "Just wait. Our day is almost here. God will exact vengeance. Remember Pharaoh? Remember the plagues and the devastation? It will be nothing compared to this day of the Lord's vengeance!"

And so they waited.

They had God's promise to rest on. No matter who was oppressing them as God's people, they knew that their day was coming. They had the words of the prophet Jeremiah.

> "Behold, the days are coming," says the LORD,
> "That I will raise to David a Branch of righteousness;
> A King shall reign and prosper,
> And execute judgment and righteousness in the earth.
> In His days Judah will be saved,
> And Israel will dwell safely;
> Now this is His name by which He will be called:
> THE LORD OUR RIGHTEOUSNESS." (Jer. 23:5–6)

And they waited.

HE IS HERE

How is it possible to wait so long and then to miss the miracle so completely? It happened on that first Christmas night, remember? All but a few shepherds and a ragtag bunch of animals missed the miracle.

Then it was thirty years later. Jesus had just spent forty days in the wilderness, fasting, praying, resisting the enemy by the power of the Word of God. Coming out of the wilderness, Jesus returned to Galilee. People heard about the unusual man who was saying things they never heard before. He taught in the synagogue and people loved it.

Luke recorded for us their response to Jesus. He spoke well and wisely.

"They were astonished at His teaching, for His word was with authority" (Luke 4:32).

Jesus moved on. He returned home, to Nazareth. On that first Sabbath back in town He stood up to read the Scripture lesson for the day. What was about to happen was outrageous. Listen in:

> [Jesus] stood up to read. And He was handed the book of the prophet Isaiah. And when He had opened the book, He found the place where it was written:
>
> "The Spirit of the LORD is upon Me,
> Because He has anointed Me
> To preach the gospel to the poor;
> He has sent Me to heal the brokenhearted,
> To proclaim liberty to the captives
> And recovery of sight to the blind,
> To set at liberty those who are oppressed;
> To proclaim the acceptable year of the LORD."
> Then He closed the book, and gave it back to the
> attendant and sat down. (Luke 4:16–20)

Think about that! He stood up in the temple to be the reader for that service, and the passage assigned for that very day was about Him.

Let me try to find a modern comparison. This is not great, but it'll give a hint of the drama. It's Friday night at a Women of Faith Conference. The arena is packed. I get up on stage with microphone in hand, pull out a book on the history of Women of Faith, and begin to read a passage from it:

> After some time God will send another to be with the core team—watch for her. She will be a forty-seven-year-old Scottish woman. She'll have a son named Christian and a husband named Barry. Her shoes will have four-inch heels. She'll eat a lot of ice cream and almost immediately regret it. She will live in Nashville and write for Thomas Nelson Publishers. She will love the New King James Version of the Bible!

Then I roll the paper up and sit down.

The audience would think that it was a joke or that I was trying to come off my medication again. Here's the wild thing. The crowd in the temple that day didn't get it at all. They just stared at Jesus.

So He continued and told them that today, that very text was fulfilled in their hearing. Can you imagine the muttering?

"What did He say?"

"He said that those words are fulfilled today."

"Oh! My goodness. Well, how nice. But isn't that Joseph's boy?"

There is a saying in Scotland that is supposed to reduce anyone who thinks too much of herself back to proper size: "She can't be famous. I knew her father!" That was what was happening that day in the temple.

Jesus handed the scroll back to the "attendant," whose job it was to handle the venerated scroll. After that was replaced in its cabinet or ark, the reader took the customary sitting position to teach or make comments on the passage. Luke began to record the response of the congregation, which at first concentrated attention and ultimately hostility. There was the sense of "Who does He think He is?"

Jesus continued, "You will surely say this proverb to Me, 'Physician, heal yourself! Whatever we have heard done in Capernaum, do also here in Your country'" (Luke 4:23).

They stared at Him. From Christ's response it's clear that they were looking at Him as if to say, "Well, do something. Do some of Your tricks here. If You can heal the neighbors, then why don't You heal us? Where's Your loyalty? What about the people You grew up with?"

Jesus answered the questions and accusations that were rumbling around their hearts and minds. He knows us so well that even the soft internal mutterings are known to Him. He told them that during the long three-and-a-half-year famine in Elijah's time, there were many widows in Israel who were hungry. Elijah didn't go to them and perform the miracle of grain and oil that wouldn't run out. He went to Zarephath, a town in Sidon about fifty miles away from Nazareth, and blessed a gentile woman with this gift. There were many afflicted with leprosy in Elisha's time, many Israelites, but the only one God healed through Elisha was Naaman, a Syrian.

Well, by then the people in the silent, staring crowd were furious. How dare He suggest that God would have more compassion on Gentiles than on His own people? A house of worshipers became a violent mob, and they drove Him out of the synagogue, through town, and to the top of the hill on which the city of Nazareth was built. Nazareth lies among the ridges of the southern slopes of the Galilean hills.

Jesus allowed the crowd to drive Him out of the town. But as they got Him up the hill and were ready to throw Him off, we read, "Passing through the midst of them, He went His way" (Luke 4:30). It doesn't say what happened. Perhaps angels walked Him out. Perhaps He looked at them with such disconcerting honesty or fierce love that they backed off. But they would be back. I imagine Satan in that crowd crying, "Do it!" Suddenly Jesus was gone.

THE GIFT OF GRACE

It was not His time to die yet. There would be another day when He would let the crowd drive Him through town, but not yet.

I wonder if anyone in the synagogue that day noticed that Jesus omitted a part of the text? The passage that Jesus read was from the prophet Isaiah but He left out one line. The fact that He left out that particular line is extremely significant. *It's about you and me.* It's about grace.

First, here is the original passage from Isaiah 61:

> He has sent Me to heal the brokenhearted,
> To proclaim liberty to the captives,
> And the opening of the prison to those who are bound;
> To proclaim the acceptable year of the LORD,
> And the day of vengeance of our God.(vv. 1–2)

Now, this is what Christ read:

> He has sent Me to heal the brokenhearted,
> To proclaim liberty to the captives
> And recovery of sight to the blind,
> To set at liberty those who are oppressed;
> To proclaim the acceptable year of the LORD. (Luke 4:18–19)

He omitted, "The day of vengeance of our God."

Why? Grace. Grace. Grace.

The Jews were waiting for Messiah, who would come in vengeance and wipe out all their enemies. They wanted Old Testament law, but Christ came to bring New Testament grace. Jesus was telling them that whoever will come can be saved, Jew, Gentile, male, female, prostitute, and priest. *Grace is offensive because it allows no one but Christ to shine.*

I think of the woman caught in the act of adultery and brought before Christ as if she were a traveling sideshow. The whole encounter was such a setup, but in the encounter between Christ, the woman, the Sanhedrin, and the crowd lie the heart and the message of this book.

The members of the Sanhedrin, which was the highest Jewish tribunal during the Greek and Roman periods, forced their way into the center of the group that Jesus was teaching in the temple court at dawn one morning.

It might be helpful to get a little background on the makeup of the Sanhedrin. Then we will better understand the impact of what Christ said to them. The members of the Sanhedrin were drawn from three classes: the chief priests, the teachers of the law, and the elders. The men were the wealthiest, most respected members of the Jewish community.

The *chief priests* included the acting high priest, those who had been high priests in the past, and members of the aristocratic families from which the high priests were chosen. The *teachers of the law* were the Pharisees. The *elders* were mostly the secular nobility of Jerusalem; the president even bore the impressive title of "prince."

Imagine the scene. It was very early in the morning, and a small crowd had gathered around Jesus. He began to teach them. Suddenly their attention was ripped away by a throng of very imposing men pushing their way into the center of the group with one woman in tow. Without as much as a "please excuse us," they started in: "Teacher, this woman was caught in adultery, in the very act. Now Moses, in the law, commanded us that such should be stoned. But what do You say?" (John 8:4–5).

They thought they had Him trapped. If Jesus refused to condemn her, then He would stand guilty of contradicting the law of God. If, on the other hand, He confirmed their verdict, what would happen to His reputation for being a man of compassion?

Jesus bent down and began to write in the dirt with His finger. That's the only record we have of Christ ever writing anything, and we don't know what He wrote. Perhaps He just scribbled in the sand as they spat out the rest of their questions. He stood up again and said, "He who is without sin among you, let him throw a stone at her first" (John 8:7). Then He bent down once more and continued writing in the dirt. Slowly, one by one, the eldest first, they began to disperse, not just the Sanhedrin, but the whole crowd. That was too much. How could He insult those men and survive?

Finally just the woman and Jesus remained.

"Woman, where are those accusers of yours? Has no one condemned you?"

"No one, Lord," she said.

"Neither do I condemn you," Jesus declared. "Go and sin no more" (John 8:10–11).

She began her day being dragged through the streets, exposed, humiliated, and shamed. She ended that same day having looked into the face of God and found that He was smiling.

A COMMON NEED FOR GRACE

Jesus put everyone in the crowd into the same boat as the woman. The high priest, the prince, the Pharisee, and the adulterous woman were leveled at the feet of Christ by grace. Grace does not say that it is inconsequential that we have sinned. Grace says that all sin matters, but grace also says that a God of grace can forgive all sin.

Every time I write, I am aware that books have lives of their own. They are passed from friend to friend, sister to sister. Someone may have thrust this on you, and much to your amazement, you've made it this far. You may be a chapter flipper, and there was something about the idea of grace that intrigued you. I don't know, but God knows. God knows all that is true about your life, all of it, and He loves you more than I can say.

We tend to categorize sin. Those of us who commit the more private, internal sins of anger, bitterness, greed, and judgment tend to stand in the public square of our hearts and look to stone the one who has committed adultery, had an abortion, or struggled with homosexual sin or alcohol or drug abuse. Whatever your struggles might be today I want you to put yourself in the position of that woman and see Christ deflect your accusers and give you back your life.

What Christ did for that woman was an act of grace, but she still had to live out the rest of her life. There would still be those who pointed at her in the street or moved away from her in the synagogue if she had the audacity to take God at His word and show up in His house.

Jesus did not rewrite the story of her life. He gave her a new chapter. The old one was taken care of at Calvary if she availed herself of that gift, but from the moment she walked away from Jesus that day, she had to choose, "How will I live now?"

If you are that woman, accept God's gift of grace, avail yourself of the forgiveness that Jesus offers, no matter what the sin. Jesus told her to go and sin no more, to live differently. You are not trapped. You can choose. So drop the overcoat of shame, and if someone walks up to you and tries to return it to you, say, "Thanks, but I gave that one to Jesus."

THE CALL OF GRACE

Something else could have happened in the temple courtyard that day. At times in the life of Christ, what He didn't say and what didn't happen are as significant as what did. He said, "He who is without sin among you, let him throw a stone at her first."

Imagine you are one of the Sanhedrin or someone at the back of the crowd who wants to see what's going on without getting too involved. You hear Jesus' words, and instead of walking away, you push your way through the crowd and take your place beside that woman. She looks at you and flinches, wondering if you want a closer shot. Instead, you smile at her and take her hand. You stand with her in as much need of grace as she is. Someone else moves forward, and another, and another. What would have happened? It would have been a greater miracle than feeding five thousand or healing a blind man. Those were things Jesus did by Himself; that's who He is.

The miracle happens when we participate in the grace process, when we become the bearers in our own bodies of what it looks like to be God's daughters. A watching world is not that impressed with miracles alone. Satan can mimic miracles. Las Vegas has miracles at eight, ten, and midnight any day of the week. A watching world is amazed when we reach out and extend grace, love, and compassion to one another.

Our hearts are broken for different reasons. We can receive a measure of Christ's healing and try to live it out alone, or we can stand together and become a healing stream. The presence of people who lived like that would change the world.

Jesus said, "By this all will know that you are My disciples, if you have love for one another" (John 13:35). "By this!" Not by gold fillings or bigger churches but by a community of grace.

Part of the reason that life is so hard even after we accept Christ's healing is, as we know, we are in a spiritual battle with Satan. But part of it is that we are at war with one another. On that early morning one woman received grace and then left to try and live it out. What would have happened if a whole community of people received grace that morning and began to live it out together? We will consider that in more depth as we move into a discussion about community. For now, I'll just comment that this is how we are wired to live.

Grace was available to all that day, but only one woman received it. Grace is offensive because it is free and not exclusive to our little club. It's like Christian's lemonade stand: "Deluxe Lemonade, $1, Free If You're Broke." We all stand at the foot of the cross without a dollar to our names, and Jesus says, "Come, drink, and you will never be thirsty again."

There is much that we could learn from the community known as Alcoholics Anonymous. I remember years ago when I was touring with my band, and I had a conversation with another Christian artist who had just been released from a drug and alcohol treatment center.

"I grew up in the church," he said. "I've gone all my life and felt like a stranger. When I stood up in that first AA meeting and said, 'Hi, my name is *Bill* and I'm an alcoholic,' I felt as if I had finally found a place to belong. No one looked at me as if to say, 'Well, how shocking!' It was as if at the bottom of the barrel of my life, I found a place to be real and honest and accepted. I finally found grace."

Bill Wilson, the cofounder of AA, reached an unshakable conviction, now expressed in twelve-step programs around the world, that an alcoholic must reach bottom before he can climb back up. He said, "How privileged we are to understand so well the divine paradox that strength rises from weakness, that humiliation goes before resurrection, that pain is not only the price but the very touchstone of spiritual rebirth."

Surely that is true for everyone who loves God. In my life it was only when I was at my weakest, my most broken, that I was able with empty hands to reach out and receive God's grace. When God has extended this kind of unmerited favor to you, it will forever change how you respond to others who stand in that same need.

Will you dress in grace? Don't you long for the freedom to stand up and say, "Hi, my name is _____, and I'm a sinner"?

Is it hard for you to accept this gift that makes no sense in human terms?

Would it be easier if there were something that you could do to feel as if you are pulling your weight?

As you sit with all that's true about your life and circumstances at this moment, will you let Jesus dress you in His grace?

In the movie *Pretty Woman* with Julia Roberts, there is a scene where Richard Gere buys her a beautiful dress before he takes her out to dinner. My girlfriends thought it was so wonderful, but it made me cringe. It poked and prodded insecurities from my past.

If I see myself in that kind of moment, here is what it looks like to me. I pull the dress out of the box. It's exquisite. The fabric is soft and it shimmers in the candlelight. But even as I hold it up, I know that it won't fit me. It will be too tight in the chest, or it won't be smooth over my hips. I go into the bathroom to try it on and remember I haven't shaved my legs. I sit on the toilet seat and cry. Shame is what I would be dressed in without Christ.

God's grace comes to us as a beautiful gift. If you hold it up, you will see that it's a perfect fit. Not only that, but as you slip it on, it covers a multitude of sins.

THE WISDOM OF PELICANS

Marlene and Frank flew in to stay with us a few days before Barry turned forty in the summer of 2003. We have been friends for years. They are our closest couple friends. Even if we haven't seen each other in months, when we get back together it's as if we kick right back in where we left off. Some of the most honest conversations I have ever had have been with them. Just before they left this time, Marlene gave me a book to read. It is called *The Wisdom of Pelicans* by Donald McCullough. I was in the middle of working on this manuscript and feeling pretty squeezed.

"Marlene, I don't have time to read a bird book at the moment," I said.

"It's not a bird book. It's a book about healing," she replied.

"Healing birds?"

"No! Healing broken hearts, you nitwit."

The book sat for a few days on the corner of my desk, pushed into the "I might get to you" pile. Then one day I picked it up and began to read. It's an honest account of one man's journey through a very dark place. Donald McCullough, a respected Presbyterian pastor and former president of San Francisco's Theological Seminary, found his life being sucked into a black hole when a private confession of an affair became public knowledge. He had confessed the sin to his wife several years before, and they had attempted through counseling and tears and prayers to rebuild the broken walls of their relationship to no avail. They divorced. Six years later he was slowly beginning to experience glimmers of hope, purpose, and forgiveness, but then the gossip wires crackled to life and his ruin spread like wildfire. Up until that point only a few trusted counselors were aware of what had taken place. His denomination formed an investigating committee and officially cut him off from fellowship. He had lost his wife and his job.

He retreated to a beach community where his only daily companions were the pelicans. The book is a walk through what happens inside a broken heart when friends, family, and fellow believers walk away. His honest dialogue rages at those who have rejected him, then turns on himself, for he was the one who chose a sexual relationship outside his marriage. Self-pity, grief, anger, sorrow, loneliness, and great sadness are soaked into the pages. Toward the end of the book he recounts a conversation with his psychiatrist in which he expresses his depression and weariness.

She asks him, "What is under that?"

"Guilt."

"What is under that?"

"Nothing! Anger I guess."

"What is under that?"

"There is nothing under that! Aren't you listening?"

"Nothing?" she asks quietly.

Rivers of tears flow down his cheeks. He has been living in hell, but in that moment it is as if all reality changes.

"No," he finally chokes out. "There is . . . God."

He writes, "Now you know, Mr. Big Shot Seminary President, you who preach and teach and write about grace, *now you know*."

You can talk about grace all your life, but it's only when you stand before God with nothing left to commend you and in that desperate place you become the one to receive that grace, then you finally understand what's so amazing about grace.

ALL THE HELP WE CAN GET

Christian has a fascination with bumps, bruises, and cuts. He is a huge fan of the first aid kit, which is very well stocked, a remnant of William's "you never know what might happen" days. One day Christian was skateboarding down the path in our backyard and I was cleaning the barbecue grill. (Can anyone explain to me why, if the barbecue is the man's domain, the woman still has to clean it?)

I heard Christian cry out and turned to see him facedown on the path. I rushed over.

"Are you all right?"

"I don't know," he said. "I think several things might be broken." He is a tad dramatic.

I cleaned him up, and the only remaining sign of the tragedy was a small cut on his right knee. I got out the antiseptic wash, some ointment, and a Band-Aid.

"It's going to need more, Mom," he said.

"What will it need?" I asked.

He pulled a large crepe bandage out of the box. "We can start here."

By the time we were finished he looked like an Egyptian mummy.

When Barry came home a few hours later, he was horrified to see his son so encased in yards and yards of bandages.

"What happened?" he asked.

"It's been a rough day, Dad," Christian replied with all the testosterone of a marine on leave. "But I'm going to make it."

"He has a little cut on his knee," I whispered.

"Christian, why do you have all that stuff on a little cut?" Barry asked.

"Dad, if you were hurt and you wanted to get well, wouldn't you take all the help you could get?"

I REST MY CASE FOR GRACE

If you are hurt and you want to get well, won't you take all the help you can get?

We have looked at the reality of the battle we are in. There will hard days, there will be failures, and there will be scars. With God's gr we survive and regroup and find the courage to get up and fight agaiı

But what if we are suffering at the hand of another believer? How we handle that? How do we forgive? Let's take a look.

✍

Father God,

Truly Your grace is amazing. Thank You that You know all that is true about my heart and yet You love me. Teach me to share that grace with others. For Jesus' sake, Amen.

APPLICATION POINTS

- *Grace* has been defined as "God's unmerited favor toward us sinners," and this precious grace is offensive because it allows no one but Christ to shine. Think about when you first understood God's grace. In what ways, if any, did you find God's grace to you "offensive"?

- Grace does not say that it doesn't matter that we have sinned. Grace says that all sin matters, but grace also says that our God of grace can forgive all sin. What unconfessed sin, if any, are you holding on to because you feel it's unforgivable? Well, it's not! Make it a topic of prayer. Confess it to God and know the grace of His forgiveness (1 John 1:9).

  How will you live now? What attitudes and behaviors do you want to characterize this new chapter of your life? Don't let anyone try to put an overcoat of shame back on you! On the cross Jesus took care of the cause of that shame.

- Bill Wilson, the cofounder of Alcoholics Anonymous, saw that it was only when an alcoholic reached bottom that he could climb back up. He said, "How privileged we are to

understand so well the divine paradox that strength rises from weakness, that humiliation goes before resurrection, that pain is not only the price but the very touchstone of spiritual rebirth." When have you experienced the kingdom truth that strength rises from weakness? That humiliation goes before resurrection? And that pain is not only the price, but the very touchstone of spiritual rebirth? Thank God for these precious lessons.

- Is it hard for you to accept the gift of grace, a gift that makes no sense in human terms? Would it be easier if there were something you could do to feel as if you were pulling your weight? As Donald McCullough and countless other believers have realized, you can talk about grace all your life, but it's only when you stand before God with nothing left to commend you that you can receive His grace. In that desperate place you finally understand what's so amazing about grace.

Community

13

CRUCIFIXION AND FORGIVENESS: BROKEN BREAD AND POURED-OUT WINE

In this manner, therefore, pray: Our Father in heaven, hallowed be Your name. Your kingdom come. Your will be done on earth as it is in heaven. Give us this day our daily bread. And forgive us our debts, as we forgive our debtors. And do not lead us into temptation, but deliver us from the evil one . . . For if you forgive men their trespasses, your heavenly Father will also forgive you. But if you do not forgive men their trespasses, neither will your Father forgive your trespasses.

—MATTHEW 6:9–15

At the beginning of 2003, the Women of Faith speaker team gathered in Dallas for our annual retreat. It's an opportunity to deliver our messages to one another before we share them with our audiences. Being together as a team for seven years has allowed the kind of trust to develop that gives each one of us a platform to make mistakes, share goofy stories, or realize we have totally missed the point of that year's theme! After we share the bare bones of our messages, we offer one another suggestions on different ways to present a point or remind one another of things that have happened that perfectly illustrate a principle. It's always very helpful, and it saves our audiences from having to suffer through some not completely thought-out ideas.

For example, I had titled my message for 2003 "The Three Golgothas." My husband was listening in on this presentation.

"What are the three Golgothas?" he asked gently.

"You will love this!" I said. "Jesus died first in the wilderness as He was tested for forty days, He died second in the Garden of Gethsemane, and then He died for the third time on the cross." I sat back and waited for applause that would probably begin small, out of awe and respect, but would build as the depth of the message sank in. There was complete silence in the room.

Finally my husband, wishing to rescue me from myself, said, "Do you think it's a little . . . heavy for a Friday night?"

I looked at him. I looked at my friends and burst out laughing. The rest quickly joined me. At times I have a tendency to be somewhat intense, and it's a gift to have people who love and respect me to balance my artsy side.

It is one thing to receive input, even criticism, from those who love us and handle our hearts with tender care. It is quite another when someone stomps across our inner sanctums with steel-toed work boots.

In the book *Bold Love*, coauthor Dr. Dan Allender described such an encounter. During a fifteen-minute break in a seminar that he was conducting, three people descended on him like a flock of vultures, pecking at him from every angle. The first was a fellow therapist who questioned Dan's basic theory of counseling and the very heart of his message. Next came an older woman who suggested people might receive him better if he tidied up his appearance. The older woman packaged her comments in the ultimate camouflage. She patted his hand and said, "God bless!" Finally a young man declared that he would come across as less arrogant if he discontinued charging for his seminars and took up a love offering instead.

In fifteen minutes, here is what he was basically told:

> Your message is wrong.
> Your appearance is wrong.
> Your heart is wrong.

He excused himself and took refuge in the rest room. He writes, "Over a few minutes break I felt discouraged, hurt, angry and nihilistic." (I looked that last one up. Among its definitions are "the belief that there is no objective basis for truth, the belief that all established authority is corrupt and must be destroyed in order to rebuild a just society." Ouch!)

All that remained to Dan as he walked through the hurt and anger was to be able to come to the place of forgiveness. He could have grabbed hold of the three word warriors and sat them down, told them how much they had hurt him, and demanded an apology. That might have worked, but it could have deepened the pain if they didn't get it and weren't sorry. More often than not, those who crucify remain unrepentant.

A NEED FOR KINDNESS

When I was sixteen years old, our church youth group decided to present a musical at the end of the summer. We thought it would give us something fun to throw ourselves into during the long school vacation. The youth leaders, Sheena and Fred, chose a musical by Jimmy and Carol Owens called *Come Together*. The theme was a call to forgiveness and unity. There were only a couple of solo parts; I was chosen for one and my friend Jenny for the other. Rehearsals were fun, and we all looked forward to the first night that we would be able to present it to the public.

The church was packed that evening, and although I was nervous, I loved the musical and believed that God would use it to touch people's lives. I just had no idea how that "touching" would affect me! Toward the end of the presentation, we provided a time for people to repent of any resentment or bitterness toward others. After a moment of quiet reflection, the audience or choir members were invited to go to those persons if they were present and ask for forgiveness. I couldn't think of anyone that I held anything against, so I just prayed that God would be with those who needed to ask for forgiveness and also with the ones who would, by God's grace, extend that to them. I had my head bowed and my eyes closed, but I became aware of someone standing in front of me, clearing her throat loudly, trying to attract my attention.

"Oh, sorry!" I said. "I didn't know you were there."

"I just want to ask your forgiveness," she began.

"Of course," I said.

"Well, let me tell you what it's for first. I resent the fact that you always get to sing the solos. I resent the fact that you made it onto the Bible quiz team and I didn't. I think you're stuck-up and I think your haircut looks ridiculous. Whew, there! I feel much better now." She walked away and sat back down, visibly lightened by the load she had just dumped on me.

The following week we presented the musical in another church. That time when I looked up during prayer, I had a line! I grew to hate that musical. I told my mom, "If one more person tells me that she can't stand me and then asks me to forgive her, I'm going to become a nun and join a silent order."

It sounds funny as I reflect on it now, but at the time it was devastating. The very work that was supposed to bring unity left me feeling as if I didn't belong and was resented by everyone I knew.

When kindness goes out the window in the name of cleaning the slate, we have missed the whole point of reconciliation. We have abandoned love. My mother's counsel to me was to forgive.

"But they're not sorry, Mom!" I said, indignant that she would even suggest I should forgive them.

"What if they are never sorry?" she asked. "Do you want to carry this hurt around with you for the rest of your life?"

BETRAYED

For some of us the issue is not that an insensitive, perhaps well-meaning person has wounded with words; it is much deeper. There is no greater cut than when you feel another believer has betrayed you or lied about you and tried to ruin your reputation.

Let's revisit my friend who described herself as an "old fool." After a few months, things began to unravel, and it was clear to her that what she thought she had been offered was not going to happen. Her e-mail to me was heartbreaking: "I wonder if I was swayed by promises and chocolate-covered carrots dangled in front of me. I would not like to think I could be so foolish; however my heart is heavy."

I have known her for a long time. I love and respect her. I've seen how she has been disappointed in the past and yet remained open to serving God and giving it another go! Now, I could tell from the tone of her note that she was desperately discouraged and felt very let down by the ministry concerned. I spent days thinking about her situation and praying for her. I wanted to be able to help, but I didn't know what to say. Then two things crossed my path in the same week that offered a different way to look at her situation.

The first was a book by Gene Edwards, *Crucified by Christians* (recently retitled *Exquisite Agony*), which I'll return to shortly. The second was one of Oswald Chambers's devotions from *My Utmost for His Highest*. The Scripture reference he used for that day was Colossians 1:24: "I now rejoice in my sufferings for you, and fill up in my flesh what is lacking in the afflictions of Christ, for the sake of His body, which is the church."

That is a complicated and much-disputed verse. What did Paul mean by "fill up in my flesh what is lacking in the afflictions of Christ"? Some theologians have asserted that the verse indicates that Christ's atonement was imperfect and that the sufferings of the saints are needed to complete His work on our behalf. I have a problem with that for two reasons. One, it is clear from all of Paul's letters to the churches that he did not believe that there is anything we can add to the finished work of Christ. These examples will show you what I mean:

> For by grace you have been saved through faith, and that not of yourselves; it is the gift of God. (Eph. 2:8)

> In Him you were also circumcised with the circumcision made without hands, by putting off the body of the sins of the flesh, by the circumcision of Christ. (Col. 2:11)

Second, the Greek word used for "afflictions" here is *thlipsis*, which means "trouble, distress, oppression, and tribulation." It refers to the hardships that Christ had in His work on earth, not to what He accomplished on the cross. There are ministerial afflictions (ask your pastor!), and there are redemptive sufferings. We have to deal with one another in the body of Christ—and that is tough sometimes—but we cannot add to the redemptive sufferings of Christ. We are called to acts of selflessness, and in that way we carry on what He began; we complete the work of Christ.

For me, a verse like that actually helps give context and grace to the hard things that happen in ministry. Christ went through it, and we go through it too. We can't touch what He did on Calvary, but we get to carry some of the load here on earth. Just as Simon stepped in when Christ couldn't carry His cross beyond the city gate, we are given the privilege of joining Jesus in the hard work of being a believer on this broken planet.

In his devotion, Oswald Chambers writes, "We are called to be broken bread and poured-out wine." The dilemma we struggle with is, Whose fingers will God use to break the bread and squeeze the juice from the grapes to make the wine? It is one thing if we recognize God's fingers in the crushing process, but what if He uses someone we don't like or circumstances that we never would have signed up for?

Chambers writes, *"We must never choose the scene of our own martyrdom."* That is hard! We pray, "Lord, I want to be more patient," and He sends someone who drives us crazy across our paths. We pray, "Lord, teach me to love as You love," and a sick relative for whom we have no time needs us to care for her. We want to cry out, "Not like that, Lord. That's not what I meant!"

I imagine that if I share these thoughts with my friend the next time we see each other, she might say, "How do I know that this is what God wanted? If God wants to squeeze me, that's one thing, but what if these people just got it wrong? Am I a victim of their poor judgment or the cruelty of others?"

Good questions. For help in answering them, I turn to this little book by Gene Edwards, *Crucified by Christians.* I don't know if you are familiar with his writings. He has a great gift of communication. His book *The Prisoner in the Third Cell* had a huge impact on my life and work. The key question in that book was, Will you love a God you don't understand, a God who doesn't always live up to your expectations?

I had resisted reading *Crucified by Christians* for some time. The title sounded like a self-pity book, but as I began to read it recently, I realized that it is far from that.

Edwards begins the book by imagining that the two of you have been invited to see a play together. The audience is small, just you and Edwards, but it is clear that you have been invited for a specific purpose. Only two actors are on stage. One sits with his face turned from the light so you can't see who he is. The other begins to talk with you about your life. He knows that you have come this evening because another Christian has grievously wounded you. The pain is so intense that it feels like a crucifixion.

HAVE YOU BEEN THERE?

Like my friend, do you feel as if you have been deceived and then abandoned?

Do you long for God to deal with that person or group as they smugly carry on with their lives and ministries while you lay bleeding in the dust? Let me ask you a few questions:

> Are you stuck?
> Can't forgive?
> Can't move on?
> Can't go back?
> Are you asking, "What can I do, Lord?"

The answer that Gene Edwards gives may be hard to take at first. It sounds extreme, even radical, but it just might change your life. He suggests that we begin by going to Christ, the only One who has been crucified and lived to tell about it. He suggests we ask Jesus: "Who did this to You?"

You might think that Satan is the one who has orchestrated your crucifixion, but not according to this book. Edwards writes that Jesus responds, "Who orchestrated my crucifixion? My Father. It was my Father."

We always feel more comfortable believing that pain comes only from the hand of an enemy. It makes sense because it's what we would expect from an enemy. When a friend, particularly another Christian, inflicts pain, we feel as if we have been stabbed in the back, and it has pierced our hearts. But to take it further than that, to suggest that God Himself, our loving Father, our first and last defense against the world, could be the One who allowed it and will use it to make us the women that we want to be? That is hard for us to welcome, but I do believe that God loves us so much that He wants us to be free from feeling like victims in this world and offer all of our lives, the joy and the pain, to Him.

DYING TO SELF

What is the point of crucifixion? The point is death, destruction. Do you think it might be possible that God's love for us is so intense, so pure, that He would allow these terrible nails to come our way so that what is dark and bitter and resentful in us could be put to death? Gene Edwards says, "Embracing a crucifixion will change your life forever."

When Jesus was in the Garden of Gethsemane, He asked His Father if it was possible for the cup of the wrath of God to pass from Him. He didn't ask for anything from Caiaphas, the high priest. He asked nothing of Pilate. The only One He talked to about the Cross was His Father. Jesus accepted fully that His life was in God's hands; in truth His Father was crucifying Him. That might sound shocking, but listen to what the writer to the Hebrews had to say:

> In the days of His flesh, when He had offered up prayers and sup-plications, with vehement cries and tears to Him who was able to save Him from death, and was heard because of His godly fear, though He was a Son, yet He learned obedience by the things which He suffered. And having been perfected, He became the author of eternal salvation to all who obey Him. (Heb. 5:7–9)

Jesus prayed to the only One who could save Him, His Father. His Father heard His prayers and allowed the Crucifixion to go ahead. He was *heard?* "But," you say, "He died. His prayer was not answered, was it?"

The Greek word used is *eisakouoœ*. It means "to be heard and listened to." Jesus asked for the cup to pass, but He also asked that the will of God be done. God heard Him. He listened to His beloved Son suffering such agony and answered Him by strengthening Him for the hill ahead.

I've often wondered what it meant when the writer said that Jesus *learned* obedience by what He suffered. A commentary suggests that the writer did not mean that He was imperfect as we think of the term: "There is a perfection that results from having actually suffered; it is dif-ferent from the perfection that is ready to suffer. 'He became,' indicates a change of relationship that follows the perfecting. The suffering that led to the perfecting did something—Jesus became 'the source [author] of eternal salvation.'"

Think of the two men executed with Christ that day. Both were guilty and were being punished for crimes they had committed. If you had offered them a way off the cross, I'm sure that they would have grabbed the chance. But as the day progressed, something changed for one of the men. In the midst of his dying he recognized Jesus and embraced Him. The best thing that ever happened to that man in his whole life was being crucified with Christ.

I don't mean to make light of your pain or the betrayal you have suffered, but if for a moment you could take your eyes off the one whom you believe put you in this place and receive it as an opportunity to let God work in the deepest place of your heart, it will free you. One thief continued to curse, but the man who saw Christ told him to be quiet. He understood the bigger picture.

The mark of a true crucifixion is that it is never mentioned again. Gene Edwards points out that after the Resurrection, Christ never referred to the cross or the pain again. There were no words of vengeance, no regret, or no cutting words—just life, forgiveness, and love. Crucifixion is God's invitation to resurrection, to a new life where the old is dead and buried.

After His resurrection, Jesus never said to Peter, "I told you that you'd deny Me!"

He never said to the disciples, "So where were you when I was dying?"

Jesus never sought out the soldier who drove the sword into His side or Pilate or any of the players on the stage of His death.

Thy will be done!

Your heart may be broken and your hands nail pierced, but will you bow down and worship and say, "Father, I welcome this crucifixion so that I might share in Your resurrection"?

[Let us look] unto Jesus, the author and finisher of our faith, who for the joy that was set before Him endured the cross, despising the shame, and has sat down at the right hand of the throne of God. For consider Him who endured such hostility from sinners against Himself, lest you become weary and discouraged in your souls. (Heb. 12:2–3)

Father God,
I ask You to bring to my remembrance those whose lives I have wounded that I might ask for forgiveness. By Your grace, teach me to forgive those who have wounded me. Help me to see Your hand even in the most painful places. Amen.

APPLICATION POINTS

- It is one thing to receive input, even criticism, from those who love us and handle our hearts with tender care. It is quite another when someone stomps across our inner sanctums with steel-toed work boots. From whom have you received loving input? When have you had footprints from steel-toed work boots on your heart? Comment on the lasting impact of each type of experience on you.

- What impact does the phrase "crucified by Christians" have on your heart? When, if ever, have you been involved in crucifying another Christian? How close are you to being able to ask forgiveness? To whom will you turn for help in either case?

- If you feel as if you have been deceived and then abandoned, as if you have been crucified by Christians, you may be asking, "What can I do, Lord?" Writer Gene Edwards suggests that you first ask Jesus as He hangs on the cross, "Who did this to You?" Edwards writes that Jesus responds, "Who orchestrated my crucifixion? My Father. It was my Father."

  When has a friend inflicted pain and you felt as if you were stabbed in the back and pierced to the heart? If you believe that God is in control of everything in your life, He is even in control of this thing that has broken your heart.

  Take this next (difficult) step: God, your loving Father, your first and last defense against the world, is the One who allowed this injury—and the One who will use it to make you the woman He wants you to be. Spend some time in prayer; talk to God about this situation.

- As Jesus' prayers in Gethsemane reflect, the point of crucifixion is death and destruction. It's the opportunity to die to self, to your own wishes for your life. In what aspect(s) of your life are you aware of the need to die to self?

- As I wrote earlier, I don't mean to make light of your pain or the betrayal you have suffered, but if for a moment you could take your eyes off the one whom you believe put you in this place and instead receive it as an opportunity to let God work in the deepest place of your heart, you will find freedom. Crucifixion is God's invitation to resurrection, to a new life where the old is dead and buried. To what crucifixion do you need to submit? Also, are you willing to forgive, to release the offender(s) to God?

14

RESURRECTED

If she were sorry I'd forgive
With wine and bread, with love instead
If he were kind, I'd let it go,
The words the wounds; that barely show
But, Father God, as You must see
These cuts run through the heart of me
With bitter tears my daily bread
For all they've done and all they've said
I cannot let this burden go
I carry it each place I go.

Jesus said, "Father, forgive them, for they do not know what they
do." And they divided His garments and cast lots.
                                                    —LUKE 23:34

THE STRUGGLE TO FORGIVE

I will never forget my greatest battle with forgiveness. I thought it
would destroy me. When I cohosted *The 700 Club,* I loved working with Pat Robertson, founder of the Christian Broadcasting Network.
He is a brilliant man who is passionately committed to God's work. I had,
however, a personality clash with one of the staff. I had watched her inter-
act with others and been impressed with her gifts. I'm sure she watched
me with others and, I hope, thought the same, but for whatever reason
we did not connect.

When I faced my struggle with depression and left CBN for a month to receive treatment, it seemed to me that she was glad to see me gone from the show. I want to emphasize here, that is how it *seemed* to me. Whether it's true or not is irrelevant for the purpose of this discussion. I was in a desperate place. I was afraid and lonely.

After I got out of the hospital, I returned to Virginia Beach, where CBN is located. Pat was very kind and supportive and told me to take all the time I needed to rest. Here is where it gets interesting and relevant to our issue at hand. Some of my friends on staff called me or wrote to me to tell me that this person "had it in for me."

I found myself panicking, sick to my stomach with anxiety. I knew that I was not strong enough to take this issue on and try to find out which person had said what and to whom. One morning as I was walking along the beach, my lifelong place of deepest dialogue with my Father, I threw myself on His mercy and asked Him what I should do.

That day was a turning point in my life. In my spirit I heard God ask me some very basic questions:

Do you believe that I am in control of the world?
Yes, Lord.
Do you believe I am in control of everything that happens at CBN?
Yes, Lord.
Do you believe that I am in control of everything that comes into
your life?
Yes, Lord.
Even this?

I stopped, sat down on the sand, and started digging my toes in deep as I considered the question.

Even this?
Yes, Lord.
Even if you are unable to change anything about how others see you or
what they say about you?
Yes, Lord.
Will you forgive?

Not yet.

So you are still struggling on the cross? Are you unwilling to die to what makes sense to you and trust Me?

Yes, I am.

I have a strong Scottish sense of justice. I think life should be fair, people should be fair, and surely God should be fair.

As long as there has been breath in our bodies, from the moment we left Eden, we have been quick to cry, "Foul!"

Christian asked Barry and me if we would sign him up for baseball camp in the summer between kindergarten and first grade. He had been to basketball and soccer camps the year before and loved them. It was a natural assumption to him that he would shine at baseball too. He enjoyed the first day, but when I picked him up after day two, the sky was dark across his forehead.

"Rough day?" I asked.

"I can't even talk about it," he said, proceeding to do just that. "I hit the ball, I mean, really hit it, Mom. It landed beside a kid who picked it up and said he caught it, so I was out. He didn't catch it!" he spluttered. "The nerve!"

"What did the coach say?" I asked.

"That's the huge, big problem," he said. "He wasn't looking. How can you be a coach if you're not looking? It's illegal!"

Have you ever felt that way about God?

"How can You be God if You're not looking?"

"If You were looking, then why didn't You stop her?"

"Can't You do anything with him?"

"Where were You, God?"

I told Christian that he would have to let it go if he wanted to enjoy the game. That's hard enough in baseball, but in relationships it's like trying to pry a stubborn goat off the end of your coat.

THE GOAT WHO WOULDN'T LET GO

When I was a little girl, my sister and I had been petting goats in our neighborhood park. One of the goats was hungry and became convinced that I was holding out on him. He stuck his head in my pocket and bit on something that smelled vaguely like food to him. He couldn't get his nose out, and he wouldn't let go. My sister told me to take off my coat, but I refused because it was my cool new green duffel coat. I ended up having to go home through the park with a goat attached to my coat.

When you won't let go of unforgiveness or bitterness, it will take you places that you don't want to go. It will keep you tethered to an event that is long gone, but you remain attached to the carcass.

In my situation as long as I was unwilling to let go and forgive, there was still a nail in my wrist, and every time I talked to someone about the situation, the nail cut in a little deeper.

I went through all sorts of stages in my struggle on the cross. I thought if I just kept moving, then I wouldn't have to die. I went through a bargaining stage. I would hear that this person had said something about me, so I would call a friend and talk it all out until she had pulled me back to a place where it seemed as if I was all right and the other person was all wrong. I had such a strong compulsion for someone to tell me that I was all right. I went through stages of feeling so angry, I could have punched a hole in the wall, but since I was living in a rented apartment, that didn't seem wise. I wallowed in spiritual self-pity.

I questioned, "Lord, how can You let this happen? Haven't I given my life to You, served You? I could have been an opera singer, You know!" It was pathetic.

Finally I came to a place where I said, "Lord, I am stuck here. Every time I think about this person I wish You would get her good! I know that this is not what You want for me. I want to please You. I want to honor You. I want to let this all go and stop trying to defend myself. So I'm going to start where I am and drag my will in line with Your will. I choose to forgive, even if my right eye is twitching at the prospect."

I made it a daily discipline. I got down on my knees morning and night and lifted this person before the throne of grace. I prayed that God's blessing and favor would rest on her. Within a few weeks I could even pray without grinding my teeth. If I had waited until I *felt* like it, I would still be waiting. If I honestly believe that God is sovereign, then nothing comes into my life that has not passed through His loving hands.

WHERE ARE YOU, GOD?

When we use our human eyes and understanding to view our situation, it can often look as if God has forgotten where we live.

Are you familiar with the story of Joseph? It is found in Genesis, beginning in chapter 37. When we first meet him, he is seventeen years old. His father, Jacob, was ninety years old when he was born. Jacob adored the boy, and it was clear to the other ten sons that he was their father's favorite. Jacob's favor was shown in Joseph's coat of many colors. That coat separated him from his brothers. It seemed to indicate that it was Jacob's intention to make Joseph the head of the tribe on his death.

As you can imagine, the brothers were furious. We follow this young boy through a series of disasters brought about at the hands of others. His brothers sold him to a caravan of Ishmaelite slave traders heading for Egypt. The brothers then slaughtered an animal, dragged Joseph's coat through the blood, and reported to their father that a wild animal killed Joseph. Jacob was heartbroken.

But the young man did well in Egypt. He was given a prominent position in the house of a man named Potiphar, an officer of Pharaoh. Joseph proved to be so reliable, innovative, and hardworking that he was soon running most of Potiphar's business. Potiphar's wife decided that she wanted the young Hebrew man. She asked him to come to bed with her, and when he repeatedly refused, she turned on him and told her husband that Joseph tried to rape her. He was thrown in prison. Year after year he languished in a dark, dank cell with no opportunity to defend himself.

How heartbreaking it must have been for Joseph to know that the first betrayal was at the hands of his brothers and his current incarceration happened because he made an honorable choice. He had told Potiphar's wife that he could not dishonor God or her husband. Her husband had thrown him in prison, and God allowed it. Did that eat at him? We don't know what went on in Joseph's heart and mind during those long dark years. I imagine him saying,

"Lord, I chose to honor You, so why didn't You come to my defense?"

There were so many things that Joseph did not know. He had no idea that in a few years he would be taken out of jail to interpret a dream for Pharaoh. He didn't know that Pharaoh would be so impressed with him, he would make Joseph prime minister of all of Egypt. He had no idea that all the years in prison learning the Egyptian language were actually preparing him for the rest of his life. He didn't know, but God knew.

A phrase keeps cropping up as we follow Joseph's life, and I've emphasized it with italics here. Luke recounted it in Acts: "The patriarchs, becoming envious, sold Joseph into Egypt. But *God was with him*" (7:9). We hear it again in Genesis:

> The LORD *was with Joseph.* (39:2)

> The keeper of the prison did not look into anything that was under Joseph's authority, because the LORD *was with [Joseph];* and whatever he did, the LORD made it prosper. (39:23)

Let's think about that for a moment. Joseph was brutalized by his jealous brothers and sold into slavery—and God was with him?

He was falsely accused of raping a woman and thrown into prison—and God was with him?

It's tempting to think that if God is with us, everything will work out as we desire. That's obviously not so. What matters is how we handle our crucifixion. We read that no matter what happened to Joseph, he found favor even in a dungeon because of how he lived. He accepted the death of his dreams and waited for the fulfillment of God's plans.

But what about exacting revenge? What about the brothers? The tables turned when there was a famine in the land. Egypt was the only place with grain, and Joseph was in charge of distributing it. One day as he surveyed the crowd lined up to buy grain, he saw his brothers. They didn't recognize him because it had been thirteen years since they last saw him. But he recognized them.

After various tests to determine if they developed any character since they abandoned him, Joseph revealed his true identity to them. The brothers were devastated. Joseph was the only one who could save their lives, but why should he? They were the ones who tried to kill him.

> Then his brothers also went and fell down before his face, and they said, "Behold, we are your servants." Joseph said to them, "Do not be afraid, for am I in the place of God? But as for you, you meant evil against me; but *God meant it for good,* in order to bring it about

as it is this day, to save many people alive." (Gen. 50:18–20, emphasis mine)

Joseph moved the issue away from blame and asked the crucial question: "Am I in the place of God?"

He said, "You meant evil against me." *God can take the most evil act perpetrated on you and use it to prosper you in body, mind, soul, and spirit.*

That is the bottom line. Look at your situation at the moment. Even if you have found yourself in a devastating place because of the evil intent of someone else, can you say, "But God intends this for good"?

Do you believe that God is in control? Is He bigger than your enemies?

That became the question for me: Am I in the place of God? If God is sovereign and good, then I rest in the place I am and worship there.

That is all that matters. I have no idea in the middle of the process what God will do in and through me or where He will take me.

THE LESSON OF THE BUTTERFLY

When Christian was four years old, a friend gave him a coupon to send to a butterfly farm. The coupon said that he would receive a butterfly garden in a box and caterpillars that, if God was good and the creek didn't rise, would become butterflies. I was dubious. We had tried an ant farm and ended up with the only colony of ants in America that refused to move. They sat in a dazed stupor inside the ant colony. I read and reread the directions to see if I had omitted anything vital, but all seemed to be in order. We came to the conclusion that we had been sent a depressed colony from a psych ward with no will to live.

Before our butterfly kit arrived, I decided to do a little research. I discovered that the transformation of the dull caterpillar into an elegant and colorful butterfly is one of nature's spectacular miracles. To become butterflies requires complete metamorphosis. To grow into adults, they go through four stages: egg, larva, pupa, and adult. I read that as adult butterflies, they live only one to two weeks. I made sure that Christian knew that and didn't start preparing for a lifelong relationship with these winged wonders.

Finally they arrived, and Christian was not too impressed with the caterpillars.

"Look at them! All they do is walk round and round, and then they eat. Then they walk some more and eat some more," he said.

"Do you know that some types of butterflies are born with no mouths so they live out their lives on the energy they stored as caterpillars?" I asked him.

"No way! Eat up, guys," he said, pushing another cabbage leaf into the box.

One morning when Christian came down to breakfast, he looked in the garden box and was horrified to see that the caterpillars were gone.

"Mom, they're dead!" he said, pointing to the three brown sacks that were all that remained of our many-legged friends.

"Well, yes and no," I said. "The caterpillars are dead, but inside that hanging sack, something is going on."

"Well, it's something quiet," he said.

When the butterflies finally emerged from their quiet crucifixion, they were a sight to behold. We watched them unfurl their wings and then decided it was time to let them go.

"Have a good life!" Christian called. "You've only got two weeks."

The comparisons are obvious, but let me unpack them a little anyway.

The only concern of a caterpillar is itself. It runs around on all its little legs, meeting its needs. It eats and eats and eats. When its time has come to an end, it looks as if it is dead. One night we had three caterpillars, but by the next morning we had three little brown pods. As they lay in their silent tombs, my son mourned their passing, but they would never become butterflies unless the caterpillars died. It was a quiet crucifixion. After their resurrection, their passion is to reproduce. For caterpillars, life is all about them. For butterflies, life is all about others, and everywhere they go they bring brilliant color. You see them only in the light. You will never see butterflies in the dark.

Perhaps you have felt for some time that you have been in a deep, dark place. You find yourself thinking, *It's so quiet here.*

You have resented the ones that you believe placed you there. Are you willing to open your heart to the fact that even in those places, you can say with Joseph, "And God was with me"?

Dear Father,

There are many things that have happened in my life that I don't understand, but I trust You that You have been with me every moment of my journey and will continue with me. I know that whatever has come into my life, meant for evil, You will use it for good. Amen.

APPLICATION POINTS

- As you read the opening poem, what wounding experience(s) came to mind? What was your greatest battle with forgiveness? What did you experience when you were able to let go—or are you still not quite there yet? As I heard our heavenly Father ask me, "So you are still struggling on the cross? Are you unwilling to die to what makes sense to you and trust Me?"

- Remember the goat that was attached to my green coat, convinced I had food for it? What lack of forgiveness or bitterness is attached to you? Be aware that it will take you places that you don't want to go; it will keep you tethered to an event that is long gone.

- Sometimes we have to choose to forgive despite what we're feeling. So make any unforgiveness in your heart the focus of daily prayer—and then see what God does. After all, if you honestly believe that God is sovereign, then nothing comes into your life that has not passed through His loving hands.

- It's tempting to think that if God is with us, everything will work out as we desire. That's obviously not so. What matters is how we handle our crucifixion.

   How well are you handling your crucifixion? Are you in a situation similar to Joseph's in that you need to accept the

death of your plans and wait for the fulfillment of God's plans? Explain your answer.

Even if you find yourself in a devastating place because of someone else's evil intent or actions, can you—like Joseph—say, "But God intends this for good"? Do you truly believe that God is in control of your life? Is He bigger than your enemies? Support your answer with God's promises in Scripture.

- At this point of your spiritual life, are you a caterpillar, a pupa, or a butterfly? Explain your answer.

15

A CHURCH DIVIDED ON HEALING

Rejoice with those who rejoice, and weep with those who weep.
Be of the same mind toward one another. Do not set your mind
on high things, but associate with the humble. Do not be wise in
your own opinion. Repay no one evil for evil. Have regard for
good things in the sight of all men. If it is possible, as much as
depends on you, live peaceably with all men. Beloved, do not
avenge yourselves, but rather give place to wrath; for it is written,
"Vengeance is Mine, I will repay," says the LORD. Therefore "if
your enemy is hungry, feed him; if he is thirsty, give him a drink;
for in so doing you will heap coals of fire on his head." Do not be
overcome by evil, but overcome evil with good.

—ROMANS 12:15–21

A NEW BEGINNING

When I left the hospital in 1992, I wasn't sure what the next step in my life should be. I knew that I didn't want to go back into television. I needed space and peace to work through all that God was teaching me about life and about my relationship with Him.

I found that leaving the hospital was almost as traumatic as going there. I had been harbored in a safe place for a month. It was a place to be open and honest, and frankly I wanted to set up shop and stay. I talked to one of my counselors about how I felt.

"That's perfectly natural, Sheila," she said. "Many patients feel that way. But this is not a place to tether your ship. We have given you a com-

pass to show you which way is true north. Now you just have to keep sailing in the right direction and have mercy on yourself if you get a little off course."

Over the next few weeks I worked with a Christian therapist who helped me to figure out how to make good decisions each day based on the Word of God and how to have appropriate boundaries in my life. *Boundaries* was a new word to me. I have since been greatly helped by the best-selling book of the same title by Dr. Henry Cloud and Dr. John Townsend. Beginning to understand this concept was life changing for me.

Childhood pain or abuse sets a child up to accept that it is normal to have others invade her space and dictate her choices. Even when I grew into an adult, I still felt like a child inside. I felt an overwhelming obligation to please others, so I would do what they thought I should do whether I agreed with it or not, but often I held great resentment in my heart. I began to learn that I get to choose whether to say yes or no to someone, and that's okay. By God's grace I was slowly learning to let go of my need for others' approval.

My counselor helped me see that God had come not to get me out of the pain and heartache of life but to live in me through it all and teach me to love in the process: "You need to know who you are in Christ, not what job you do. Who you are in Christ is everything."

As I prayed and talked to friends and family, I made the decision to go back to seminary and pursue a master's degree in theology for no other reason than the good of my own soul. I applied to Fuller Theological Seminary in Pasadena, California, and was accepted. I remember so clearly the day that I left Virginia Beach in early 1993 to begin the five-thousand-mile drive from the East to the West Coast. I went down to the beach one last time just as the sun was rising and stood at the water's edge. I had spent many hours there, bent over in despair. I lifted my hands up to my Father and worshiped: "Lord, I praise You today, for You have rescued my life from the pit. Now that You have placed my feet on a rock I give You back this life to use as You will."

I had no idea when I prayed that prayer what God had planned to make out of the broken pottery of my life. A couple of weeks before I left Virginia Beach, I had made a final appearance on *The 700 Club* to say good-bye. I discussed with the producers of the show just how much I should share with the audience. They said, "It might be best not to mention the hospital. You could just say that you were overworked, took a break, and now feel that God is calling you to further study."

I appreciated their concern, but I knew that I had to tell the truth. I had spent so much of my life hiding from the truth, and now I wanted to embrace it. Pat interviewed me as I talked about God's grace and mercy toward me.

As Frederick Buechner wrote in *Godric*, "God had daylight mercy on my midnight soul."

Then it was time to leave. I love to drive, and I relished every moment of the five-day journey. I drove through the warm and friendly heartland of America, over the Rocky Mountains, and through the dry heat of the desert. When I arrived in California, I settled into my new little apartment that would be home during my seminary days and began to get organized for the beginning of school. I was nervous at the thought of returning to a formal classroom. One of the symptoms of depression is difficulty in concentrating, and I hoped I would be able to study well and retain what I was learning. The next few months were some of the happiest and most peaceful I had ever known. I loved my classes, loved studying, and had a new beach to walk in Laguna Beach, California.

One day my friend Marlene called and asked if I would speak at a women's luncheon in Palm Springs.

"Not a chance, Marlene," I said. "I'm not doing anything in public."

"Come on, Sheila. You'll love it. Palm Springs is beautiful this time of year," she said.

"Marlene, I'd rather stick my hand in a blender."

"Look, Sheila," she continued. "Here's the deal. I have to find a speaker for Saturday. I've asked everyone else. You are the last one on my list. Will you do it as my friend?"

When she put it like that, she took the pressure off me. I was not the great white hope; I was the bottom of the barrel! I said that I would, but as I drove out to the desert that day, I could have kicked myself.

"Why did you have to open your big mouth and say yes? What are you going to talk to a bunch of perfect Palm Springs women about—plastic surgery in the Bible?"

I found the idea of standing in front of a group of perfectly groomed and coifed women very intimidating. I arrived at the country club, parked my car, and went in. Marlene greeted me at the door.

"This is great. Thanks! Can you speak for about an hour? Do you want to sing?"

"Marlene, I don't know how this is going to go," I said. "I'm really nervous."

Marlene prayed for me, and we took our places at the head table. As I looked out across a sea of lovely faces in exquisite outfits, I asked Jesus to give me His eyes to see, His heart to feel, His ears to hear the cry of every woman present that day. I know what it feels like to hide behind a suit and enough concealer and foundation to repaint the kitchen.

It's a day I will never forget. I decided that instead of speaking on some safe, impersonal subject, I would simply tell my story. As I moved through the corridors of my journey, there was silence in the room, no sounds of tinkling of spoons on saucers or shifting in chairs. I talked about my experience with depression, which was still fresh and present, and I became aware of people crying. Tears streamed through perfect makeup, and tissues were passed across tables as we women always do for one another. When I was finished, I said, "I'm sure many of you have to rush off, but I'll be here if anyone wants to talk."

No one left the room, so I sat down on the edge of the platform. A woman in her fifties came up and sat beside me. She whispered some of her story in my ear: "I have struggled with depression for years, but I'm so ashamed. I've never talked about it to anyone."

Another woman joined us. She said, "My daughter struggles with depression too, but her church thinks that it's wrong for a Christian to take medication so she won't take it. I can't reach her."

I stayed for hours that day, listening and talking, praying, laughing, and crying with a group of women that I thought I would have nothing in common with. God opened a curtain in my soul that day, and I saw that just beneath the surface of perfectly coifed lives are broken hearts. Then I wondered, Was it just because these women were rich and awake to the lie that "stuff" can make you happy?

I soon saw that was not the case. I was asked to tell my story at a small Hispanic church in a very poor area of Los Angeles, then to one of my classes at Fuller. Again I encountered the silent community of the broken. *The 700 Club* forwarded more than five thousand letters from viewers who saw that last show and wanted to tell me their stories. I was honestly stunned by the response. If so many Christians were struggling with depression, why hadn't I heard more about it? Why didn't we talk about it? Where were the resources to help us through it? Why were we so ashamed of our brokenness?

Do you remember the woman we visited with in the Introduction? She shared the devastating story of her daughter's suicide.

"She would have been thirty-five this week," she began. "She worked full-time in a large church but had been struggling with depression for some time. She asked the pastor for a short leave of absence to get some help. He told her they didn't believe that a Christian should seek help from a psychiatrist. My daughter killed herself. She loved God but she killed herself."

DIVIDED ON HEALING

It's clear that the church is divided on how we should seek our healing for some of our struggles, and that very division has cut through the hearts of many suffering people. If you have a brain tumor, few would question the wisdom of getting all the medical help you can get, but if you struggle with depression, the issue is much cloudier. The trouble is that far more women deal with depression than will ever deal with a brain tumor. So where are we to go for help?

I understand the reluctance of some to turn to the offerings of the pharmacist. Should a believer in a healing God take medication? If we are healed by Christ's wounds, then why would we need the pharmaceutical community's help?

My first appointment in the hospital was with the psychiatrist. He asked me if I understood what had brought me to this place.

"I don't know. I just know that I feel as if I'm disappearing a little more every day. I can't concentrate. I can't eat. I can't sleep. I am so sad. I find it hard to even speak."

"It seems clear that we need to stabilize your brain chemistry. I'm going to prescribe some medication that will . . ."

"Stop right there!" I said. "I'm not taking any happy pills! I'm in enough trouble without an injection of Joy to the World!"

"Is that what you think it would do?"

"Sure, I've read stories of people who walk around with an inane grin on their faces, totally oblivious to what is going on around them. I don't want to do that."

He seemed to be used to that kind of knee-jerk response. He gave me a basic lesson that day in Brain Chemistry 101.

Here is a layman's take on what he told me that day. God has designed the most intricate messenger system within the brain. Neurotransmitters are the chemical messengers that facilitate communication between nerve cells. They're like FedEx for your thought processes. There are three primary players that are believed to play a role in mood regulation: norepinephrine, dopamine, and serotonin. Serotonin seems to be a particularly key player in contributing to the symptoms of depression. When serotonin levels are low, the brain cannot function well. It can become depleted for a variety of reasons:

1. The brain is simply not producing enough serotonin.

2. Not enough receptor sites are active in the brain to receive it.

3. Serotonin is being taken back up too quickly before it can reach receptor sites and do its job. Imagine two nerves in your brain, nerve A and nerve B. For the brain to function well, messages need to be able to be passed from A to B. Serotonin leaves nerve A with an important message for B, but before it gets there, nerve A absorbs it again.

The doctor explained to me that morning that brain chemistry is an inexact science. If you have a brain tumor, an X-ray will reveal that, and surgery, chemotherapy, or both will be administered. Further X-rays reveal whether the treatment is being effective or not. But with brain chemistry there is no such medical plumb line. Research has been done extensively over the last few years with drugs called SSRIs, selective serotonin reuptake inhibitors. Here is how it works: after the message has left nerve A, the SSRI closes the front door and won't let the message back in. The message gets to B, and life continues as normal. That is a very crude illustration and wouldn't stand up in the *New England Journal of Medicine,* but perhaps it will clarify the clinical reality behind depression.

If there is a breakdown anywhere along the path, neurotransmitter supplies may not be sufficient for your brain's needs. Inadequate supplies lead to the symptoms that we know as depression. Depression is not a sign of weakness or a character flaw. It is a medical condition.

We all get bad days. There are times when we are down because we are out of fellowship with God or others. We might be in a job we don't enjoy, or we might be fed up waiting for Mr. Right to come along. (He got lost and refused to ask for directions!) These are situations that we can do something about without the need for medication. But clinical depression is a medical condition that needs specific help, and it is very treatable. Usually your family doctor can refer you to a reputable psychiatrist.

One of the most important things for me to understand during my initial consultation with the psychiatrist was that the medicine simply helps the brain to behave normally. I had a mental picture of the drugs turning my brain into a nightclub with Barry White music playing all night!

So I started taking the medication. Within a couple of weeks I could tell a huge difference. I didn't feel as emotionally vulnerable all the time. I was able to think and read and pray. The most amazing gift was the return of hope. It was a faint glimmer at first, like a stray shaft of sunlight through a thunderous sky. Even as I was beginning to appreciate the value of the treatment I was receiving, I received a letter from a friend who basically told me to pull myself together.

Saying to a person who is struggling with severe clinical depression that she should snap out of it or pray more would be the same as telling a diabetic to skip his insulin and join a Bible study.

Have we become too dependent on pills in our culture? I think we probably have. When I sign on to check my e-mails, I always have at least two from sites offering me everything from Viagra to Prozac. It is easy to pop a pill rather than deal with what might be going on in our lives that we need to deal with. My only plea is for those who do need help. Let's not condemn them or further shame those who are already drowning. I'm sure many people have been put on medication when they simply needed to be able to talk openly to someone about their lives.

We, as the church, have contributed to the overuse of medication by our lack of grace and unwillingness to say to each other, "Come as you are. We will love you and walk with you." I know of many women who are on medication just to make it through their encounters with God's people. But many others genuinely need medical help so that they can be returned to their husbands and children, their churches and communities, and be the people they are in Christ. It would be a wonderful thing to see the medical and the church communities walk hand in hand to care for people. For someone who is already sinking fast, dealing with disapproval from her brothers and sisters in Christ is heartbreaking and leads to despair.

FACING THE TRUTH

Part of my journey was dealing with the disapproval of others and recognizing that the church is divided on how we view many issues related to healing. One very close friend withdrew her friendship when she knew that I was on medication. I have tried several times to open up a conversation with this person, but she remains closed twelve years later. I struggled with feeling rejected, but I was angry too. I wanted my friend to be in this process with me, but she would not. I was stuck. Then I put into place the lessons that I was learning on my journey. Part of life is dealing with disappointment with God, with myself, and with others.

"With God!" you say. "That sounds a little strident."

Part of the process of embracing all that is gloriously true about God is letting go of all our illusions. It's necessary to relinquish our quid pro quo mentality where we think, *I will do this for God and God will do this for me.*

Facing the truth about others has to start with facing the truth about God. I found it helpful to sit down and write a letter to God about the things I didn't like in my life and the things that made no sense to me. I told Him that I thought it was a really bad idea to take my dad when He did because I would have been a different girl if he had lived. I used to dread Father's Day because it was an annual reminder of a missing piece in my life.

What about you? What would your letter look like? It might be a helpful exercise to write out everything that you wish God had made happen or stopped happening.

I read my letter out loud to God and then said, "That's the part I don't like, but I love You and I trust You. If that's the path You chose for me, then I trust You. You have such a track record with me, Father."

Facing our disappointment with ourselves is an exercise in grace. It is a crucial step if we are to be able to face our disappointment with others. If we are perfectionists or those who have been addicted to the approval of others, it's very hard to extend grace to ourselves, but it is a form of pride that has to be crucified in Jesus' name.

What in your own life do you constantly beat yourself up about?

What are the internal tapes that play again and again, speaking harshly to your soul?

Remember the truth of this promise,: "If we confess our sins, He is faithful and just to forgive us our sins and to cleanse us from all unright-eousness" (1 John 1:9). I could be wrong, but I think that verse says "all." That means all, not everything apart from that one thing you keep doing.

Facing our disappointment with ourselves gives us grace to deal with our disappointment with others. I have found a few steps helpful when I have struggled to forgive.

I allow myself to feel the hurt rather than pretend that it didn't really bother me. When I pretend, it seems to form a callous over my heart. An honest wound can be healed.

I accept that forgiveness is God's gift to me to help me live in a world that's not fair. Remember, we don't want to be tethered to that dead carcass for life.

Start where you are. Don't wait for a wave of warm emotion. Line up your will with the will of God, and start. Don't expect to feel overwhelmed with love for the person, particularly if the offense was great. Forgiving does not mean that what happened to you was okay or that you ever have to let that person into your life again. Forgiveness is a way of lining up your will with the will of God and simply being obedient.

So we return to the question of a church divided on healing.

On one side of the fence you have those who say that we should not look outside the doors of the church for any sort of help. All of our struggles are spiritual in nature and should be addressed that way. There must be unconfessed sin or a deficiency in the sufferer's prayer life. The bottom line is, it's *your* fault. There may well be times when that is true, but even in those times we need grace and love to help us see, not judgment.

On the other side are those who say that people are broken and hurt-ing and need help. They perceive that help is not available in the church, and they turn to psychology.

As I have said, I have been greatly helped by counselors and, when I needed it, by medication. I am very grateful to God for that. But as I moved on in my life, I discovered what I had really been looking for deep in my soul. I found community. I've been surrounded by people most of my life. God's people have encircled me, but I've not always lived in com-munity. Being part of the Women of Faith team has changed my life.

In the past I have paid for the very thing that should be our gift as believers. I have paid someone eighty dollars an hour to listen to the truth about my life and help me get on the path back home. I don't regret one cent of it, but that is the job of the church. We are supposed to be a healing community, bathed in grace and love, unbinding one another so that we can walk.

As I learned to face disappointment with myself, I am learning to face disappointment with others and forgive. Many times I have tried to convince someone of the validity of seeking professional help, but to no avail. She, too, had firmly held convictions. That's where grace is a gift to us again. I don't need everyone to agree with me, understand me, or support what I believe. If we differ in our opinions but we both love Jesus, we can walk together and be part of a healing community. In the next chapter let's look at what that can be like.

Father God,

Thank You that Your grace is available to me every day, for myself and for others. Help me to walk with those who understand my pain and with those who don't. In Jesus' name, Amen.

APPLICATION POINTS

- I spent a month in the hospital. As I left, one of my counselors said, "We have given you a compass to show you which way is true north. Now you just have to keep sailing in the right direction and have mercy on yourself if you get a little off course."

  Where did you get your compass?

  Why do you struggle—or have you struggled—to have mercy on yourself if you get a little off course?

  Why is this wise counselor's advice worth heeding?

- What about my synopsis of Brain Chemistry 101 did you find especially helpful?

- Part of the process of embracing all that is gloriously true about God is letting go of all our illusions. Sit down and write a letter to God about the things you don't like in your life and the things that make no sense to you. What do you wish God had made happen or had kept from happening? Read your letter out loud to God. You might even be able to use my P.S.: "This is what I don't like, but I love You and I trust You even if I don't understand the path You've chosen for me."

- We need to face our disappointment with ourselves and with other people as well as our disappointment with God.

    What do you find hard to forgive yourself for? What do you constantly beat yourself up about? What internal tapes play again and again, speaking harshly to your soul? With what truth(s) from God's Word could you replace those internal messages?

    Review the steps for dealing with disappointment with others (page 188). What, if anything, do you think God wants you to do in response to this discussion?

- It would be wonderful for the church and the medical community to work together to care for people, but at the moment the church is divided on how believers should seek healing for some of life's struggles.

    In what ways, if any, has this division caused you pain or resulted in isolation or greater depression? When, for instance, have you felt judged by God's people as you sought healing?

- What point(s) from the closing discussion (pages 187–89) did you find especially helpful? Basically, what role does grace play among believers who love Jesus but disagree about where to go for help and healing?

16

TAKE OFF THE GRAVE CLOTHES!

And Jesus lifted up His eyes and said, "Father, I thank You that You have heard Me. And I know that You always hear Me, but because of the people who are standing by I said this, that they may believe that You sent Me." Now when He had said these things, He cried with a loud voice, "Lazarus, come forth!" And he who had died came out bound hand and foot with graveclothes, and his face was wrapped with a cloth. Jesus said to them, "Loose him, and let him go."

—JOHN 11:41–44

SEVEN SIGNS

In John's gospel there are seven signs that point to the divine authority of Christ:

1. Turning water into wine at the wedding in Cana

2. Healing the official's son at Capernaum

3. Healing the sick man at the pool of Bethesda

4. Feeding the five thousand in Galilee

5. Walking on the stormy Sea of Galilee

6. Healing the man born blind in Jerusalem

7. Raising Lazarus from the dead in Bethany

The account of the raising of Lazarus is the culmination of these signs; *semeion* is Greek, meaning "a sign, a signal or mark." It says, "Take notice. Are you paying attention? Please don't miss this!"

Each of Jesus' seven signs illustrates a particular aspect of His divine authority. Every one is an involvement in a different area of human experience. Christ's life was a demonstration of the kingdom of God embracing the brokenness of man. I am constantly amazed that God saw our sin and desperate need for a Savior, yet He cares for even the smallest details of our lives. Think of the signs that John recorded.

A family was embarrassed to run out of wine at a wedding. Jesus stepped in (at the prompting of His mother!) and changed water into wine. Even the things that are not life-changing events are important to God. The message is, Bring Me what you have and I'll exchange it for what you need.

A man in authority was brokenhearted as he watched his son slip away from him. Jesus was touched by the man's absolute faith and honored his request. It was rare in Christ's ministry on earth for someone to recognize that He could speak a word and it would change the world. He honors that kind of faith.

A man lay by the edge of the pool, unable to get in quickly enough to be healed. Jesus came to him. When it seems as if we are never going to be the one to be in the right place at the right time to receive a touch from Christ, He comes to us.

He turned bread and fish into an all-you-can-eat buffet. We are human, and even though we long for words of life, we need sustenance too. It is all right, after all, to be human.

Jesus walked across the stormy waters of Galilee to reach a boatload of frightened men. Why were they afraid? Most of them were fishermen. I guess they were afraid because it was very unusual for a storm to blow up on the lake. The message is clear: Christ will be there when the unthinkable happens.

He healed a man who was blind and cut off from so much of life. The bigger message is, I can give you eyes to see what you miss every day of your lives.

Then He raised Lazarus from the dead. That was Christ's last miracle before the Cross. It was a declaration that Jesus is Lord over our greatest enemy, death. The last miracle was a two-edged sword.

It was the final straw that led to His death: "Then, from that day on, they plotted to put Him to death" (John 11:53).

Imagine being there that day! Lazarus had been in the tomb four days. He was buried in a cave cut into the limestone hill, and a stone was rolled over the entrance. The Jews did not embalm bodies, so there would have been the beginnings of significant decay. The first one whom Jesus encountered as He arrived at the village was Martha.

Jesus said to her, "Your brother will rise again."

Martha answered, "I know that he will rise again in the resurrection at the last day."

Jesus said to her, "I am the resurrection and the life. He who believes in Me, though he may die, he shall live. And whoever lives and believes in Me shall never die. Do you believe this?"

"Yes, Lord," she told him, "I believe that You are the Christ, the Son of God, who is to come into the world." (See John 11:21–27.)

> *Martha, do you believe?*
> *Yes, Lord.*
> *Take away the stone.*
> *Lord, he's been dead four days.*
> *Did I not tell you that if you believed, you would see the glory of God?*

There we see the gap between heaven and earth. *Yes, I believe, but do I believe enough to roll the stone away?*

They rolled the stone away that day. Jesus thanked God for what He had already done. Then He addressed Lazarus. He spoke to a dead Lazarus, just as He would speak to a living Martha.

In another part of John's gospel, Jesus told us, "Do not marvel at this; for the hour is coming in which all who are in the graves will hear His voice" (John 5:28).

OUR PART

Here is where you and I come in. Here is the whole point of this story for us in the context of this message on community.

Jesus said to them, "Loose him [from the graveclothes], and let him go."

Here we have the participation of heaven and earth, of God and His people working together. Jesus called Lazarus out of the tomb, and then He asked those who were watching to remove the grave clothes. There is a world of meaning in that simple command. Jesus could have taken off the grave clothes. He must have been the only One there who was not afraid. But what happened that day is huge. Jesus did the part that only He can do, calling us from death to life; then He asked us to step in and do the part that we can do. He asks us to care for one another, to get involved, to get messy, to unbind one another.

Jesus was talking to us all the time that He was on earth. He talked by what He said and did. He talked by His silence and what He did not do. He talked by the things He invited us to participate in and the things He waited to see if we would understand and say yes to on our own.

Let's return to that early-morning encounter between Christ, the Sanhedrin, the woman caught in adultery, and the crowd. We thought about what could have happened that day. If each person in the crowd had recognized that his need for God's grace and mercy was as great as that of a woman caught in an adulterous relationship, a miracle would have taken place. As it stands, we don't know what happened to everyone in the crowd. The woman went home and began to try to make sense of what happened in light of all the other events in her life. People assume she was a prostitute. She might have been, but she might have been a woman who was married to someone she didn't love and who didn't love her. She left that encounter, and then what? With whom was she supposed to work out the detangling of her life?

The crowd went home. Did they clear out quickly before the woman, if she was a prostitute, exposed any of them? What did they think that night? All the rules were changing, it seemed. Where would that leave them? What would it have been like if they had all encountered grace that day and then left together to work out how to live as a community of sinners touched and changed by the grace of God? Isn't that what we all long for? Don't we want to be in a place where we are known as we are but not left there?

A NEW DAY

Christ's invasion into the ways of man threw everyone. If women like *that woman* are welcome to come to God, what about me? Have the tables turned completely, and those of us who have played by the rules are no longer welcome?

It's very difficult when out of the blue someone changes the rules. I encounter that every time I play a game with my son. His latest passion is Junior Monopoly. It's different from the original game in that instead of purchasing houses or hotels, you buy rides at a fun fair. Every time you land on a ride that another player purchased, you have to pay the fee to enjoy that ride. The last time we played I landed on his carousel. It was supposed to be four dollars to ride.

"That will be five dollars," he said.

"I think that's four dollars."

"Sorry about that, lady. We've had to do some repairs and it's bumped the price up."

Then he landed on my hot air balloon ride.

"Four dollars, please!" I said.

"I'm afraid I can't ride on hot air balloons. They make me sick. I could get a note from my doctor if you need one."

His rule changes are innovative, if disorienting.

It's much more difficult when God turns the tables and suddenly everything that seemed right is wrong and those who are wrong are given the opportunity to be made right. Brennan Manning says in *Lion and Lamb* that what makes us happy and what makes us sad are good gauges of where we are in our relationship with God. Do we celebrate His outrageous grace or pout like spoiled children when someone else receives a gift on Christmas morning?

IT'S NOT FAIR!

Take the parable of the vineyard owner who needed workers to pick his crop. There is a huge lesson for us here if we will receive it. It could set us free!

> The kingdom of heaven is like a landowner who went out early in the morning to hire laborers for his vineyard. Now when he had agreed with the laborers for a denarius a day, he sent them into his vineyard. And he went out about the third hour and saw others standing idle in the marketplace, and said to them, "You also go

into the vineyard, and whatever is right I will give you." So they went. (Matt. 20:1–4)

We read that he did the same at the sixth, ninth, and eleventh hours. Then it was time to pay.

When evening had come, the owner of the vineyard said to his steward, "Call the laborers and give them their wages, beginning with the last to the first." And when those came who were hired about the eleventh hour, they each received a denarius. But when the first came, they supposed that they would receive more; and they likewise received each a denarius. And when they had received it, they complained against the landowner, saying, "These last men have worked only one hour, and you made them equal to us who have borne the burden and the heat of the day." But he answered one of them and said, "Friend, I am doing you no wrong. Did you not agree with me for a denarius? Take what is yours and go your way." (Matt. 20:8–14)

It was a familiar story to Christ's audience. It was a story told by rabbis, and they said that the workers who came at the end were paid the same as the ones who began the day because they worked harder than the rest. In their story man was rewarded for working hard and keeping all the rules. Jesus told the story, but He changed the ending. In Christ's story the thing to celebrate was the goodness of the owner of the vineyard, God. It was a picture of His kingdom, and it was shocking to the people.

You've changed the rules!

You're letting anyone in these days!

This is ridiculous!

God's generosity is scandalous.

Brennan says that our reaction to God's scandalous ways tells us how close we are to His heart. Are we thrilled that even those who straggled in at the last minute received the same generous grace of God as those of us who were slogging away all day? Do we stand in line offended by God's generosity?

"All right," we say. "Pay them a full day's wage, but don't we deserve a bonus?"

God's love says to celebrate My grace and take off their grave clothes. I can't imagine that it was a pleasant job to remove Lazarus's grave clothes. He had been in there four days. The love of God compels us to reach out to one another in the midst of the mess and see not the mess, but the face of the one who is being set free. You can do that only if you have made peace with the fact that Christ embraced you when your grave clothes came off. Sin is not pretty; death is a poisoned enemy, but we come to one another in the name of Jesus, bringing the fragrance of Christ.

UNWRAPPING WITH LOVE

It's unlikely that we will ever be called on to literally remove death clothes from another human being, so how does Christ's command to those who were present at Lazarus's return to the land of the living affect us?

A few years ago a friend invited me to a ballet being performed by a new avant-garde troupe from New York. I am a fan of traditional classical ballet, so I wasn't sure that I would appreciate the production. I enjoyed some of the pieces and found others a little strange (twelve people dressed up as organs in the body—a dancing kidney I can live without!), but one number had a profound effect on me.

A man completely wrapped in strips of cloth was lowered from the ceiling of the stage onto the floor. He lay there for a few moments and then began to struggle. All he could do by himself was roll over. He rolled and rolled, and finally in frustration he stopped moving and became still again. The other dancers came on stage, spinning and jumping around him, encouraging him to join in. Two male dancers lifted him up onto his feet. He was still tightly bound, so he simply stood there, incapacitated. Another dancer approached him and took the end of a piece of the cloth and began to unwrap him. Then another joined her and another until all the dancers were in a chain behind the first woman, all pulling on the cloth.

The man who was bound began to spin round and round as the cloth freed his legs, his body, his arms, and then his head. (I sat there, thinking, *Lord, please let him have something on under the cloths!*) When he was finally free, the troupe embraced one another and left the stage, leaping and spinning together. It was simple, but very powerful. The man could not get out by himself, no matter how much he wanted to. He could hear the music, but he couldn't join in. It was only when someone connected with him and began to unbind him that he was finally free to dance. We encounter people all the time who need help in getting rid of the grave clothes.

In his letter to the church in Galatia Paul wrote, "You, brethren, have been called to liberty; only do not use liberty as an opportunity for the flesh, but through love serve one another" (5:13). Part of our sinful nature is that we are selfish; we don't want to get involved in the lives of others who seem a little messy.

Is there someone in your church or circle who makes the same mistakes again and again? Perhaps no one has ever shown her how to live differently and make better choices.

Take off her grave clothes!

Is there someone coming to your group as a new believer, and all you can see is how secular her appearance, her language, or her outlook seems to you?

Love her as she is. Let the love of God through you take off her grave clothes!

We are called to be present in the lives of others not in a frantic attempt to meet everyone's needs, but in love and grace and mercy.

IN A HOUSE CALLED HOPE

Since I was a child, I have heard people talk about the love and grace of God. Every now and then I am given the gift of meeting someone who lives it out twenty-four hours a day. Sara Trollinger is a woman who has spent many years taking the grave clothes off America's broken teenagers. The passage that motivates her heart is this:

> To preach the gospel to the poor;
> . . . to heal the brokenhearted,
> To proclaim liberty to the captives
> And recovery of sight to the blind,
> To set at liberty those who are oppressed. (Luke 4:18)

I first met Sara when I was cohost of *The 700 Club*. As Sara talked about her heart for teenagers who are lost and the parents who don't know what to do with them or how to parent, I heard the heart of God. It's amazing what one woman and a passion to share the love of God with kids can do.

In 1985, Sara Trollinger, a former schoolteacher, established House of Hope, a residential home where hurting, troubled teens can learn about the love of God firsthand. Sara began with five people praying and two hundred dollars. Today, House of Hope has changed the lives of thousands of young people. Barry and I are very involved with the ministry. There is now a home for teenage boys too. Every time Barry and I visit the campus, one of the boys or girls shares his or her story with us. Here is a little of Grace's story (name changed for privacy):

> At seventeen she made the decision to end her life. She was a high-school dropout with problems that started when she was just seven years old. As a young girl walking home from school one afternoon a man in a car pulled up beside her and asked her to help him look for his dog. He threw her into his car and drove to a secluded area where he proceeded to rape Grace.
>
> By the time she entered middle school, her Dad was destroying himself with drugs and alcohol. Then he abandoned the family. Grace decided it would be better to end it all, so she swallowed between fifty and one hundred ibuprofen pills.
>
> She survived and was shipped to a juvenile mental hospital, locked down with other adolescents. Finally, the judge placed her into a residential program at the House of Hope. Grace says, "What I've learned since being at the House of Hope is that by believing in God, I am going somewhere and I am somebody. God really cares who I am. Jesus has given me back my self-respect and has promised to restore what was brutally taken from me—my childhood."

Grace gets the message: *It's never too late to be who you might have been!* God's rules are not our rules. His ways are not our ways. Thank God! They are so much greater and higher.

When we find God's heart in human flesh, a small part of us has found what it feels like to live in His kingdom. Sara and her staff lovingly peel off the rotten rags that cling to the kids who come to them for help.

I have found that grace with my Women of Faith team. At forty, I finally found a place to be right and wrong, happy and sad, and know that in all those moments I would be loved and received. We need one another. We find God's healing and grace in the company of one another. Just as the Father, Son, and Holy Spirit live in relationship with one another, we are called to emulate the beauty that exists in the Trinity.

Gracious God of heaven and earth,
Thank You today that Your love calls us back to life.
Give me Your eyes to see, Your ears to hear, and Your heart to feel
the pain of others.
In Jesus' name I will take off the grave clothes. Amen.

APPLICATION POINTS

- In the seven signs found in the gospel of John, Jesus embraced all aspects of the brokenness of human beings. Give examples of how He has touched different aspects of your life, ranging, for instance, from meeting your everyday needs, to coming to you when you need His touch, to being there when the unthinkable happens, to opening your eyes to all that He is doing around you every day of your life.

- Jesus wept at the tomb of Lazarus, and I think one reason He wept was that the perfect world He had created was never supposed to be like what He saw or like it is today. What events in your life reflect the truth that the world "was never supposed to be like this"? (Do you think Jesus might weep over some of the items on your list?)

- Whose grave clothes have you been privileged to help take off? Describe the situation and your sense of God's involvement in the process. Who has helped you or is helping you take off your grave clothes?

- Writer Brennan Manning notes that what makes us happy and what makes us sad are good gauges of where we are in our relationship with God. Are you thrilled that even those who straggle in at the last minute receive the same generous grace of God as those of us who have been slogging away all day? Or are you offended by God's generosity? Give specific instances from your life to support your answer.

- Part of our sinful nature is that we are selfish. We don't want to get involved in other people's messy lives. Confess this to God (He already knows it about you anyway!) so that, forgiven, you can more easily hear His call on your life to serve others and be filled with His love and power so that you can help take the grave clothes off suffering individuals.

17

The Joy of Community: An Alternate List of Miracles

I say to you, he who believes in Me, the works that I do he will do also; and greater works than these he will do, because I go to My Father. And whatever you ask in My name, that I will do, that the Father may be glorified in the Son. If you ask anything in My name, I will do it.

—John 14:12–14

There is a balm in Gilead
To make the wounded whole;
There is a balm in Gilead
To heal the sin-sick soul.

—"There Is a Balm in Gilead"

Every now and again, when I've managed to convince myself that the protein diet is a good thing, I spend a couple of hours in our local Waffle House. I order a cheese omelet and coffee, and I listen to the voices around me.

One day in particular stayed with me for a long time. I was aware of several conversations going on at surrounding booths. In one corner there were a man in a dark wrinkled business suit and a woman in a peach silk blouse, short brown skirt, and high-heeled pumps. Their whispers became louder as the distress level at the table escalated. The man looked about to make sure that no one was listening in. I wanted to say, "I can hear you, but it doesn't matter. I don't know your wife and I've no desire to turn you in, but do you know how miserable you look?"

A trucker at the counter pulled out a photo and showed it to the waitress. She was busy, but she took the time to look.

"That's my grandbaby! The wife and I are raising him."

"He's a fine-looking boy," the waitress replied.

"He's a good boy too," he added. "Let's hope he stays that way."

Two women were chain-smoking to my right.

"They're all losers!" one said.

"I thought things were working out," her friend added.

"He got Jesus and moved out!" she said indignantly before they both burst into a wheezy fit of laughter. "I never thought I'd get dropped for another man!"

A man walked past my table talking in staccato, broken sentences. I looked up and saw that there was no one with him. He went into the rest room, and I heard him let out a cry like a wounded animal caught in a trap. The woman at the table opposite mine looked up, alarm in her eyes. She picked up her coffee and moved away from the path of the noise. When the man reappeared, he was quiet. He ordered coffee to go and slipped out into the busy street.

The preceding snapshots are borrowed moments from lives that have crossed paths with mine just for a moment but long enough to feel a little of their pain and sadness. Our world is full of lonely, broken people. We live on a planet that seems to delight in taking our hopes and dreams and smashing them before our eyes. Divorce, death, disappointment, and despair are at epidemic levels not just in the Waffle House, but in the house of God as well.

What had happened in the life and mind of the man who screamed out his anguish in a public rest room, then collected himself enough to try to blend in again? What will become of the clandestine couple drowning in the mire of their choices or the little boy being raised by grandparents? Will their love be enough to erase the pain of his questions as he gets older? Will they live long enough to see the fruit of their love poured into his tiny heart?

LONGING FOR NORMAL

I received an e-mail recently from a woman who attended one of our conferences. She feels as if all grace and kindness has gone from her life:

I recently attended one of your conferences. This year everything in my life changed. My grandmother died and my dad died and I said to my Mom, let's just skip the WOF thing. I will pay the church for our tickets and room and we can just stay home. She said no let's go. I can say that I sat next to my beautiful Christian mom and looked to see if the things you were saying made her sad, happy, or anything. Boy, there were almost a few moments that weekend that we seemed normal. Oh, how I long to feel normal and not to ask God why would He take my wonderful, loving dad.

Look around you and you will see people try to get through one more day without falling apart. There seem to be unprecedented levels of cancer and disease attacking families everywhere we turn. How are we to walk through these times?

THROUGH IT ALL

One of my favorite books to read to Christian at night is *Toot and Puddle: You Are My Sunshine* by Holly Hobbie. Toot and Puddle are two little pigs who are best friends. Previous books have detailed all sorts of wild adventures, but in this book Toot is in a bad place. Nothing that used to make him happy seems to touch him anymore. Puddle tries everything he can think of to restore a smile to his friend's face. He arranges a picnic and invites all their friends. It changes nothing. Puddle jumps through hoops trying to help his friend, but in the end only one thing made a difference.

The thing that helped was that Puddle stayed beside Toot through it all. Isn't that what we really long for deep in our souls, after all is said and done? We long for those who will not only take off our grave clothes but will also stay with us for the rest of the journey on this earth. We need one another. We are the body of Christ, but more often than not we live at enmity with one another.

God composed the body, having given greater honor to that part which lacks it, that there should be no schism in the body, but that the members should have the same care for one another. And if one member suffers, all the members suffer with it; or if one

member is honored, all the members rejoice with it. Now you are the body of Christ, and members individually. (1 Cor. 12:24–27)

That is a familiar passage, but we struggle with the working out of it in contemporary life. Our humanity rebels in so many ways that cause division where there should be love and unity. Many issues chip away at our call to love one another—jealousy, fear, judgment, insecurity, or hurt feelings. We are offended when one person is honored over another. We assume it says something about that person or about us or about God's favorites. It is hard work to love one another. It is easy to take offense, and even if we don't confront the persons who hurt us, we withdraw from them as a way to punish them.

God's word is crystal clear: "This is My commandment, that you love one another as I have loved you" (John 15:12).

That's a tall order, but it is Christ's command to us. I found that passage very challenging in regard to the person I clashed with at CBN. I had no desire to love her. I believed that she had purposely tried to hurt me, so why should I reach out to her in any way? I wanted to move ahead with my life but nurse a little grudge inside. But I couldn't get away from Christ's command to love, whether I felt like loving or not. It's not a suggestion; it's a command.

Not long after God's Word had convicted me of the hardness of my heart, I bumped into this person. By God's grace I dragged my stubborn will in line with the will of God and spent some time talking with her. It was such sweet release to let go of my anger and genuinely pray that God would bless her. It was not a one-time, quick-fix thing for me. I had to keep bringing any residual trash from my heart before God and one more time pray that He would bless this person. It has become my daily prayer that God would give me a heart of compassion for everyone I meet, not just those I like and immediately feel warm toward.

PEOPLE OF COMPASSION

How do we live as the body of Christ in these times in which we have been placed? What are the hallmarks of a changed life? One word that immediately comes to my mind is *compassion*. One of my favorite psalms is Psalm 103. You might want to read it out loud as the children of Israel did in the desert. There is something powerful in speaking the truth aloud so that our own ears can hear and our own souls can cry out, "Amen!"

I love to take a psalm like this one and read it out loud at the top of my voice!

> Bless the LORD, O my soul;
> And all that is within me,
> bless His holy name!
> Bless the LORD, O my soul,
> And forget not all His benefits:
> Who forgives all your iniquities,
> Who heals all your diseases,
> Who redeems your life from destruction,
> Who crowns you with lovingkindness and tender mercies,
> Who satisfies your mouth with good things,
> So that your youth is renewed like the eagle's . . .
> As a father pities his children,
> So the LORD pities those who fear Him.
> For He knows our frame;
> He remembers that we are dust.
> As for man, his days are like grass;
> As a flower of the field, so he flourishes.
> For the wind passes over it, and it is gone.
> And its place remembers it no more.
> But the mercy of the LORD is from everlasting to everlasting
> On those who fear Him,
> And His righteousness to children's children. (Ps. 103:1–5, 13–17)

That is such a wonderful promise! It's full of life and hope. Why, then, are so many of us in the church still so wretchedly unhappy?

The whole gospel can be summed up in these words: "'You shall love the LORD your God with all your heart, with all your soul, with all your mind, and with all your strength.' This is the first commandment. And the second, like it, is this: 'You shall love your neighbor as yourself.' There is no other commandment greater than these" (Mark 12:30–31).

My book *All That Really Matters* is built around this text. Jesus came to show us how to love God and how to love our neighbors. Every step of

Christ's walk on this earth was a demonstration of the compassionate heart of a Father who is consumed with love for His children. We are called to live as He lived. But what does that actually mean? What would that look like?

> Most assuredly, I say to you, he who believes in Me, the works that I do he will do also; and greater works than these he will do, because I go to My Father. And whatever you ask in My name, that I will do, that the Father may be glorified in the Son. If you ask anything in My name, I will do it. (John 14:12–14)

What do you think of when you consider doing greater works than Christ did on earth? In the process of finishing up this book someone questioned me on my assumption that most people connected this passage with miracles. I thought about that for a while, but I have to say that I have never heard anyone connect it to anything but miracles. We are attracted to the spectacular and quick fixes. But is it possible that Jesus was giving us an opportunity to understand a greater privilege, a different way to live?

So what do you think of when you read Christ's words? Do you think of the miracles?

Jesus turned water into wine, He raised the dead, He took a lunch box and made it into a feast fit for thousands, He restored sight to the blind, He made the lame walk, He pulled money for government taxes from the mouth of a fish, and as if that wasn't enough, He came back to life after being brutally crucified.

Or do you think of the selfless way that Jesus lived? He returned love for hate. He turned the other cheek and forgave those who betrayed Him and left Him to die.

The miracle list would certainly be the easiest to live out because miracles require little of us and all of God, but what would be a greater challenge and witness to a watching world?

THE GREATER MIRACLE

I want to present another way to look at this passage and see if it rings as true in your heart as it does in mine. I have prayed over this text and asked God to help me understand what Jesus was saying. What did He mean by "greater works than these"?

The Gospels give an account of thirty-five miracles performed by Christ. They can be divided into three groups: miracles of healing, command over the forces of nature, and raising the dead. Let's think of these miracles as the A list.

I want to suggest a B list. They are the heart of this book.

Jesus resisted the enemy with the power of the Word of God:

> Then Jesus said to him, "Away with you, Satan! For it is written: 'You shall worship the LORD your God, and Him only you shall serve.'" Then the devil left Him, and behold, angels came and ministered to Him. (Matt. 4:10–11)

Jesus reached out and touched the unlovely:

> A leper came and worshiped Him, saying, "Lord, if You are willing, You can make me clean." Then Jesus put out His hand and touched him, saying, "I am willing; be cleansed." (Matt. 8:2–3)

Jesus recognized broken hearts and turned toward them with love:

> And when Jesus came to the place, He looked up and saw him, and said to him, "Zacchaeus, make haste and come down, for today I must stay at your house." So he made haste and came down, and received Him joyfully. But when they saw it, they all complained, saying, "He has gone to be a guest with a man who is a sinner." (Luke 19:5–7)

Jesus forgave the unforgivable:

> When they had come to the place called Calvary, there they crucified Him, and the criminals, one on the right hand and the other on the left. Then Jesus said, "Father, forgive them, for they do not know what they do." (Luke 23:33–34)

Jesus gives those who make the worst choices in life a second chance:

> He said to him the third time, "Simon, son of Jonah, do you love Me?" Peter was grieved because He said to him the third time, "Do

you love Me?" And he said to Him, "Lord, You know all things; You know that I love You." Jesus said to him, "Feed My sheep." (John 21:17)

I could list many more incidents, but my point is simple: don't you think that if we lived as Jesus lived, loved as Jesus loved, it would be a greater miracle than cancer cells disappearing for a few years, only to lose the inevitable battle with death at some point? What if living like that is what Jesus meant when He said that we would do greater works? Instant miracles are easy. Either God shows up and a miracle occurs, or He doesn't. Sharing the heart of Christ for this broken world is an act of grace and a greater miracle, for we have to say yes to it. These kinds of "miracles" change the world. These miracles bind up the brokenhearted and put the lonely in families.

What would that look like for us?

We don't count on our human flesh to be strong or our human minds to come up with a good retort; we rest on the Word of God. *When the devil tempts us, we resist with the power of the Word of God.*

We reach out and love the unlovely. We reach out to those who have lost their place in our world. Our passionate commitment at Women of Faith in 2004 in partnership with World Vision is to reach out to women and children who are HIV positive. I had the privilege in 2003 of beginning to work on this project. My first encounter was with a mother and two children. All three were dying from AIDS. The mother's prayer was simple: "I pray that God will spare me to hand the children to Him." God answered that heartbreaking prayer, and the children died first, then the mother.

We recognize broken hearts and turn toward them with love. I remember talking with a woman at one of our conferences when she suddenly ducked down.

"What's wrong?" I asked.

"It would be terrible if those women who just passed saw me here. They know how I have messed up. I was in their church, but I had an affair and I left. I don't belong anywhere anymore."

We forgive the unforgivable. Forgiveness is a hard but necessary discipline if we long to live in relationship with one another. Rather than divide us further, being able to humble ourselves and ask for and receive forgiveness will make our bond stronger than ever.

We give those who have made the worst choices in life a second chance. We choose to reach out to those who have made a mess of their lives by the choices they have made. When it seems to them that all the doors of grace should slam in their faces, we open up the door and invite them in to kneel with us at the throne of grace.

We invite them in because we have been there too. Real community is founded on recognizing that each one of us stands in need of the grace and mercy of God.

THE COST OF LOVE

A wonderful one-act play by Thornton Wilder is called *The Angel That Troubled the Waters.* The play takes place by the pool of Bethesda. The sick and dying lie waiting for the angel to trouble the waters. They know that whoever gets into the water first will be healed. The angel appears at the top step and surveys the crowd waiting below. A new invalid approaches the pool, crying out in his heart to be healed of an internal torment. Another man wakes from a nightmare, and imagining that once more he has missed the angel's touch, he throws himself in the pool. His friends mock him, "Crazy fool!"

The new invalid gets close to the edge, but the angel tells him to draw back. The man cries out for mercy. His wounds might not be as noticeable as those of the disabled beggars who live in desperate hope that someone will get them to the water in time, but he knows that if only he could be healed from his internal torment, he would be a more effective servant of God. The angel tells him to step away. She says,

> Without your wounds where would your power be? It is your very remorse that makes your low voice tremble into the hearts of men. The very angels themselves cannot persuade the wretched, blundering children on earth as can one human being broken on the wheels of living. In love's service only the wounded soldiers can serve. Draw back!

The angel stirs the water, and the man who had awakened from his nightmare tumbles in and is healed. As he gets out of the pool, he sees the newcomer and recognizes him as the one who has helped his son out of a dark depression. He asks the man to come home with him: "Only you have ever lifted his mood."

Our very wounds, when offered to Christ, become beacons of hope to others. When you have had your heart broken, you understand what it's like to suffer, to feel despair. You recognize that drowning look in the eyes of someone else.

Now is the time to live as Christ lived. Now is the time to love as Christ loved. You don't have to be perfect, just perfectly convinced that love is the only way to reach a broken heart.

We have walked through a lot of stuff together in this book. I pray that you have found it as helpful to read it as I have to write it. I know that there is so much joy offered to us as God's children when we bring our wounds to Him to heal. Then we are able to arm ourselves against the wickedness of a defeated enemy. What a blazing neon sign it would be to our world in these difficult and uncertain times if we would reach out in love to one another and those around us and live as a community of grace!

Jesus had only a few short hours left to live. He had just enjoyed His last meal with His friends before He would be led through a mocking crowd and executed. The sand was rapidly disappearing from His hourglass. In those last few moments of private conversation with His closest friends, this is what He told them: "A new commandment I give to you, that you love one another; as I have loved you, that you also love one another. By this all will know that you are My disciples, if you have love for one another" (John 13:34–35).

A new commandment? Surely that was always the way. Didn't Jesus tell them again and again to love God with all the heart, soul, mind, and strength? But look at what Jesus said: "As I have loved you, that you also love one another."

As I have loved you.
As I have loved you.
As I have loved you.

211

Dear Father God,

Give me Your eyes to see, Your heart to feel, Your ears to hear and let me be Your fragrance in this world. For Jesus' sake, Amen.

APPLICATION POINTS

- Snapshots from my visit to the Waffle House showed people dealing with divorce, death, disappointment, and despair. What similar snapshots have you noticed around you at your Waffle House? In the house of God you call home? I shared with you the Holly Hobbie story *Toot and Puddle: You Are My Sunshine.* The thing that helped Toot smile again was Puddle staying beside him through the bad times. You and I long for people who will not only take off our grave clothes, but who will also stay with us for the rest of the journey on this earth.

- When have you had the privilege of staying at someone's side through his or her dark times? Reflect on what you learned from that experience about God, pain, healing, or community.

- When have you been blessed to have someone stay by your side through your dark times? Again, reflect on what you learned from that experience about God, pain, healing, or community.

- If you haven't had one or either experience, think about why that may be—and what you might do to find opportunities for such rich relationships. Jesus commands us to "love one another" (John 15:12). This is not a suggestion!

- Who in your life is hardest to love? That person probably is in great need of love!

- Who can help you obey this commandment in regard to that person? (Hint: His initials are H. S.) Think about the selfless way Jesus lived. He returned love for hate. He turned the other cheek and forgave those who betrayed Him and left Him alone to die. What a witness to a watching world we would have if we lived this way!

- In your mind, walk through your day imagining what living selflessly as Jesus did would look like—and then, after you close this book, continue the experiment in real time! When offered to Christ, our very wounds become beacons of hope to others.

- When has someone else's woundedness enabled her to be a beacon of hope in your life?

- What will you do to make yourself available for Jesus to use you, your woundedness, and your story of God's grace to be a beacon of light for others? "Here am I" is a good start.

A Final Thought:
Don't Hide Your Heart

I have not hidden Your righteousness within my heart; I have declared Your faithfulness and Your salvation; I have not concealed Your lovingkindness and Your truth from the great assembly.

—Psalm 40:10

On a missions trip to Thailand in the 1980s I had the honor of meeting a doctor who works with people in a leper colony on the border between Thailand and Cambodia. His heart was not only to minister to the physical needs of those who suffered so, but also to minister to their spiritual needs.

Leprosy has afflicted humanity since time immemorial. It once affected every continent, and it has left behind a terrifying image in history and human memory—of mutilation, rejection, and exclusion from society. Today there are more than half a million cases in Southeast Asia alone. There are two kinds of leprosy, and I asked the doctor what is the most difficult type of leprosy to cure.

"The hardest thing to cure is not the disease. Today, with multidrug therapy, leprosy is much easier to treat. What is hard to treat is what the disease does to a man's, a woman's, or a child's soul. The first thing I noticed as I made my way through the leper colony was that no one wanted to make eye contact with me. There is great shame associated with this disease," he said.

"How do you treat that?" I asked.

"The same way you treat it anywhere, with the love and compassion of Christ."

He told me that he and another doctor started a church in the leper colony.

"What we began to see take place there was far greater than what we saw take place in our clinics. We saw the grace and mercy of Christ wash over wound sites, disfigured faces and bodies. We saw smiles return to faces that had forgotten such a thing was possible."

I asked him if there was one moment that stood out above all others.

"Yes. I will never forget the day that a man came into my clinic who we had treated before. He had always refused to look at me, but on this day he stood as straight as his body would allow and extended his right hand to me. He looked in my eyes and smiled. He said just one thing: 'Loving Jesus has given me my life back.'"

That is the call of this book. Come to Jesus and get your life back. Do you feel disfigured by life? Are you afraid to really live? Are you lonely but too ashamed to open up?

Real healing is offered to you if you will come to Jesus, just as you are right now. It's easy to believe that God is love, so therefore God must love me. But I like Brennan Manning's question in *The Wisdom of Tenderness:* "Do I wholeheartedly trust that God likes me? And do I trust that God likes me, not after I clean up my act and eliminate every trace of sin . . . but in this moment, right now, right here, with all my faults and weaknesses?"

If you answer yes, then you are living in the grace of those whose hearts have been broken, crucified, and resurrected by a living Lord Jesus.

I plead with you in the name of the Wounded Healer who gave everything so that we could live, come to Jesus, and live a life worth living.

In Jesus alone, there is real healing for a woman's wounded heart.

Come to Me, all you who labor and are heavy laden, and I will give you rest. Take My yoke upon you and learn from Me, for I am gentle and lowly in heart, and you will find rest for your souls. For My yoke is easy and My burden is light. (Matt. 11:28–30)

✍

Father God,
I come to You now in Jesus' name. I give all of me to all of You. I

bring my brokenness, my disappointments, my joys and fears. I give You my heart. Thank You that in You there is healing for my brokenness. Because of Jesus, Amen.

APPLICATION POINTS

When asked how he treated the shame associated with leprosy, the doctor who worked in the Southeast Asia leper colony said, "The same way you treat it anywhere, with the love and compassion of Christ."

- In what ways have the love and compassion of Christ brought you healing? One of his patients had always refused to look at this good doctor, but one day he stood as straight as his body would allow and extended his right hand to the doctor. He looked in the doctor's eyes (something his shame had never let him do before) and said just one thing: "Loving Jesus has given me my life back."

- Since coming to know Jesus as your Redeemer and Healer as well as your Savior and Lord, in what ways have you received your life back?

I'm sure that, like me, you are well aware of tender places that still need God's healing touch. Continue to turn to the wounded Healer. After all, He gave everything so that you and I could live. In Him alone there is real healing for a woman's wounded heart.

Bible Study

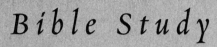

BIBLE STUDY

An Introduction:
Our Hidden Pain

Read Matthew 11:28–30, reprinted here from Eugene Peterson's *The Message:*

> Are you tired? Worn out? Burned out on religion? Come to me. Get away with me and you'll recover your life. I'll show you how to take a real rest. Walk with me and work with me—watch how I do it. Learn the unforced rhythms of grace. I won't lay anything heavy or ill-fitting on you. Keep company with me and you'll learn to live freely and lightly.

- Choose a Bible other than *The Message.* To whom does Jesus extend His invitation, "Come"?

- Is Jesus talking about you when He refers to someone weary and burdened? Why are you weary? What burdens are you carrying—and which ones have you carried for an especially long time?

- Weariness comes when we try to earn God's love. In what ways, if any, are you trying to earn God's love or to prove to Him your love for Him?

- Why do you struggle to receive and to rest in God's grace?

- What is appealing about Jesus' invitation to you?

  Holy Spirit, please help me understand not only in my mind, but also in my heart God's immeasurable love for me despite my sinfulness. I believe He loves me; help my unbelief. Amen.

Chapter 1:
Broken Hearts and Shattered Dreams
Read Job 3:20–26.

- Turn to Job 1 and read the chapter. What events have prompted the words and emotions of Job 3:20–26?

- When, if ever, have you felt the way Job felt in chapter 3? What statements from this passage express feelings you have had?

- What events in your life have prompted you to ask, "Why, God?"

- What does it mean to you that we serve a God to whom we can speak so openly, honestly, and freely?

Read John 20:24–28.

- What opportunity did Thomas want and—by God's grace— have?

- Christ carried the scars of the Crucifixion with Him as He rose from the dead, but His wounds were healed. What hope for your wounded heart does that physiological truth offer you?

  Lord God, I pray as David prayed so long ago: "Restore to me the joy of Your salvation, and uphold me by Your generous Spirit" (Ps. 51:12). You alone have the power to heal and transform a wounded heart and a crushed spirit. So I humbly turn to You once again. Amen.

Chapter 2:
God, Do You See My Pain?
Read John 11:1–44.

- What did Jesus arrive too late to do? When was He first contacted about Lazarus's need for Him?

- When have you been puzzled about the timing of God's answer to your prayer? Be specific.

- God did something far greater than Mary and Martha could have imagined: He raised their brother from the dead. What does God's timing here reveal about Him?

- What hope do you find in the account of Lazarus? Note especially that neither the way God answered the sisters' prayers for their brother nor His timing was at all what they had in mind.

- What message does God have for you in Isaiah 55:8–9?

Lord God, Your ways are not human ways, and Your thoughts are higher than ours. Thanks for reminding me about this truth. I don't need a smaller God, One who answers prayers according to my timing and my idea of "good." But, Lord, I do need help in trusting You. Amen.

Chapter 3:
The Truth About Our Shame
Read Luke 8:40–48.

- Imagine the scene of jostling, noisy humanity that Luke reported here. Despite the urgency of His mission and the crushing crowd all around Him, what small, easy-to-miss action stopped Jesus as He hurried to heal Jairus's daughter?

- According to Jewish law (Lev. 15:19–30), this woman's bleeding had made her ceremonially unclean for twelve years. In light of that fact, what kind of existence do you think this woman had known for more than a decade?

- What question did Jesus ask the crowd?

- What response did He receive?

- Keeping in mind that it was a male-dominated culture, comment on the strength of both the woman's character and her faith as well as the boldness of her action.

In John 8:31–32, Jesus said, "If you abide in My word, you are My disciples indeed. And you shall know the truth, and the truth shall make you free." As I wrote in the chapter, Jesus can help us know freedom from sin and fear, freedom from the dark cellars of our lives, and freedom from the dictates of our inner events.

- What do you most desire to be free of? Make that a topic of prayer this week.

Read Romans 8:31–34.

- Rewrite this marvelous passage in your own words, and personalize it. Use *I* and *me* ("If God is for *me*, who can be against *me*?") as well as your own name. Then read it out loud and hear these great truths about God's love for you.

    Lord God, please give me the grace and courage to bring the heartache no one sees into Your light. Help me to trust in Your love for me so that I may know freedom in You. Amen.

Chapter 4:
The Lies We Have Believed

What did you learn about Satan when you were young?

1. He was presented as a very real force to be reckoned with.

2. He was reduced to a cartoon character with a trident and pointy tail.

3. He was ignored; or

4. He was credited with every mishap that came along.

Why does Satan like the second and third choices?

Get to know your enemy and his strategy by looking up the following verses. Write down the name of Satan and/or the description of him you find there.

- Genesis 2:25–3:6 (Notice how subtly the serpent changed God's words and sowed seeds of doubt about God's character. And don't miss his bold lie about the consequences of Eve's action.)

- Zechariah 3:1

- John 8:44

- 1 Peter 5:8

- 1 John 3:8

Your enemy the devil was also Jesus' enemy. Read about Jesus' forty-day temptation in Matthew 4:1–11.

- With what three things did Satan tempt Jesus?

- What was Jesus' weapon against Satan's temptations?

- What image for God's Word do you find in Ephesians 6:17?

- What are you doing or could you be doing to be sure you are wielding that sword with strength and skill? Be specific.

Turn to page 52 and reread the contrasting statements of Satan and Jesus. Which of the truths Jesus spoke do you need to believe with your heart, not only your mind? Memorize the corresponding verse (listed below) so that the truth is hidden in your heart and can take root there.

- "In Me you are strong" (2 Cor. 12:9).

- "In Me you are found" (Ps. 23:1; Luke 15:6).

- "In Me you are a victor!" (Ps. 60:12; 1 Cor. 15:57).

- "You are beautiful" (1 Peter 3:3–4).

- "In me you are treasured" (Deut. 7:6).

- "In me you are safe" (Prov. 18:10).

- "You are healed by My wounds" (Isa. 53:5).

- "I love you!" (John 15:9).

Because you are a child of the King, the enemy has no business whispering his lies into your ear. Remind him of that by stating boldly and aloud: "Be quiet, Satan, and leave! I am the Lord's; you don't belong here!" Remember, too, that Jesus is standing at the right hand of God praying for you (Rom. 8:33–34).

Lord God, thank You that in You I have victory over my enemy—over his lies and his deception, over the ways he uses our culture's and even the church's false messages, and over the way he manipulates the pain and loss of my past to keep me chained. Amen.

Chapter 5:
Longing to Be Loved

Read 1 Corinthians 13:1–13. Perhaps this passage is familiar to you, but have you ever read it as a description of God's love?

- What traits of God's love are especially significant to you right now?

- Why?

God's love is not only described in the Bible; it is illustrated again and again, supremely in Jesus Christ.

- According to John 15:13, what is the clearest sign of one person's love for another?

- According to 1 John 3:16, what sign of His love has Jesus given us?

We've touched on the fact that one reason God sent Jesus into the world was to show you and me what God is like. Read Philippians 2:1–11.

- What picture of God's love did Paul describe there?

- Comment on its connection with Jesus' teaching in John 15:13.

Read 1 John 3:1.

- What further indication of God's love for you did John mention there?

Father God, my prayer is the prayer of the psalmist: "Deal with me for Your name's sake; because Your mercy is good, deliver me. For I am poor and needy, and my heart is wounded within me" (Ps. 109:21–22). I long to know Your love not just with my head, but in my heart as well. Amen.

Chapter 6:
The Wounded Healer

Read Isaiah 53:3–5 printed here. Highlight the details about the Messiah and your Savior that surprise you. Also note the details that you don't fully understand and need to learn more about—and do just that.

> He is despised and rejected by men,
> A Man of sorrows and acquainted with grief.
> And we hid, as it were, our faces from Him;
> He was despised, and we did not esteem Him.
> Surely He has borne our griefs
> And carried our sorrows;
> Yet we esteemed Him stricken,
> Smitten by God, and afflicted.
> But He was wounded for our transgressions,
> He was bruised for our iniquities;
> The chastisement for our peace was upon Him,
> And by His stripes we are healed.

- What does it mean to you that Jesus is "acquainted with grief"?

In many ways through the Bible, God says, "I am here." Note beside each passage listed what He did to reveal His presence and His power.

- Genesis 19:11
- 2 Kings 19:35

- Mark 14:22–24
- Acts 5:19

Think of a time or two when God has revealed His presence and/or power to you. Let that encourage you now. If you can't think of an example, ask God to open your eyes to His presence and His power with you in the next twenty-four hours.

A much-loved statement about God's great love for us and His presence with us is Psalm 23.

- What image is especially appealing to you today? Why?

- Hardly the smartest of God's creatures, sheep have no natural ability to defend themselves, they cannot right themselves if they fall over, and they are subject to disease and torment by insects. In this psalm what kinds of provision and protection does God promise us, His people and—yes—the sheep of His pasture?

Remember Christian's lemonade stand? His deluxe lemonade was $1 a glass, but "free if you're broke." Your heavenly Father makes a similar offer in Isaiah 55:1: "Ho! Everyone who thirsts, come to the waters; and you who have no money, come, buy and eat. Yes, come, buy wine and milk without money and without price."

- In what ways are you broke or feeling broke?

- What does the offer of free food and drink say to you about the One making the offer?

- What, if anything, is keeping you from receiving that gracious offer? Make any obstacle a topic for prayer.

Lord Jesus, it is humbling and amazing to realize that You let Yourself be wounded and killed in order to be my Healer. Thank You for the gift of Your presence with me always as I wait for the kind of healing You want to give me and the time You want to do so. Amen.

Chapter 7:
If I Have Enough Faith, Will God Heal My Body Too?

Read James 5:16: "Confess your trespasses to one another, and pray for one another, that you may be healed. The effective, fervent prayer of a righteous man avails much."

- What command do you find here?
- What hope do you find?
- What guarantee do you wish were included here?

Now read 2 Corinthians 12:7–10.

- What was the apostle Paul dealing with?
- What good purpose did he find in it?
- What was God's answer to Paul's prayer to remove the thorn from his side?
- In light of God's answer, what did Paul rejoice in—and why?
- As you wait for God's healing touch on your life, what can you do to know His strength in your weakness?

Remember what I learned about the Hebrew word for "commit"? It means "to roll; to roll away," and it was used to describe the way a camel gets rid of its burden. A camel first kneels down and then, as it rolls to the left, its burden falls off its back.

- What burden are you carrying?
- Think about times you've knelt before the Lord in prayer about this burden. Did you take the next step? Did you let the burden roll off your back? If not, why not? If so, what happened? And if so, have you picked up your burden again?

Proverbs 16:3 reads, "Commit your works to the LORD, and your thoughts will be established."

- What else besides your healing, if anything, do you want to commit to the Lord? Don't hesitate to do so now.

God's ways and thoughts are outside my human capacity for reason, and, as you saw in the Bible study for Chapter 2, I'm hardly the first to notice that! Read Isaiah 55:8.

- What observation did the prophet share?
- What does this truth say to you about healing that doesn't come—or doesn't come in the way or the time that you hoped and prayed?

God moves in many different ways, and who are we to say how He will manifest His presence in a given situation? What troubles me is that we seek what God might do instead of seeking God Himself.

- What do you see about yourself as you look into the mirror of that last sentence?

Lord, Your ways aren't our ways, and if I truly call You "Lord," I need to submit to Your often inscrutable ways. Please help me to trust You and to trust in Your love even when life doesn't go the way I would script it. Please also help me, as an act of trust, to release to You those burdens I'm carrying. And may I know Your strength in my weakness. Amen.

Chapter 8:
How Can You Mend a Broken Heart?
Read Matthew 27:57–61 and John 19:25; 20:1, 10–18.

- At what key places do we find Mary Magdalene?
- According to Mark 16:9, what earlier contact had Mary Magdalene had with Jesus?
- What do the verses in Matthew and John suggest about Mary's response to her Healer and Savior?

Think back to the chapter discussion of Mary.

- At what points of agony and loneliness could you identify with Mary?

- What do her deliverance and devotion mean to you personally?

Read Philippians 1:6. Now write it here, replacing *He* and *you* with *God* and *your own name,* respectively.

- What evidence that God has indeed begun "a good work in you" do you see in your life? A trusted friend may be able to help you answer that question, and I might be able to help too. Here are some thoughts: you picked up this book according to God's sovereign plan. You've read to Chapter 8 without giving up on the book or, even more important, without giving up on the God of healing and hope I'm pointing you toward. Right now, while you may be struggling to believe in God's love for you and His desire to heal you, you're letting me believe for you that God can and will heal you. That's all evidence that God has begun a good work in you!

- Is God going to give up? Answer this question with facts from Scripture, not your own feelings or ideas. Here's some help: Psalm 100:5 and Lamentations 3:22–23.

The defining moments I'm most concerned about in this book are the painful moments that etch a deep trench through our hearts. These defining moments can have a lifetime of repercussions if we are not able to bring those always fresh wounds into the light of God's grace to be healed.

- List some key defining moments, some of the instances in which time seemed to stand still as the pain seared your soul. At the bottom of your list, write Luke 1:37, and remind yourself that nothing you've experienced is beyond God's redemptive and healing power.

It's time to invite Christ into these broken places and let Him make you whole. Read Psalm 6:2–4.

- Which of David's words could be yours? You might also choose to use some of the words from the prayer in Chapter 8, found on page 108.

Some of our wounds are so great and so painful that it would be wise to find a godly counselor to help us deal with them. Don't be ashamed to ask for help—and keep looking until you find the right person to help you. God wants you restored, strong, and full of His life and love. Only Christ can heal broken hearts, but He often chooses to do so through people. Read James 1:5, and then, in faith, ask God to give you wisdom about whether and where to seek help.

Read 2 Corinthians 1:3–5.

- According to verse 4, why does God comfort "us in all our tribulation"?

- When, if ever, has someone who has suffered been able to comfort you "with the comfort with which [he/she was] comforted by God"?

- What happens in your heart as you consider being able to be used by God to comfort others? That's His plan for you!

We are healed so that we can go to others in Jesus' name and offer them the healing we've received. Those of us who have been broken and restored by Christ have a God-given ability to connect with others in pain

230

and to offer them hope and healing. It is one of the greatest privileges of my life to watch the way God uses what was a nightmare to me as a candle in the darkness for others.

> *Lord Jesus Christ, thank You that You have come that I might have life. I bring all the broken pieces of my heart to You, knowing that You will lovingly put them back together. Lord, I do want to get well. I want You to be able to use me to offer healing to others who are broken. Amen.*

Chapter 9:
It's a Minefield out There!

We have a very real enemy who would love to undo the healing work of Christ in our hearts. Read Ephesians 6:10–13.

- What do these verses teach about who your enemy is?

- Why is or isn't this list frightening to you?

- When did you first become aware that the spiritual battle rages all around you, not just in Washington, D.C., or the Middle East?

Fighting this battle requires the armor of God (Eph. 6:14–18), and we'll look closely at that in Chapter 10. You could start memorizing those verses now, though, so that every morning you can put on the armor God provides us! Right now, consider Romans 8:11.

- Who is living in those of us who have named Jesus as our Savior and Lord?

- What do we learn of His power in this verse?

- What hope does that fact give you as you face your enemy in the minefield of this world?

Remember Chapter 4's discussion of Satan's forty-day temptation of Jesus? We saw that Jesus wielded the sword of the Spirit with great skill.

- Considering that your enemy is also known as the father of lies and the deceiver, why is it important to know Scripture?

- What kind of Scripture study and/or memorization program would be helpful to you—and when will you start it?

There is no doubt that Satan's rage is intense, but we can take heart, for he can do only what God will allow.

- What did Jesus tell Simon Peter in Luke 22:31?
- What do Jesus' words teach about the limits on Satan's action?
- What encouragement do you find in this single verse?

The New Testament offers many rich promises of God's presence with us and of the power of the Holy Spirit within us. Read the following and be encouraged! (You might even choose one as a good starting point for your sword-sharpening, Scripture-memorization program!)

- Matthew 1:23
- John 14:16
- 1 Corinthians 1:8
- Ephesians 1:17–20
- Ephesians 3:17–21

Thank You, Lord, for providing me with Your armor so that I can stand strong in the spiritual battle that rages in this world. And thank You that no matter what Satan may throw at me, You will never let me go! What amazing love! Amen.

Chapter 10:
Dressed to Kill

Turn to Ephesians 6:10–18 for a closer look at the pieces of armor God has provided for us, His children.

- Twice God tells us to put on "the whole armor of God" (vv. 11, 13). Why do we so easily ignore these clear instructions and instead, figuratively speaking, show up in the lobby in our pink capris and stiletto sandals?

- What is the first piece of armor listed in verse 14, the first piece a Roman soldier would put on to prepare for battle? Why is this piece so important? (Consider the names of our enemy!)

- What other piece of armor does Paul mention in verse 14? Why is it appropriate that the breastplate symbolizes the righteousness of Christ that covers us believers? (See Romans 3:21–22.)

- What is the next piece of armor mentioned (v. 15)? Explain in your own words what "the gospel" is and why it makes us ready for battle against Satan.

- What piece of armor is identified in verse 16? Faith is not only the action of obeying what we believe God has called us to do, but also the content of what we believe. Why is content key to being able to extinguish the deceiver's fiery darts?

- What is the next piece of armor we are to put on (v. 17)? Why is it important for us to protect our heads in our battle against the father of lies? Also, give an example of when the knowledge in our minds (perhaps about God's love as described in Romans 8:38–39) can help us counter our inaccurate feelings ("God can't love me").

- What final piece of armor does God provide us (v. 17)? What is this weapon, the one offensive weapon God gives us, used for? Give an example.

I ask You, Holy Spirit, to reveal to me any area of my life where I am dealing in lies. I renounce all lies as tools of the enemy, and in Jesus' name I put on the belt of truth. At the same time, please show me my sin so that I can confess it, ask forgiveness, and stand in the righteousness of Christ. I thank You for Scripture and the truth found there so that I can recognize the enemy's lies and extinguish his fiery darts. I praise You for the gift of salvation and the fact that nothing can separate me from Your love. And I thank You for Your Word, a powerful and effective weapon against the great deceiver. Thank You for preparing me so well for battle. Amen.

Chapter 11:
Walking by Faith
Read Hebrews 11:1.

- What is God's definition of *faith*, and what encouraging call to perseverance do you find in that definition? Hear that definition as a call to set sail in response to God's call instead of remaining safe on the dock.

Read Isaiah 43:2.

- What is communicated by the use of *when* instead of *if*?
- What floods and fires have swept through your life?
- What promise does God make here?
- Either at the time or looking back on the situations, in what ways were you aware of God's presence with you? Be specific.
- What hope do you find in this verse and/or in looking back over your life?

Read further in Hebrews 11. Skim through this great "Hall of Faith."

- These forerunners in the faith believed that the Messiah would come, but they never saw His birth. Who stands out to you in this parade—and why?
- Do you think it would have been easy for you to believe in Jesus had you lived in Jerusalem when He did? Why or why not?
- What expectations that you have for how Jesus should or might act may be keeping you from seeing Him at work in your life?

Turn to Genesis 22:2–3.

- What did God command Abraham to do?
- What was Abraham's response?

- In the chapter, I shared my theory. Now it's your turn. Why do you think Abraham was able to arise in obedience to God's commands?

- Abraham's faith was based on what he knew of God's character and ways. What do you know about God's character and about how He does things? Why can that knowledge strengthen your faith just as Abraham's knowledge of God strengthened his faith?

Read the words of Jesus in John 14:1. Take some time to note the context.

- What was the context of Jesus' statement in John 14:1?

- Why did He need to call His disciples to "believe in God"?

- What, if anything, is causing you a troubled heart? What will you do about that "anything" and about that troubled heart?

Lord, someone has said that courage is just fear that has said its prayers, so I'm prayin'! I believe and still I fear, so please help my unbelief! May I, like Abraham, hope against all hope and act in faithful obedience to what You command because I know that You are faithful. Amen.

Chapter 12:
Grace and Truth

Review Luke 4:16–20 and the words of Isaiah, so familiar to His Jewish audience, that Jesus quoted there.

- What did the Jews in Roman-occupied Jerusalem expect as a fulfillment of that prophecy?

- What are your hopes for this Redeemer's work in your life?

- In what ways have you already been blessed and redeemed by His preaching good news to the poor, binding up the brokenhearted, proclaiming "liberty to the captives and recovery of sight to the blind"? Be specific—and thankful.

Read John 8:2–11.

- What no-win situation was the Sanhedrin trying to put Jesus in?
- What was Jesus' response to their question in verse 4?
- Why is this response a demonstration of grace?
- To whom do you need to extend such grace today? Do so!

Now read Romans 3:23, keeping in mind Jesus' words to the crowd in John 8:7.

- In the scene from John 8, who was in need of grace and forgiveness?
- Why should each one—and you and I as well—have stepped into the circle with the woman?
- Why is coming alongside someone in his or her sin a way of participating in God's grace? (See Galatians 6:2.)

As Christian so wisely put it, if you are hurt and want to get well, won't you take all the help you can get? Here are some passages that offer help:

- Psalm 51:7
- Psalm 51:17
- Psalm 103:12
- 1 John 1:9

Amen!

Lord God, Your grace truly is amazing. Thank You for helping me see that. Please grant me a humble spirit that I may never take for granted the love and forgiveness You extend to me, a sinner in need of Your grace. Amen.

Chapter 13:
Broken Bread and Poured-Out Wine

Read Ephesians 4:15. As I said earlier, it is one thing to receive input, even criticism, from those who love us and handle our hearts with tender care. It is quite another when someone stomps across our inner sanctums with steel-toed work boots.

- Where, if at all, is God calling you to offer input to a fellow believer?

- What will "speaking the truth in love" look like in that situation? Or, perhaps an easier starting point, what will "speaking the truth in love" not look like?

- Why is "speaking the truth in love" essential to healthy and godly community?

Turn to Matthew 6:14 and read what Jesus said there.

- What command did Jesus give His followers?

- In addition to the fact that we are to obey God (which is definitely reason enough to forgive those who sin against us!), why is forgiving others a good thing for you to do? Think about times when you or someone you know has carried a grudge rather than extending forgiveness to the one who caused the hurt.

In his devotional based on Colossians 1:24, Oswald Chambers wrote, "We are called to be broken bread and poured-out wine." But, I ask, whose fingers will God use to break the bread and squeeze the juice from the grapes to make the wine?

- Whom has God already used in your life?

- In what ways has God used you since those painful experiences of breaking and squeezing?

Read Hebrews 5:7–9.

- What was the focus of Jesus' prayers?

- What was God's response to His Son's passionate plea?

- What pain have you been asking God to remove or help you avoid?

- What can you learn from Jesus' experience?

Turn to Hebrews 12:2–3.

- What are some benefits that come from fixing our eyes on Jesus?

- What do you think Jesus was thinking of as He "endured the cross"?

- What truths can help you stand strong in the pain of your crucifixion, your dying to self?

Dear Jesus, my hands have not been pierced by nails as Yours were, but my heart is broken. So I come before You to worship You and, by Your power, to say, "I welcome this crucifixion so that I might share in Your resurrection." Please take me to a deeper place where I can truly recognize Your hand in everything that comes my way. Then, please help me move from acceptance to forgiveness, extending to others the forgiveness You have extended to me. Amen.

Chapter 14:
Resurrected

We've all had hard things to forgive, and Jesus knows that. He also knows a lot about forgiveness. Read Luke 23:32–34.

- What is your reaction to Jesus' words in verse 34?

- What message does God have for you in His Son's words?

Sometimes we have to forgive certain sins that are committed against us again and again. Read Matthew 18:21–22.

- What situation or person from your own life comes to mind when you read Peter's words?

- Why do you think Jesus answers the way He does?

- Who can help you (and me!) forgive and forgive and forgive—seventy times seven times?

Review the story of Joseph in this chapter or in Genesis 37; 39–45.

- Whom might Joseph have had a hard time forgiving? (It's not a short list!)
- What fact, reported in Genesis 39:2, 23 as well as in Acts 7:9, helps enable Joseph—and you and me—to forgive evil done or spoken against us?

Now turn to Genesis 50:18–20.

- What did Joseph understand about God (v. 20) that helped him forgive his brothers?
- What do you appreciate about the story of Joseph and his example?

Thank You, Lord, that You are with me always, even as You were always with Joseph. Thank You that You are sovereign over my life, that You are in control of all that happens, that You are bigger than my enemies, and that You can take the most evil act perpetrated against me and use it to prosper me in body, mind, soul, and spirit. You can also help me forgive those who are hard to forgive—and I ask Your help in doing just that. Amen.

Chapter 15:
A Church Divided on Healing

[15] Rejoice with those who rejoice, and weep with those who weep. [16] Be of the same mind toward one another. Do not set your mind on high things, but associate with the humble. Do not be wise in your own opinion. [17] Repay no one evil for evil. Have regard for good things in the sight of all men. [18] If it is possible, as much as depends on you, live peaceably with all men. [19] Beloved, do not avenge yourselves, but rather give place to wrath;

for it is written, "Vengeance is Mine, I will repay," says the Lord. [20] Therefore,

"If your enemy is hungry, feed him;
If he is thirsty, give him a drink;
For in so doing you will heap coals of fire on his head."

[21] Do not be overcome by evil, but overcome evil with good. (Rom. 12:15–21)

What guidance does this passage offer the church today, divided as it is about avenues of healing that are appropriate for believers?

- Verse 15

- Verse 16

- Verse 18

- Verse 21

In what ways do paid professionals do for some of us what verse 15 calls fellow believers to do for us? Why do you think we believers aren't always there in that way for each other?

What does verse 16 say to believers who disagree with each other about an issue, any issue?

God commands us to "as much as depends on [us], live peaceably with all men" (v. 18). What action step, if any, is this verse calling you to take? Be especially aware of any lack of peace that has resulted from disagreement over where believers "should" seek healing.

What does verse 21 say to us believers?

Do you remember the praise chorus, "And they'll know we are Christians by our love, by our love; yes, they'll know we are Christians by our love"? What does this truth suggest about what each one of us, as a member of God's body, the church, can do to bring unity and community where there is division? More on this in the next chapter!

Lord, the Christian community can indeed be a bright light and a powerful witness to Your love and Your truth—but not if we're arguing with each other and adding to each other's pain. If and when I encounter someone with whom I strongly disagree, teach me—in that context and every other context of my life—to overcome evil with good. Use me, Lord, to help others to first recognize our love for them and for each other for what it is—a reflection of Your love—and then to come to know You. Amen.

Chapter 16:
Take Off the Grave Clothes!

In the gospel of John, seven acts of Jesus Christ point to His divine authority. I commented that every one reveals Jesus' involvement in a different area of human experience. Clearly He demonstrated that the kingdom of God embraces every aspect of the brokenness of man. Skim the biblical accounts of each miracle and review my discussion of those seven signs. Then next to each of the first six, write what you personally find most significant or encouraging about what Jesus reveals of Himself in each setting.

1. Turning water into wine at the wedding in Cana (2:1–11)

2. Healing the official's son at Capernaum (4:46–54)

3. Healing the sick man at the pool of Bethesda (5:1–15)

4. Feeding the five thousand in Galilee (6:1–15)

5. Walking on the stormy Sea of Galilee (6:16–24)

6. Healing the man born blind in Jerusalem (9:1–7)

Now let's look more closely at Jesus raising Lazarus from the dead (John 11:1–44), the culmination of these signs. Summarize in your own words what this miracle teaches us about the importance of community. Verse 44 is key!

Turn to Matthew 20:1–16, and read Jesus' parable of the workers in the vineyard.

- Remember what I said about the way the rabbis ended this story when they told it? What is different about Jesus' ending?

- What does the story the way Jesus tells it celebrate about God?

- When have you been blessed by God's scandalous generosity? Be specific.

Paul wrote, "You, brethren, have been called to liberty; only do not use liberty as an opportunity for the flesh, but through love serve one another" (Gal. 5:13).

- Into what arena(s) has God already called you to serve?

- To what place of need might He be calling you now? If you're not sure, the next question may help.

Read Luke 4:18.

- Specifically identify some of the following in your world:

> The poor
> The brokenhearted
> The captive
> The blind
> The oppressed

- For which group do you have a special concern? If that question is hard to answer, ask God to give you eyes to see and a compassionate heart for the needy people He puts in your path.

- What do you respect most about Sara Trollinger's response to this passage?

- What might God want your response to this passage to be? Make it a topic for prayer.

Gracious God, thank You that Your love calls us back to life. Thank You for those sisters and brothers You've provided—and will provide—to help take off my grave clothes. Please give me Your eyes to see, Your ears

to hear, and Your heart to feel the pain of others so that You might use
me to help take off their grave clothes. Amen.

Chapter 17:
An Alternate List of Miracles

We who name Jesus as our Savior and Lord are the body of Christ on earth—and that metaphor is rich in meaning. Reread 1 Corinthians 12:24–27.

- When have you suffered because a brother or sister in Christ was suffering? Be specific.

- When have you rejoiced when a sister or brother in the Lord had cause to rejoice?

- When, if ever, have you sensed the compassion of someone who suffered with you as you suffered? What impact did that person's presence have on you?

- When, if ever, has someone rejoiced as you have rejoiced? What impact did that person's response have on you?

In John 15:12, Jesus said, "This is My commandment, that you love one another as I have loved you." With whom do you especially struggle to obey this command? Even if you don't feel like it, pray and ask God to give you a heart of compassion for that person and the ability to forgive. Also ask God to bless this person.

If you didn't do so as you read the chapter, read Psalm 103:1–18 aloud.

- What image do you find especially powerful? Why?

- What promise is especially meaningful to you right now? Why?

When asked what law is most important, Jesus responded, "'You shall love the LORD your God with all your heart, with all your soul, with all your mind, and with all your strength' . . . And the second, like it, is this: 'You shall love your neighbor as yourself.' There is no other commandment greater than these" (Mark 12:30–31). Read John 14:12–14 for an idea of what living in obedience to these commands might look like.

- When you read this passage, do you think of miracles, or do you think of the selfless way that Jesus lived?

- After reading this chapter (and feel free to go back and review), what do you think Jesus meant by "greater works than these"? Explain.

Sharing the heart of Christ is an act of grace and the kind of great miracle that changes the world. Consider now this list of such great miracles:

- Jesus resisted the enemy with the power of God's Word (Matt. 4:10–11).

- Jesus reached out and touched the unlovely (Matt. 8:2–3).

- Jesus recognized broken hearts and turned toward them with love (Luke 7:36–50).

- Jesus forgave the unforgivable (Luke 23:33–34).

- Jesus gives second chances to those who make the worst choices in life (John 21:15–19).

Which of these miracles can you be a part of today? Tomorrow? What impact might miracles like these have on people around us? To God be the glory!

Father, Your love is overwhelming . . . Your grace is amazing . . . Your hope never fails . . . Teach me to live as Jesus did—in total dependence on You . . . And teach me to love as Jesus did—with a serving, sacrificial love for the people around me. Amen.

A Final Thought:
Don't Hide Your Heart

In Psalm 40:9–10, David praised God. Rather than keeping to himself his knowledge of God's goodness, David proclaimed God's great faithfulness to the assembly. He shared openly about God's love and truth.

- When has someone's proclamation of God's goodness and faithfulness been an encouragement to you? Be specific about how you benefited from that person opening, rather than hiding, her heart.

- What examples of God's faithfulness to you can you point to?

- What evidence of God's saving love and very personal love are you aware of?

- What impact has God's truth had on your life? Specify the statements of truth that have been especially significant.

- Be ready to open your heart the next time you have the opportunity to share with someone what God has done and is continuing to do in your life. Don't hide your heart!

Lord God, help me boldly proclaim Your goodness and faithfulness to those who need to hear about Your healing love and healing presence. In You alone is there real healing for wounded hearts. I praise You for calling me to know You and love You, to be healed by You and to be blessed by You. And I praise You that You who began a good work in me will see it through to completion! Amen.

ABOUT THE AUTHOR

*S*heila Walsh says, "Words are powerful, whether sung, spoken, or written," and her career as a communicator highlights the unique combination of singer, talk-show host, and author. Formerly cohost of *The 700 Club* and host of her own show, *Heart to Heart with Sheila Walsh*, Sheila is also the author of *Honestly*, *Unexpected Grace*, *Life Is Tough But God Is Faithful*, and *All That Really Matters*. She is a featured speaker at the Women of Faith™ conferences and recently released the album, *The Best of Sheila Walsh*. She and her husband, Barry, live in Nashville, Tennessee, with their son, Christian.

Irrepressible Hope
Devotions to Anchor Your Soul and Buoy Your Spirit

THE 2004 WOMEN OF FAITH® DEVOTIONAL BOOK,
BASED ON THE YEAR LONG THEME OF "IRREPRESSIBLE HOPE"

If you experience feelings of confusion, doubt, insecurity, and fear, always remember this: Regardless of what goes on in the world or our lives, we can have hope! Hope is the unbreakable spiritual lifeline that connects us straight into the heart of God. In this dynamic 60-day devotional, the Women of Faith speakers identify the emotions that come from a life void of hope and direct us to the source of all hope—Christ. What better remedy for a troubled world than to offer huge doses of Irrepressible Hope?

ISBN: 0-8499-1804-9

Unexpected Grace
Comfort in the Midst of Loss

WOMEN OF FAITH® SPEAKER SHEILA WALSH SHARES THE
LESSONS OF LOVE AND GRACE SHE LEARNED WHILE CARING
FOR AND LEARNING TO LOVE HER DYING MOTHER-IN-LAW.

Some experiences change your life. Some relationships do too. As Sheila
Walsh walked with her mother-in-law through her last moments, the two
women learned lessons of life—ones that had previously eluded them.
These memories have changed Sheila's relationship with Christ and her
perspective forever. And they become a blessed chronicle that will change
readers' lives as they too are plunged into God's river of mercy.

ISBN: 0-7852-6530-9